Elizabeth Sirriyeh was until her retirement Senior Lecturer in Islamic Studies at the University of Leeds. A specialist on dream interpretation in Islam, she has also written on Sufism and Islamic reform, religion in Ottoman Syria, Muslim ideological disputes and the interface between Islamic and modern Western thought. Her previous books are *Sufis and Anti-Sufis: The Defence, Rethinking and Rejection of Sufism in the Modern World* (1999) and *Sufi Visionary of Ottoman Damascus: 'Abd al-Ghani al-Nabulusi, 1641–1731* (2005).

'To study the history of Muslim dreaming is to enter an enthralling meta-world in which believers sought authenticity, authority and salvation through their nocturnal encounters with the Prophets and Saints. Elizabeth Sirriyeh is a judicious and expert guide to over twelve centuries of deliberations on the credibility and meaning of dreams. Her book will appeal to anyone interested in this under-studied topic.'

— **Nile Green**, Professor of History, UCLA, author of *Sufism: A Global History*

'Elizabeth Sirriyeh's authoritative book on dreams and visions in the Islamic tradition concerns what might be termed "mysticism", and as such relates to the very heart of the Sufi tradition. It provides a comprehensive and lucid account that commences in the pre-Islamic period and brings readers up to the present era with discussions of the topic within the contemporary Middle East. For students of Sufism and Islamic spirituality this book is indispensable, because it provides a clear account of the potency and significance that dreams and visions have had, and continue to have, in the region.'

— **Lloyd Ridgeon**, Reader in Theology and Religious Studies, University of Glasgow

'The Prophet Muhammad received revelations from God in his dreams and he himself interpreted the dreams of his companions. And after his death, and the end of Qur'anic revelation, Muslims believed that God would continue to reveal himself to them through their dreams. In this fascinating book, Elizabeth Sirriyeh explores the role that dreams and visions played in the religious lives of pre-modern Muslims. She ranges widely: from the earliest biographical sources on the life of the Prophet, through formal manuals for the interpretation of dreams and philosophical treatises on the nature of dreams, to the visionary accounts of Muslim mystics. She devotes special attention to the unexplored dreams of Muslim women. Her analysis is masterful and eminently accessible, and there is much here to delight both the specialist and the general reader.'

— **John C. Lamoreaux**, Associate Professor of Religious Studies, Southern Methodist University, author of *The Early Muslim Tradition of Dream Interpretation*

Dreams & Visions
in the World of Islam

A History of Muslim Dreaming
and Foreknowing

Elizabeth
Sirriyeh

I.B. TAURIS
LONDON · NEW YORK

Paperback edition published in 2018 by
I.B.Tauris & Co. Ltd
London • New York
www.ibtauris.com

Hardback edition first published in 2015 by I.B.Tauris & Co. Ltd

Copyright © 2015 Elizabeth Sirriyeh

The right of Elizabeth Sirriyeh to be identified as the author of this work has been asserted by the author in accordance with the Copyright, Designs and Patents Act 1988.

All rights reserved. Except for brief quotations in a review, this book, or any part thereof, may not be reproduced, stored in or introduced into a retrieval system, or transmitted, in any form or by any means, electronic, mechanical, photocopying, recording or otherwise, without the prior written permission of the publisher.

Every attempt has been made to gain permission for the use of the images in this book. Any omissions will be rectified in future editions.

References to websites were correct at the time of writing.

ISBN: 978 1 78831 093 2
eISBN: 978 0 85773 820 2
ePDF: 978 1 78673 964 3

A full CIP record for this book is available from the British Library
A full CIP record is available from the Library of Congress

Library of Congress Catalog Card Number: available

Typeset in Garamond Three by OKS Prepress Services, Chennai, India

For Hussain, Ala and Reema

CONTENTS

Preface	viii
Introduction	1
1. Seeing Gods and Angels before the Rise of Islam	9
2. The Prophet as Model Visionary	32
3. Scholars and Saints in the Path of the Prophet	58
4. The Dream Must Be Interpreted	83
5. Muslims Dreaming of Christians, Christians Dreaming of Muslims	103
6. 'And if a Woman Dreams'	118
7. Envisioning God and His Prophet	140
8. Contacting the Righteous Dead	158
9. Visionary Traditions and the Impact of Modernity	174
Notes	195
Bibliography	223
Index	233

PREFACE

In a survey of Muslim academics, undertaken at the International Islamic University of Malaysia early in the twenty-first century, all the participants reported their belief in the possibility of receiving true guidance from God in their dreams. Many said that they performed rituals before sleep in the hope of receiving such dreams, had consulted expert dream interpreters and had experienced dreams of great importance for their lives. A number of those surveyed mentioned that the dreams had helped them in solving problems, had served as a warning of dangers and some believed that they had been given clear instructions via dreams. For example, one woman academic claimed that she had seen her deceased brother-in-law in a dream and that he had asked her to take care of his children.[1]

Anyone may be regarded as being able to 'see' the truth in their night visions, but those who are especially pious are generally considered to be more open to receiving and understanding divine communication. Consequently, they are commonly consulted for guidance as to the meaning of dreams and may even dream on behalf of more ordinary dreamers. A Turkish academic recounted his own experience from 1991 when he was seeking to marry into a pious family, who were associated with one of the Sufi orders in Istanbul. The family decided to consult their shaykh as to the suitability of the marriage. The shaykh then performed the ritual known as *istikhara*, in which he prayed to God to supply an answer before he went to sleep. He dreamt, but told the family that he had seen an unfavourable outcome if the marriage were to go ahead. The family accepted the shaykh's interpretation of his dream as a divine warning and rejected the proposal of marriage.[2]

Those who do not have ready access to a skilled interpreter of dreams frequently turn to dream dictionaries for guidance. Some of the classical keys to dreams remain remarkably popular, although modern abridgements and compilations are also available. These works are easily identified as offering a method of foreknowing similar to that of the Greek dream interpreter Artemidorus (second century CE). They claim to foretell the future rather than seeking to provide the dreamer with psychological insight. John Lamoreaux, writing of the early development of Muslim dream interpretation, explains this approach to interpreting dreams: 'Dream interpretation offered Muslims a royal road that led not inward, but outward, providing insight not into the dreamer's psyche but into the hidden affairs of the world.'[3] Nevertheless, I have been surprised, on visiting a Middle Eastern bookshop, to find such works placed in the psychology section next to modern books in the field. There appears to be a trend in some quarters to claim the medieval Muslim authors of guides to dreams as precursors of modern psychoanalysis. The organisation of the above bookshop reflects this trend.[4]

How did the situation arise in which dreaming and other visionary experience became so important to highly spiritual men and women as well as many Muslims with more mundane interests? This book is principally occupied with seeking an answer to this question. The major focus is on the emergence and flowering of literature in Arabic relating to dreams and visions, principally, but not exclusively, designed as a means of foreknowing future events. A variety of forms of divination were in use among the Muslims and had the goal of knowing the future, such as astrology, sorcery and reading the meanings of shapes and lines drawn in the sand (*'ilm al-raml*). However, they never gained the respected status of the veridical dream or vision, which was elevated above humbler divinatory practices and acknowledged as constituting a part of prophecy.

Therefore, despite the interest of various branches of Islamic divination for their contribution to traditional culture, they fall outside the coverage of this book.

Arabic writings are the most prominent sources, since they are of critical importance for studying the evolution of the Muslim visionary tradition and Arabic is the Islamic language with which I am most familiar. It has also been necessary to control the geographical scope of the work. Therefore, the study focuses in particular on the place of dreaming and waking visions in the lives of Muslims from the formative period of Islam until the eighteenth century, mainly in the Arab lands with limited coverage of other areas in the later part of the book. Finally, there is some discussion of the Muslims' encounter with Western modernity and its impact on their attitudes to dreams and visions.

Chapters 2 to 8 of the book endeavour to see the visionary world through the eyes of pre-modern Muslims, accepting that we can only partially hear their voices and enter into their concerns at this remove in time and space. In places the focus is primarily, or even exclusively, on dreaming, for example in discussing the development of guides for interpreting the symbolism of dreams. Elsewhere dreams and visions are treated together as part of the same basic phenomenon and because in many writings it is hard to know for certain whether a narrative describes a dream or a waking vision or even, at times, a physical miracle, as in the case of the Prophet's night journey to Jerusalem and ascension to Heaven. Guy Stroumsa has remarked in relation to early Christians' visionary experience that 'any study that focuses on dreams while ignoring visions is bound to remain deeply flawed'.[5] The same conclusion may often, although not always, be applicable in studies of pre-modern Muslims' records of such experience.

Following an introduction to Muslims' perceptions of dreams and visions, Chapter 1 considers the Pre-Islamic context out of which they arose. Dream interpretation is a notoriously conservative occupation. Did Muslims simply continue a pattern that had actually been established in the ancient Near Eastern, Greco-Roman, Jewish and Christian traditions? The chapter provides a short survey of certain aspects of the ancient traditions that appear to have had the greatest influence on the Islamic tradition.

Chapter 2 opens the main body of the book with a study of the Prophet Muhammad as the model for Muslims of a perfect dreamer, visionary and interpreter of dreams. It is observed how dreaming lies at the very foundations of Islam because Muhammad was said to have received his earliest revelations in dreams for a period of six months before the beginning of the waking revelation of the Qur'an. The chapter discusses the major role played by both dreams and visions in his life's work as the God-guided Prophet of the Muslim community. Finally, it examines the record of the Prophet as an interpreter of others' dreams, establishing a basis for the high value placed on dream interpretation in later generations.

Chapter 3 explores how leaders, scholars and pious figures followed in the path of the Prophet in assigning great importance to dreams and visions and their proper interpretation. Attention is paid to this formative period of Islamic scholarship from the late eighth to early tenth centuries, examining the role of *hadith*s and other anecdotal reports concerning dreaming and its interpretation. The chapter concludes with a discussion of the visionary theory of the philosopher al-Kindi (d. *c*.870) and the visionary experience of the mystic Abu Yazid al-Bistami (d. 875).

Not all dreams contained clear messages, whose meaning was immediately obvious to the dreamer. Chapter 4 focuses on the compilation of manuals by dream interpreters, intended to provide guidance for making predictions as to the possible meanings of images seen in dreams. The chapter looks at developments in Muslim dream interpretation before and after the Christian physician Hunayn b. Ishaq (d. 873 or 877) translated the famous Greek dream manual of Artemidorus into Arabic. Given that Muslim dream manuals provide a valuable picture of common information, misinformation and social attitudes, Chapter 5 explores some views of 'the other' that they present and is primarily concerned with medieval Muslim views of Christians exhibited in an influential dream manual of the eleventh century and a Christian view of Muslims as represented in a rare Byzantine compilation of roughly the same period. The chapter has previously appeared in a fuller version as a journal article in *Islam and Christian-Muslim Relations* xvii/2 (2006), pp. 207–21. I would like to express my thanks to Taylor and Francis for permitting the reproduction of the work in a modified form in order to fit the structure of the book.

Most of the Islamic literature discussed up to this point is concerned with the dreams and visions of male dreamers and visionaries. Chapter 6 explores some narratives of Muslim women's dreams and visions alleged to have taken place in the seventh to early tenth centuries and recorded in history, *hadith*s, moralising anecdotes and spiritual biography. These accounts are compared and contrasted with the views on interpreting women's dreams contained in dream manuals up to the seventeenth century.

The higher levels of vision form the subject of Chapter 7, especially dreams and visions of God and the Prophet experienced by Sufis from the late twelfth century onwards, notably the Iranian Ruzbihan Baqli (d. 1209) and the great Andalusian mystic Ibn 'Arabi (d. 1240). The latter part of the chapter examines reports of Sufi dreams and visions of the Prophet from North and West Africa and the Sudan in the fifteenth to nineteenth centuries. Chapter 8 extends the discussion to consider visionary contacts with other righteous figures, in particular the Imams of Shi'ism and the saints, giving special attention to beliefs and practices in seeking to encounter the holy dead at their graves.

Chapter 9 discusses the impact of Western modernity on Muslim attitudes to the visionary life in the twentieth and twenty-first centuries in a range of geographical and social settings. It includes an examination of those who have preserved relatively traditional ways of connecting with their dreams and, on occasion, waking visions, those whose outlook has altered in modern conditions and those who have lost an understanding of their dreaming as a means of divine communication.

The transliteration system used in the book for proper names and terms in Arabic, and occasionally other Islamic languages, is that of the *International Journal of Middle East Studies* with some modifications. Diacritical marks have been excluded throughout the text and notes. The Arabic definite article 'al-' is used only at the first mention of a proper name and dropped subsequently (for example, 'Bistami' instead of 'al-Bistami'). Transliteration is generally standardised except in the case of quotations. However, a number of place names and a few modern personal names are given in the form in which they are most familiar in English. In the case of some more common words, the English form of the plural is used in preference to the Arabic (for example, *mawlids* rather than *mawalid*). Translations are my own where they are not otherwise referenced.

The research for this book was begun while I was working in Theology and Religious Studies at the University of Leeds and has been brought to completion during my retirement. I should like to take this opportunity to thank former colleagues for their interest along the way, especially Kim Knott for advice in the early stages of the project. I also wish to thank Philip Mellor and Séan McLoughlin for enabling me to complete the work through an honorary lectureship at the present School of Philosophy, Religion and History of Science. I am particularly grateful to Alex Wright of I.B.Tauris for inviting me to write the book and for his support throughout its preparation. As ever, I owe a special debt of gratitude to Hussain, Ala and Reema for their constant encouragement over the years and to all the family for their patience when I have been preoccupied with the world of dreams and visions.

INTRODUCTION

Visions of the Night and Day

The Arabic term *ru'ya* is given to the true dream that is understood in Islamic tradition to be sent from God. True dreams are identified as visions because they are 'seen' in a vivid manner by the dreamer. Usually they are visions of the night. Such dreams are often described as remarkable for their clarity. Dreamers are said to awaken quickly and remember every detail.[1] During a period of her anthropological fieldwork in Pakistan, Katherine Ewing, also a trained psychoanalyst, was astonished when she experienced an amazingly clear dream of a white horse, a dream from which she woke suddenly and with the strong sense that she had been sent this dream through the intervention of a Sufi shaykh. She was surprised to find that, despite her training and her social and academic background, she was on the edge of being drawn into the belief world of those for whom the spiritual dream and visions were very real.[2]

Other visions have been reported as occurring in a waking state, whether by day or night, and still others are noted as taking place in a state between sleeping and waking. Such waking visions have generally been accorded a high status and regarded as a sign of the believer's remarkable piety. Although almost everyone dreams, not everyone has true dream visions. An even more select group are those who have true waking visions. The general view of pre-modern

Muslim writers was that such visions were granted only to the prophets and the most righteous of the believers, frequently those who were regarded as saintly mystics or martyrs. The Prophet Muhammad served as the model for later visionaries in that the reception of the Qur'an came about through his vision of the angel Gabriel as well as many subsequent visual and auditory encounters in which he heard the divine word. His famous journey by night to Jerusalem and ascension to Heaven offered an example of visionary experience to encourage the most spiritually advanced of Sufi mystics to aspire to follow in his path on their own journeys towards God. Many Muslims accepted these events as literal, physical miracles, in which the Prophet travelled in the body until he reached the highest heaven. However, the extraordinary stories also gave rise to much discussion as to whether the Prophet had actually experienced his heavenly journey in a veridical dream or in a waking vision.

As visions were so closely linked to prophecy, they came to be highly valued in Muslim society and increasingly frequent. The great spiritual author al-Ghazali (d. 1111) noted of Sufi mystics:

> From the beginning of the Way they experience unveilings and visions, so that in their waking state they see the angels and the spirits of the prophets. They hear their voices and benefit from their advice. They then progress from the vision of forms and images to degrees beyond description.[3]

Nile Green has observed the apparent obsession of certain medieval spiritual writers with visions to the point that dreams were effectively downgraded:

> The fact that many sufi writers had been more concerned with the amazing subject matter of the spellbinding visions of their early mentors suggests that they allowed themselves, at times, to leave the more trifling category of the dream to the chattering classes of Baghdad.[4]

The 'chattering classes of Baghdad' had indeed become absorbed with dreams and their interpretation, but, despite fluctuating fashions in the literature, many mystics over the course of Islamic history appear to have appreciated the value of both dreaming and waking visionary experience.

The Importance of 'Seeing' the Unseen World

In 1937 Carl Jung delivered the Terry Lectures at Yale University, which were published a year later under the title *Psychology and Religion*. In his opening remarks Jung admits: 'Being a doctor and a specialist in nervous and mental diseases my point of departure is not any creed, but the psychology of the homo religiosus.'[5] He discusses, in particular, the situation of one of his patients, a man whom he describes as an intellectual, a 'Catholic by education', but lapsed and not 'interested in religious problems'. The patient was deeply disturbed by his extraordinary dreams, 400 of which he recorded at Jung's request. Jung, as psychoanalyst and modern-day dream interpreter, wrote with what seems like an element of wistfulness:

> The modern mind has forgotten those old truths that speak of the death of the old man and of the making of a new one, of spiritual rebirth and similar old-fashioned 'mystical absurdities'. My patient, being a scientist of today, was more than once seized by panic when he realized how much he was gripped by such thoughts. He was afraid of becoming insane, whereas the man of two thousand years ago would have welcomed such dreams and rejoiced in the hope of a magical rebirth and renewal of life.[6]

Certainly many a medieval Sufi mystic would have welcomed such dreams, although the fear of insanity does not appear so much of a modern phenomenon as Jung depicts it here. The Prophet was supposedly confronted by such a fear on receiving his first overwhelming vision of the Angel Gabriel. Awareness of the potentially devastating power of visions to unhinge the mind became deeply rooted in the Muslim consciousness and can be encountered to this day in many Islamic subcultures from Morocco to Pakistan. However, where Jung's patient was confronted by fear of a mundane mental illness, those Muslims succumbing to visions of the unseen world that were too powerful for their minds to bear would commonly be described as 'drawn' to God (*majdhub*). The everyday world around them was ripped apart and they were 'opened' to the world of divine reality in a way that only the righteous and spiritually prepared could handle. Effectively, waking visions and even veridical dreams were accepted as significant divine interventions in human affairs. They were welcomed, but also treated with the caution and respect owed to those events that are beyond the ability of humans to control.

Dreams and visions, with their capacity to disrupt the everyday world, could affect far more than the human psyche of an individual, although they could also do just that. They could predict the rise and fall of dynasties, foretell the outcome of battles and wars, identify those who were saints and martyrs and tell of their burial places. They provided a means by which the righteous could contact the Prophet and the most saintly lay claim to conversations with God. Although these messages, when understood as divine communications, might serve to resolve a personal spiritual crisis, they had a far wider effect on public as well as private life. Until the impact of Western modernity from the late nineteenth century, and later in many Muslim communities, the assumption prevailed that the unseen world was at least as important as the seen world of everyday life. Pre-modern Muslims normally considered the events of dreams and visions to be just as real as the ordinarily visible and supposedly real events that occurred in their lives. Despite the fading of belief in the importance of the unseen under the pressures of globalisation, there are still very many Muslims worldwide for whom dreaming and, more rarely, waking visions provide a pathway to access the reality of the divine.

Was This Dream Really Dreamt?
Was This Vision Really Seen?

Writing with reference to the dreams of classical antiquity, William V. Harris remarks:

> An expert on the extensive dream-literature of Byzantium has said that we have no single trustworthy dream-narrative anywhere in the history of that whole culture. Some classical scholars would probably say that the same is true for Greek and Roman times, yet scholars also make exceptions for their own favourites, whether it is the martyr Perpetua or the emperor Constantine. Since we cannot even be entirely sure about the truth, let alone the exactness, of the dreams we hear about from our own acquaintances, the possibility of finding out what the Greeks and Romans dreamt may seem practically nil.[7]

The same logic applies equally well to Islamic dream narratives and makes it reasonable to argue that, while some may be 'trustworthy', the chances of determining which ones fit into this category are severely limited. Yet Harris was admittedly a little more hopeful of peeling away the layers of 'fibs, lies and fantasies' to expose the inventions and conventions of the Greeks and Romans and perhaps to unmask a degree of the real experience of dreaming that lay behind them.[8] Some of the reasons for inventing dreams in classical antiquity appear remarkably similar to those present in the pre-modern Muslim world. When so much credence is given to the idea that dreams can bring to light truths that are otherwise concealed from humans, there is a strong temptation to create dreams that claim to reveal the truth. There may also be added to this belief a desire to elevate particular individuals or groups of people (whether rulers, religious scholars or saintly mystics) by relating a supposedly true dream or vision concerning them; the temptation then to fabricate narratives is even greater. Accounts of dreams and waking visions are also liable at times to have propagandist purposes. They can make it possible to articulate minority viewpoints, including juristic, theological or sectarian ideas, with less fear of repercussions because the narrator is suitably distanced from the content. Yet, because it may contain that hidden truth, the dream or visionary narrative can also lend force to an argument.[9] There may, of course, be pious and sincere motives for producing such a narrative, but they do not in themselves guarantee its authenticity.

Even when it is possible to suspect a fake, it is far harder to demonstrate the suspect nature of the account beyond a shadow of doubt. C. F. Beckingham has warned of the difficulties to be encountered in seeking to establish the 'reliability of travel narratives and geographical descriptions written in classical Islamic times'.[10] He sees the problem as extending well beyond the 'stories of miraculous phenomena and events' that they often contain and being applicable also to more mundane narratives. He cautions especially against being attracted by 'the ring of truth' in accounts of this kind. The same caution can reasonably be exercised in relation to those stories of dreams and visions that often border on the miraculous and, following Beckingham's advice, those that seem perfectly credible.

A twentieth-century story from Egypt serves to illustrate this need for caution. During her fieldwork there in the 1980s, Valerie Hoffman recorded an alleged critical turning point in the life of an Egyptian Sufi, 'Izz al-'Arab al-Hawari, regarded as a living saint by many who came in contact with him.[11] He had spent his early years in a religious environment in Upper Egypt, but moved to Cairo with his family at the age of 15. There he lost touch with his religion and even neglected the basic duties of prayer and fasting. In 1963 he joined the army and married in 1966. Shortly afterwards he fell ill, was diagnosed with an abscess in the right lung and entered a military hospital for surgery to remove half the lung. It was there in the hospital that he recorded an extraordinary experience. He was alone in his room late at night when he heard the call to prayer coming from the River Nile, although it was well past the time for the call and there was no mosque there. 'Izz had not been accustomed to pray for a number of years, but he performed major ablutions, prayed the evening prayer and additional prayer before sitting in bed to read the Qur'an.[12] He told Hoffman:

While I was reading the Qur'an, I found the wall that looked out over the river had opened up. I saw a strong beam of light, stronger than the sun. I covered my eyes. When I uncovered them, I looked and saw that doctors had come in, wearing surgical clothes. They rose out of the water. An old man was at their head and he said, 'Don't worry, we are going to do the operation now.' The operation was supposed to be Saturday. This was Thursday. I couldn't see any surgical tools. Twelve people came in, men and women. One man came forward, not the old one who had come first, and he opened the buttons of my shirt and rubbed my chest and closed the buttons again. That was the operation.[13]

'Izz recalled that X-rays the following day showed no signs of any abscess and he was soon discharged from the hospital. That was the climactic moment that led to his reversion to Islam, initially to become a Muslim preacher in the army, but later to return to the Sufi form of faith of his childhood.

This is 'Izz's story, but what exactly happened? It appears to be an account of some kind of vision. Perhaps 'Izz fell asleep and dreamt the event. He admits that it was late at night. Perhaps he was hallucinating or experiencing visual disturbance as a result of heavy medication before he underwent an operation. The incident may have become magnified in his mind and increased in significance as he related it to others, including Hoffman. Why was it so important to tell the vision? The reading of the Qur'an immediately lent the experience 'the ring of truth'. A widespread belief maintains that the appearance of the Qur'an in a dream or vision testifies to its truth as divine communication. The timing of the event was also critical, as it occurred on a Thursday night, a time to visit the graves of the saintly deceased when they might be expected to be present for those who were spiritually prepared to meet them. The light, reported as 'stronger than the sun', is frequently associated in visions with the arrival of figures of great importance. 'Izz identified the people 'wearing surgical clothes' as all members of the Prophet's family, for whom Egyptian Sufis exhibit deep love and devotion. The old man at their head was said to be the Prophet Muhammad's grandson, Husayn, while the surgeon was Husayn's son, 'Ali Zayn al-'Abidin. Acceptance of the narrative as being one of a true vision was evidently valuable in asserting 'Izz's status because to be granted such a vision was an important sign of his purity of heart and potential for saintliness. This contemporary example shows the very great difficulty of establishing the reliability of these narratives. Consequently, the assumption in this book is that accounts of pre-modern, and modern, Muslims' dreams and visions may be invented, relayed in accordance with the conventions of the society or retold sincerely by those whose memories are not always reliable or who may be affected by the influences of prolonged fasting, illness or medication. They may also be genuine and trustworthy, but that will be beyond our means to confirm. Hence we will not be as negative as the expert on Byzantine dreams who asserted that there was 'no single trustworthy dream-narrative anywhere in the history of that whole culture', but we will merely point to the possibilities that exist in relation to tales of a visionary nature and observe that it is indeed hard to be 'entirely sure about the truth' of any given narrative. Our investigation, therefore, begins with this word of caution.

CHAPTER 1

SEEING GODS AND ANGELS BEFORE THE RISE OF ISLAM

Many of the Muslims' ideas about dreaming and visionary experience derived from the peoples and cultures of the pre-Islamic Near Eastern and Mediterranean regions, although the channels through which they received these ideas have, in most cases, been lost. Only occasionally, for example in the reception of Artemidorus' famous dream manual, is it possible to identify the route by which a particular idea reached the scholars of the medieval Islamic world.[1] This chapter looks selectively at some features of the ancient traditions relating to dreams, including their methods of describing and analysing them, whether in literary narratives or manuals for deciphering dream images. It does not presume to be comprehensive, but considers those characteristics that appear to have been absorbed into the broader dream culture and are often shared by Jews, Christians and Muslims. Records of the waking vision are noted with reference to the experiences of the early Christians before the chapter concludes with some comments on Muslims' adaptation of the pre-Islamic beliefs and practices.

Dreaming in the Ancient Near East

A Symbolic Dream Tale from Mesopotamia

Dream texts from Mesopotamia provide some of the most important and extensive material on dreaming in the region, but they have proved notoriously hard to classify.[2] They include a range of literary and historical accounts as well as others of an oracular or ritual nature. Some texts have clear meanings and need no interpretation, whereas some contain 'enigmatic visual images that require an interpreter upon awakening' and are commonly described as symbolic dreams.[3] Still other dreams may contain symbolism that is sufficiently obvious not to require specialised interpretative skill or may consist of a clear message with occasional symbolic elements. It is not clear that the Mesopotamians made strict distinctions between dreams of a symbolic and non-symbolic variety,[4] but they would bequeath a variety of dream forms to successive peoples in the Near East.

Acknowledging the complexity of the situation, we will first examine the example of a famous literary narrative of a symbolic dream from southern Mesopotamia. The oldest extant version of the dream of Dumuzi has been dated to around 1800–1700 BCE, although it is likely to originate from even older versions.[5] The dream narrative forms a section in a cycle of mythic accounts concerning Dumuzi, whose name appears in the list of kings of the city of Uruk in ancient Sumer and is thought to have lived in the third millennium BCE. Dumuzi is depicted in the myth as a god-king and shepherd who falls foul of Inana, goddess of sexual love and fertility, the Queen of Heaven (known in Akkadian as Ishtar). A cycle of stories tell of Inana's journey to the Underworld, from which she is permitted to escape on condition that another will take her place. Her lovers, the kings of the cities of Sumer, go into mourning for Inana during her absence in the Underworld. However, Dumuzi does not conform. Instead of mourning, he enrages the goddess by engaging in drunken partying. Inana orders demons to seize Dumuzi so that he will be the one to take her place in the Underworld. Before the demons come to carry him off, Dumuzi lies down in a drunken state to sleep in his sheepfold, but he wakes terrified from a dream. He relates the dream to his sister:

> A dream, my sister! A dream! In my dream rushes were rising up for me, rushes kept growing for me; a single reed was shaking its head at me; twin reeds – one was being separated

from me. Tall trees in the forest were rising up together over me. Water was poured over my holy coals for me, the cover of my holy churn was removed, my holy drinking cup was torn down from the peg where it hung, my shepherd's stick disappeared from me. An owl (?) took a lamb from the sheep house, a falcon caught a sparrow on the reed fence, my male goats were dragging their dark beards in the dust for me, my rams were scratching the earth with their thick legs for me. The churns were lying on their sides, no milk was being poured, the drinking cups were lying on their sides, Dumuzid [Dumuzi] was dead, the sheepfold was haunted.[6]

There is a sense of tension building in Dumuzi's description of his dream with the piling up of symbolic image after image presaging his terrible fate. The symbolism is largely related to the natural environment and an agricultural lifestyle, involving plants, animals and birds, their movements and interactions with one another and with the life of the shepherd.

Dumuzi calls on his sister to interpret the evil dream and her response is noteworthy. She repeats that it is 'not favourable' and asks her brother to tell her no more of it.[7] Her reaction heralds an attitude that will become deeply embedded in Middle Eastern society; it is better not to speak of terrifying night visions. In Mesopotamia the common outlook on such evil dreams was that they were either sent by a deity as a punishment for the dreamer's sins or provoked by the dreamer's enemies, who felt more able to attack a dreamer who had lost divine protection.[8] In Dumuzi's case, he was defenceless against the wrath of the goddess Inana. His sister, however, does offer an interpretation of the nightmare, which is remarkable because many later interpreters would not wish to emulate her example. She deciphers each symbolic image in turn, a practice that has parallels in much later periods when interpreting symbolic dreams. For instance, she predicts that the male goats 'dragging their dark beards in the dust' signify that her own 'hair will whirl around in the air like a hurricane' in mourning for her brother, while the rams 'scratching the earth with their thick legs' show that she will tear her cheeks with her fingernails for him 'as if with a boxwood needle'.[9] Some meanings are obvious, while others are obscure, but all the symbols herald death and destruction, an evil fate for Dumuzi.

In Mesopotamian literature these types of dreams were regarded as 'symbolic messages sent by a god and understood intuitively by the dreamer or a dream-interpreter'.[10] Sudden awakening from a dream, as in the case of Dumuzi, would be taken as a sign of the divine origin of a dream. Those who possessed intuitive knowledge of the meanings of dreams might be thought to contain an element of the divine, as in the case of Dumuzi's sister, her brother being regarded as a god-king. Alternatively, they could be those with priestly links to deities as well as other natural ecstatics or seers. Females appear prominent in the role of dream interpreters, but it is not clear whether gender was a significant factor in predisposing someone to develop an intuitive ability.

Biblical Records of Symbolic Dreams

To what extent were influences from Mesopotamia absorbed into the Old Testament narratives of symbolic dreams? Notable symbolic dreams are recorded with reference to Joseph as both dreamer and interpreter of dreams in Genesis 37 and 40–1 and striking narratives of such dreams are also included in the Aramaic chapters of Daniel, 2, 4 and 7. Central to these accounts is the message that both the righteous and the wicked may receive veridical dream communication from God, but it is the Israelites who are enabled by God to understand the divine messages.[11] Notably, the servants of the Lord, Joseph and Daniel, are sent with the true interpretation of enigmatic dreams. Both the Pharaoh and Nebuchadnezzar wake from their dreams in an anxious, troubled state, which has led to the suggestion that this is an indication of 'contemporary interpretative practices, such as those evident in Mesopotamia'.[12] The interpretation of the dream acts in a way similar to exorcism so as to release the dreamer from the powerful and evil hold of the uninterpreted dream.

The Genesis accounts of symbolic dreams may or may not bear the marks of Mesopotamian influence, but it is of interest to note certain shared views observable from biblical accounts and Mesopotamian epic. All the narratives support a belief in symbolic dreams as messages sent by a deity to a variety of human dreamers, including those with an element of the divine in them or a special relationship to the deity. All such dreams can be interpreted by those who receive divine guidance, the gift of intuitive insight into the true meanings of dreams. In the Mesopotamian context, female interpreters of this type are present, although inspired dream knowledge may not be an exclusively female prerogative because males also interpret. In Israel males are the inspired interpreters. In all cases, the symbolic dream narratives suggest the superiority of intuitive, divinely guided interpretations over deductive human systems of divination based on the following of inherited technical knowledge. However, the technically trained, if uninspired, forms of dream interpretation were also highly popular over thousands of years. Information on these deductive systems in the ancient Near East has been most fully preserved from Egypt and Mesopotamia.

Guides to Symbolic Dreams in Egypt and Mesopotamia

In Egypt the earliest references to dreams occur in a series of texts described as 'Letters to the Dead' and dating mainly from the time of political division known as the First Intermediate Period (*c.*2150–2055 BCE).[13] The letters were placed in the tombs, usually in order for living relatives and friends to make requests that the dead offer their help; they include reference to the desire to see the dead in a dream. It is noteworthy that the ancient Egyptians speak of 'seeing in a dream' rather than referring to 'dreaming'.[14]

The only work on dream interpretation surviving from Egypt before the Greco-Roman period is thought likely to date from the reign of Ramesses II (1279–1213 BCE), possibly from around 1279–1257.[15] Only 11 pages of the papyrus are preserved in a reasonable condition and they include a collection of dream omens, in which there is an attempt to divide humanity into two broad categories of dreamers: those who have good dreams and those who have nightmares. Those having good dreams are identified as the followers of the god Horus, but, unfortunately, the description of them is missing from the text. Those who experience nightmares are said to be the followers of his adversary Seth, god of disorder, and their characteristics include red hair, bad manners, aggression and rowdy drunken behaviour.

Each dream omen in the Egyptian papyrus opens with the words, 'If a man sees himself in a dream'. However, the dreams are then divided into a set of 143 good dreams of the Followers of Horus and 91 bad dreams of the Followers of Seth. There is no obvious organisation by topic. An example of a good dream reads: 'Sitting in an orchard in the sun: good: it means pleasure.' A case of a bad dream reads: 'Drinking warm beer: bad: it means suffering will come upon him.'[16] The list of bad dreams is followed by advice on a purification ritual to rid the dreamer of their evil effects.

Within the ancient Near Eastern region the arts of dream divination were at their most technically accomplished in Mesopotamia, and it is the Mesopotamian system that appears to have had the greatest long-term influence in the area. Foretelling the future through dreams formed just a small part of an extensive system of divination that comprised many different methods of foreknowing, including the observation of natural phenomena, such as unusual animal births, the movement of birds and insects and the configurations of the stars. The divination discussed earlier in the chapter, with reference to the symbolic dream narratives of Mesopotamia and Israel, may be classed as 'natural' or 'inspired', since it depends on natural abilities to understand divine messages. However, in Mesopotamia, as in Egypt, trained practitioners were also considered as able to comprehend certain divine communications through the use of deductive methods. Consequently, they could be consulted on the meanings of dreams, among other phenomena, in the hope that a dream might contain a propitious omen and that the evil consequences of nightmares might be averted.

The earliest written tradition of deductive divination of dreams from Mesopotamia has been dated to the Old Babylonian period from around 1800–1700 BCE. Perhaps the earliest example of this type of technical interpretation occurs with reference to a nightmare: 'If a man while he sleeps [dreams that] the town falls again and again upon him and he groans and no one hears him', then the

Seeing Gods and Angels before the Rise of Islam 15

interpretation is a positive one that protective spirits are attached to his body. However, if he groans and someone hears him, there is a demon attached to his body.[17] Dream omens such as these were apparently copied for hundreds of years before being gathered into a more organised form, notably in the famous Assyrian Dream Book of the seventh century BCE. The scribal practice in Mesopotamia demanded that each dream omen be laid out on a separate line, if necessary continuing on a second indented line of Akkadian cuneiform text. The predictions opened with an 'if'-clause, following the same pattern as the nightmare omen above and similar to that of the Egyptian predictions. However, unlike the Egyptian omens, those in the Assyrian Dream Book are organised by topics, for instance a topic on going to a series of places. This group first outlines the effects on the dreamer of going to various cities and regions, then to the houses of different categories of people (parents, a gardener, tavern-keeper, sailor or ploughman) and, finally, countryside locations such as an orchard, vegetable garden or sheepfold.[18]

Dreams of all classes of people may be considered meaningful, but the same dream may result in different outcomes according to the status of the dreamer. Similarly, the meaning may vary due to variations in the description of the symbolic image seen in the dream. For example, the colour of an object may affect the interpretation. A black dog and a white dog will have different meanings. The behaviour of the image will also impact the significance; if ants are seen heading north, it will not mean the same as if they were heading south.[19] The origin of the image can also affect the interpretation; water from a river or well indicates wealth, whereas water from a ditch is a sign of quarrels. If the dreamer is given water from a canal, 'the storm-god will flood his harvest'.[20] However, some symbolism is more consistent. The right side is invariably associated with being good or fortunate, while the left side is said to be bad or unfortunate, and it does not matter what other variables are present.[21]

Near Eastern Epiphany Dreams

Egyptian and Mesopotamian guides to dreams concern the dreams received by people from a variety of classes. However, epiphanies in which the dreamer saw and/or heard deities or their messengers were usually the preserve of those in authority. The dreamer is normally described as falling deeply asleep and then hearing a message delivered in a clear manner by a divine figure or a representative of the deity, who stood at the dreamer's head. The dream's message was readily understood by the dreamer and required no interpretation. The auditory element was of key importance. There might or might not be a description of the speaker's appearance. In the dream records of the Hebrew Bible it was common for only a memory of the speaker's voice to be recorded.

However, at times there was a visual element even in the biblical accounts, a notable case being that of Jacob's dream at Bethel, recorded in Genesis 28. On this occasion Jacob famously saw angels ascending and descending a ladder between earth and heaven and heard God addressing him directly: 'I am the Lord, God of your father Abraham and the God of Isaac.'[22] Nevertheless, the most vivid accounts of dream visions accompanying spoken messages have survived in the reports of theophanies from Mesopotamia. A striking example is that of an Assyrian priest, who dreamt of the goddess Ishtar entering his room, 'quivers hanging at her right and left, holding the bow in her (one) hand, the sharp sword drawn (ready) for battle'.[23] Other accounts described a figure of amazing size and beauty, towering over the dreamer.[24] On some occasions the speaker informed the dreamer of divine favour, perhaps announcing a forthcoming victory or acquisition of power; sometimes the deity or messenger entered into a dialogue with the dreamer, in which case the dreamer was expected to respond in a spirit of submission and obedience. Across the ancient Near East the usual view was that epiphany dreams were the prerogative of males of high status, such as kings, priests and leading figures in the community. People of lesser ranks were rarely reported as witnessing epiphanies.

The usual practice was to report all the circumstances of a visionary event, including when and where it took place. Most dreams naturally occur at night, so it is often clearly stated that the dreamer has gone to bed and is sleeping. It may also be noted that the dreamer wakes, startles and realises that it is a dream, the noted mark of a true dream from a divine source, as apparent in Dumuzi's nightmare.

A famous occasion of daytime dreaming is described in the Stela of the Sphinx at Gizeh, telling of a dream of Pharaoh Thutmose IV (c.1425–1417 BCE), who fell asleep at midday in the shadow of the Sphinx.[25] The statue of the sun god Ra-Harakhty was said to have addressed him, assuring him that he would rule over the whole of Egypt:

> Thou shalt wear the southern crown and the northern crown on the throne of Geb, the crown prince (of the gods). Thine is the land in its length and its breadth, that which the Eye of the All-Lord illumines.[26]

Divine support for a king's right to rule and prediction of his future success were frequent themes in message dreams. In the case of Thutmose IV, as the son of a pharaoh's minor wife, dream news of this type was no doubt valuable in promoting his position. The message from a god or goddess could serve as a powerful tool of propaganda in a situation in which leaders needed such divine communication, and 'the complete withholding from a king of dream messages could signify little but divine disapproval'.[27]

Dreams and Visions in Classical Antiquity

In the early Greek world those favoured by the gods expected to see visions of deities in their waking life. Gods are described as visible in battles standing beside humans. In the Homeric epics of the *Iliad* and the *Odyssey* the worlds inhabited by humans and deities are very close and their paths intersect. Half-divine heroes still walk the earth; so the heroic warrior Achilles can see his mother, the goddess Thetis, even if lesser mortals cannot. After his arrival home in Ithaca from the Trojan War, Odysseus, despite being fully human, can see the goddess Athena as she guides him with her lamp past the sleeping suitors, who had come to woo his wife Penelope during the many years of his absence.[28] For Homer the visits of the deities are often regarded as propitious, giving support in times of greatest need. However, they are also to be feared and hence the divine presence, whether seen or heard or even scented, may lead to anxious efforts to propitiate the visiting god or goddess. There are reports of deities appearing in majestic human forms and accounts of mortals being anxious not to anger the divine being who appears in a likeness that is not immediately recognised.

The earliest Greek descriptions of dreams are also recorded from the time of Homer. Uncertainty about the truth-telling qualities of the dream emerges from the very earliest account of a dream told in the *Iliad*, when Zeus is described as sending 'dire Dream' to the Greek leader Agamemnon in order to deceive him into thinking that his forces will easily seize Troy. The dream figure is said to take the form of Nestor, the elder held in highest regard among the Greek warriors, and he stands at the head of Agamemnon to deliver his message in the manner of an ancient Near Eastern epiphany.[29] Even though Homer relates this dream as being sent by the king of the Olympian gods, its truth is not guaranteed. Its audience shows some reluctance to accept it and does so only because it is the dream of Agamemnon as a man of great authority. The deceptive nature of the god-sent dream heralds the development of a cautious attitude towards dreams in Greek culture.

Homeric epic, and much later classical literature involving dreams, would remain unknown to medieval Muslims, although some ideas might be absorbed indirectly as they infiltrated later classical culture. As for Greek philosophical thought on the subject of dreams, it had a more obvious influence on Muslim thinkers, who claimed a particularly high regard for Aristotle. This admiration is surprising, since Aristotle did not accept the popular Greek view that dreams could be sent by the gods. Instead, he looked for scientific explanations of the occurrence of true predictive dreams. He also devoted relatively little attention to the art of dream interpretation, despite admitting its use in diagnosing illness.[30] However, it was Artemidorus, the most famous professional representative of dream interpretation in late antiquity, who would have the greatest practical impact on dream interpretation in the world of Islam.

Artemidorus and His Interpretation of Symbolic Dreams

Despite his description of himself as being from his mother's town of Daldis, Artemidorus was a resident of the great city of Ephesus in Asia Minor.[31] It was there that he authored the one handbook of dream interpretation known to have survived from the Greco-Roman world, his *Oneirocritica*, produced at some point around the mid-second century CE. He was born into an age of prosperity and culture when the Roman Empire had reached a peak of expansion and his contemporaries included the physician Galen and astronomer Ptolemy, both of whose ideas were to have a significant influence on the medieval Islamic world. Artemidorus appears to have been highly educated, possibly quite wealthy, and well-travelled in his search for accounts of dreams and their interpretation in Greece and its many islands as well as in Italy and his home region of present-day western Turkey. He visited religious festivals and games, listening to retellings of dreams by athletes and spectators, worshippers and market-place dream interpreters. Robin Lane Fox has noted the wide social range of those whose dreams Artemidorus recorded: 'a well-to-do woman in Italy who dreamed she was riding an elephant, members of the upper classes in the Greek cities, orators, Roman knights, a tax collector, convicts and criminals, the poor, the sick and the slaves'.[32]

Artemidorus divided his work on dreams into five books. The first three of these he dedicated to Cassius Maximus, possibly a certain Maximus of Tyre known for his rhetorical writing. The last two books were for the use of his son, also called Artemidorus, and intended to assist him in his own work as a professional interpreter of dreams. Books One and Two predict the fortunes of the human being from the cradle to the grave. Artemidorus makes a clear decision to place humans at the heart of his interpretation. He openly declares: 'We shall not begin, as early writers did, with the gods, even if we strike some people as being irreverent but, observing the natural sequence of events, we shall begin first with birth.'[33] The relationship of humans to their gods is treated later as they become involved in worship as a part of adult life and along with other public roles in the community. The final images are of death. Books Three and Four both act as supplements, while Book Five is a record of 95 dreams that are alleged to have come true.

It would be easy to assume that Artemidorus was somewhat irreverent in his attitude to the gods, but, if he was, he exercised caution in his public statements. He accepts the division of dreams into the two fundamental types of the *oneiros*, thought to be predictive of future events, and the *enhypnion*, merely reflecting the dreamer's current state. His interest is solely in the *oneiros*, which 'signifies good or bad things that will occur in the future'.[34] These 'good or bad things' can be seen in a literal form, requiring no interpretation, or in an allegorical form where the dream images mask the true meaning and have to be deciphered. Artemidorus is concerned with the allegorical form of the true dream in the same way as the unknown Egyptian and Mesopotamian compilers of dream guides, but with a greater degree of subtlety. However, he is reserved as to the causes of the alleged true dream:

> Those dreams [...] which visit people who are not anxious about anything and which foretell some future good or misfortune are called god-sent. I do not, like Aristotle, inquire as to whether the cause of our dreaming is outside of us and comes from the gods or whether it is motivated by something within, which disposes the soul in a certain way and causes a natural event to happen to it. Rather, I use the word in the same way that we customarily call all unforeseen things god-sent.[35]

His tone suggests a practical outlook in his efforts to predict human fortunes and a readiness to suspend judgement as to the ultimate cause of dreaming.

Artemidorus encourages careful observation of the individual dreamer, insisting on the importance of knowing the dreamer's occupation and social status, and considers it important to know about the dreamer's state of mind when experiencing the dream. Was the dreamer happy or unhappy? If s/he was happy, then the good things seen in the dream are more likely to come true and, if unhappy, then bad fortune is more probable. However, Artemidorus is only interested in the dreamer's psychological state in so far as it affects the outcome of the dream. He also believes it necessary to know not only about individual characteristics, but also about the customs of particular communities. Among several examples he observes that, while people usually eat fish, the Syrians do not because they are worshippers of Astarte.[36] The implication is that a dream of eating fish may signify something different for a Syrian dreamer than for other people having the same dream.

As with earlier and later keys to dreams, Artemidorus is principally concerned with the dreams of ordinary men and women. For the most part, he classifies these as 'personal' dreams. However, he remarks that they may not only concern the dreamer, but may also affect the lives of others. In his experience people tend to dream about matters that they have some reason to think about in their waking lives. Consequently, although private individuals could have dreams of concern for the future public life of their city, it is more likely that such dreams will occur to a number of citizens when some great event is about to happen and involve them all. Nevertheless, they will not all tell of their dream in public. In this case, he considers the dream to be a dream of 'the people', who, in their collective capacity, become just as important as rulers and generals. Artemidorus, despite his great concern in general with social status, shows himself here as perhaps less of a snob than he may at times appear.[37] Admittedly, he does not expect a private citizen who is not normally concerned with affairs of state to be the only person to have a dream of great public import, but a single individual seeing such a dream should be 'one of the generals or a man who held some other office, or a priest, or a prophet of the city'.[38] However, there seems to be no particular reason to view Artemidorus as snobbish in making these statements. He owes much to his own practical experience in his society and also to the views of his predecessors in dream interpretation and to their judgements as to the kinds of people most likely to receive true dreams of public consequence; they include priests and prophets as well as those in high office. He appears just as interested in recording the dreams of women and of slaves as recording those of the rulers and wealthy. Artemidorus also mentions briefly the existence of 'cosmic' dreams in addition to the 'personal' and 'public' ones, noting that they predict great events in the cosmos, such as total eclipses of the sun and moon and major disturbances of the earth and sea (presumably as in earthquakes and tsunamis).[39] However, he has little more to say about them at this point and does not indicate whether 'cosmic' dreams are the preserve of any particular groups of people.

Artemidorus appears as a dedicated, even obsessive, field researcher. Yet not all contemporary scholars have been impressed with the quality of his work. William V. Harris has observed that he was 'a man of monumental gullibility (whose book would have aroused the scorn of many other ancients)'.[40] Some of the dreams described by Artemidorus are almost as far-fetched as those contained in the Egyptian Book of the Dead or the Assyrian Dream Book, but did the Greek interpreter necessarily always believe his informants? Harris is concerned with detecting what Greeks and Romans may actually have experienced in their dreams. Consequently, the presence of some highly improbable dreams in Artemidorus' descriptions is problematic. By contrast, Patricia Cox Miller has been less concerned with the lived reality of dreaming and more admiring of Artemidorus' skill in his interpretative strategy of imposing meaning on dream images by use of 'such devices as analogy, puns and wordplays, mythic associations, and numerological equivalents of alphabetic letters'.[41] Among the more incredible dreams described by Artemidorus are those in which dreamers see themselves with the head of a variety of creatures, including a lion, elephant, dog, horse and, finally, a bird. After looking for a connection between the bird and the dreamer, Artemidorus interprets the dream of having the head of a bird as signifying leaving one's homeland because birds fly or because the fledglings leave their parents.[42] It is typical of his method that he looks for such a point of similarity between the dream image and the dream's meaning even in the most unlikely situations, and sometimes with a great deal of mental agility. However, he does not claim that he actually knew anyone who had such a dream or that it was particularly likely.

Jewish Dream Interpretation in the Babylonian Talmud

The Jews of late antiquity had acquired a certain reputation as interpreters of symbolic dreams and may have been some of the experts consulted by Artemidorus.[43] While dream interpretation features elsewhere in Talmudic literature, notably in a long passage of the Palestinian Talmud, the largest rabbinic text on the subject is contained in about three folio pages of the Babylonian Talmud, *Berakhot* 55a–57b.[44] It is this text that may have formed a separate dream book before being incorporated in the Talmud, and that bears some comparison with Artemidorus' *Oneirocritica*. However, while Artemidorus' work is that of a single author and professional dream interpreter, the rabbinic dream book appears to be of composite authorship, but representing the views of rabbis often apparently seeking to assert their position in opposition to professional dream interpreters. It has been suggested that it contains a 'chorus of voices' and represents the ideas of 'informants of at least three centuries (first century CE to fourth century CE), two countries (Palestine and Babylonia), and several cultural environments (late Hellenistic, Roman, Persian, Byzantine'.[45] This could account for a greater diversity of approach than in the *Oneirocritica*, despite some similarities being observed in the principles of interpretation as well as in the content of specific dream predictions. For example, both Artemidorus and the rabbis understand a raven seen in a dream as representing an adulterer. For Artemidorus it can also signify a thief.[46] It is unclear whether any direct borrowing took place, but more likely that the parallels can be explained by a shared cultural milieu, in which a variety of informants contributed to each work from their inherited stock of experience.

While these parallels are interesting, differences are also of interest. Although the rabbis absorbed much ancient dream knowledge of the Near Eastern region and its environs, they also sought to record interpretations of dream images likely to be 'seen' by Jews. Hence it is not surprising that they included their views on dreams of the Torah and of biblical personalities such as David and Solomon. The rabbis also attempted to bring an ancient system of interpretation into line with their religious beliefs by evaluating certain dreams with reference to scripture. Ancient pagan interpretations would be given support by citing biblical verses that showed their truth in a way acceptable to religious Jews.[47]

A further idea that appears to originate in rabbinic dream theory is that the outcome of a dream is dependent on the interpretation and is somehow activated by the dream interpreter. An important principle is that 'a dream that is not interpreted is like a letter that is not read'.[48] If it is not interpreted at all, a dream cannot be predictive. Therefore, interpretation is extremely important, but it must be the best possible interpretation because a badly interpreted dream can have undesirable consequences. The rabbis relate anecdotes of negative interpretations even leading to death. Their message is essentially that dream interpretation is too dangerous a skill to be left to the unqualified or unscrupulous and that it is best in their own hands and not in those belonging to the guild of professional dream interpreters. Acknowledging the idea that a true dream is closely linked to revelation and can function as a sixtieth part of prophecy, they seem to have realised the need to control the great power that could be exercised through expounding the prophetic dream.

Early Christian Visionaries

Early Christians shared the rabbis' recognition of the potential power of dream interpreters and were anxious about their disruptive influence on believers. However, instead of trying to solve the problem by producing a Christian version of the *Oneirocritica* or the Talmudic dream book, the Church took action against the interpreters by excluding them from Christian baptism.[49] For the first three centuries of Christianity its followers were in a relatively marginal position in the Roman Empire, but, with the rise to power of the Emperor Constantine (306–37), laws were instituted against the practice of all forms of divination. Constantius II (337–61) insisted that the interpretation of dreams was included 'among the forbidden practices'.[50] Although it was acknowledged that some dreams came from God, especially those experienced by

SEEING GODS AND ANGELS BEFORE THE RISE OF ISLAM   25

monks, nuns and saintly persons, there was also a fear that many other dreams, perhaps most dreams, came from the devil. Where the Stoics had divided dreams according to their origin (from gods, demons or the soul), Tertullian (d. *c*.220) adapted this division to bring it in line with Christian beliefs and claim that dreams originated either with God or the devil or the soul (*a deo, a daemonio, ab anima*).[51] However, Guy Stroumsa has noted that it is often not possible to distinguish clearly between early Christian reports of dreams and reports of waking visions. He has observed that 'waking visions, obtained in a state of ecstasy, were reported in the same terms as dreams'.[52]

Despite, and perhaps because of, the severe anxieties of many early Christians about the nature of their sleeping and waking visions, they came to focus on the importance of constant prayer and fasting to improve the spiritual state for the reception of visionary experiences. These were practices long predating Christian tradition in preparation for seeing and hearing the divine, but they received renewed emphasis. Among the best known of the early Christian visionaries was a slave called Hermas, who recorded his extraordinary waking or sleeping epiphanies at Cumae in Italy of the late first to mid-second centuries.[53] His account is known as 'The Shepherd' and relates a series of visionary encounters in which he speaks of meeting with angels and with the Church in the form of an elderly lady because, as an angel informs Hermas, she has existed from the beginning of Creation. At times Hermas professes to be terrified by the messages given him by the Church, but also encouraged by the prospect of God's awaited rule. In a later vision he admits to being unable to recall the Church's teaching revealed to him and asks for it in a book so that he can copy it; the idea of the heavenly book confirming the vision was long established in Jewish and other religious beliefs of the Mediterranean region.[54] However, it was only after a period spent in fasting and prayer that Hermas claimed to have understood the message. He was to urge his fellow Christians to repent and assure them that their sins would be forgiven if they repented sincerely as soon as they received the message. There would be no forgiveness for those who repented at a later date after Hermas published his vision. He was also to admonish his own family, especially his wife, who was to be disciplined for 'her lying tongue', and was told that he was to live with her as with a sister without sexual relations.[55] Features of Hermas' visions have been likened to those of Jewish apocalyptic texts: angels, a heavenly book, instructions to fast and the feeling of terror in encountering the supernatural.[56]

Angels played a prominent role in early Christian dreams and visions, whether as beautiful beings who guided visionaries and explained the hidden truth or as terrifying implementers of punishment. Although they had concerns about the risks of being deceived by the devil, Christian writers also appreciated the value of recording visionary encounters. Seeing angels after a period of prayer and fasting was regarded as a sign of purity and could confer status and enhance the authority of Church leaders and their institutions. At times they could help to explain conversions or perhaps encourage them. They often served to support efforts at moral instruction of the community. One example related by Jerome (d. 420) concerns a certain Praetextata, 'who was threatened by an angel for having had the temerity to give her niece a stylish coiffure – the punishment was paralysis of the hands, shortly followed by death'.[57]

Ways of Foreknowing in Pre-Islamic Arabia

As in ancient Mesopotamia, the art of dream interpretation in pre-Islamic Arabia constituted a small part of an extensive system of divination and was intimately linked with other methods for foretelling the future. Yet, in his classic work on Arab divination, Toufic Fahd has observed that what little is known about interpretative practice from this period is both suspect and fragmentary.[58] We are left with occasional dream narratives composed by much later Muslim authors and posing an obvious problem of credibility. Fahd notes a few examples, including that of an Arab tribal leader who was accompanied on his raiding expeditions by a diviner; this diviner made predictions based on observing the movement of birds, but also acted as an interpreter of dreams.[59]

A further case concerns Rabi'a b. Nasr, a king of Yemen, who awoke terrified from a dream in a manner familiar in the ancient Near East. He had seen in his dream black men advancing from an unknown land and occupying the coastal district of his country, overwhelming its chiefs. His reaction was to consult a number of diviners: all the *kahins* (priests whose role involved the performance of sacrifices, guardianship of the sanctuary and a divinatory function), sorcerers, interpreters of omens and astrologers. They interpreted the king's dream as foretelling the occupation of Yemen from Abyssinia (Ethiopia), its liberation by Sayf b. Dhi Yazan with Persian assistance and, finally, the coming of an Arab prophet, whose rule would have no end.[60] Fahd has reasonably concluded that the dream report is a forgery. It certainly lacks 'the ring of truth' and seems very unlikely to be anything other than propaganda. The list of diviners consulted by the king may be intended to give the impression of a primitive time before the coming of Islam, after which dream interpretation became a more specialised and respected religious science on a higher level than other efforts at foreknowing.

The Ancient Legacy to the World of Islam

The legacy of the ancient Near East remains evident in the dream narratives and manuals of dream interpretation produced by Muslim writers over many centuries. They continue to record the 'seeing' of events in dreams in the same manner as the ancient Egyptians of 2000 BCE. The dream reports of Muslims contain the same variety of symbolic and non-symbolic elements as those found in ancient Mesopotamia. There are accounts full of enigmatic images, which require interpretation, even if their symbolism is not as elaborate as that of Dumuzi's terrifying dream. There are also texts that consist of clear messages, but include the occasional enigmatic image; such messages may be easily deciphered or they may be more obscure. Reports may present dreams as being understood intuitively by someone able to comprehend divine messages, notably Muhammad as God's messenger. Mystics may also be regarded as having this special insight, but on a lesser and more vulnerable level. Inspired interpreters are usually, but not exclusively, male.

The basic patterns for manuals of deductive dream interpretation appear to retain a number of similarities through the millennia. The authors of Muslim dream manuals use the same form of omen text as the ancient Egyptians and Babylonians, frequently framed along the lines, 'If a man sees in a dream...', then such-and-such will happen. As in Pharaonic Egypt, the good are expected to be more likely to receive good dreams. As in Mesopotamia, the outcome of the dream is recognised as varying according to the dreamer's status and also as a result of variations in the nature of the image. Not all dreams of water have the same significance. The right side continues to be viewed as fortunate and the left as unfortunate. The meanings of particular images may be lost or changed, the routes by which they have reached the Muslim writers may be unknown, but these basic features testify to the essentially conservative qualities of dream interpretation in the region.

The epiphany dream or vision was also to survive into the Islamic era. The focus on the auditory element continued, although the dream was often accompanied by a visual aspect. Records of dreams received by males of high status within the community were more frequent than records of females' dreams. However, it was widely recognised that women could have such dreams and, rarely, it seems that a woman might dream on behalf of a man. Occasionally, Muslim writers were more restrictive in their view as to who might receive epiphanies; the philosopher Ibn Sina (Avicenna) (d. 1037) adhered most closely to the ancient Near Eastern position, stating that kings and sages were the most favoured in this respect.[61] Certainly it was not unusual for dream messages to support rulers in need in a manner not much different to that experienced by Pharaoh Thutmose IV in his daytime dream by the Sphinx. However, there were obviously aspects of the epiphanies that would change under Islamic influence. The figure who delivered the message could no longer be one of the old deities or their messengers, but was replaced by the Prophet

Muhammad, other respected Muslim figures or angels. God's voice was sometimes heard, rarely and controversially accompanied by a visual image. Gone also were the common instructions in the old messages that a temple should be built or restored for a particular deity and in their place were others that a mosque or tomb-shrine should be erected at a designated site.

The epiphany dream, of alleged divine origin, whether sincere or deceptive, would have a long history, continuing through to late Greco-Roman antiquity and beyond into medieval Europe and the Muslim world. Its decline in Europe appears gradual from the fourteenth to eighteenth centuries, its death perhaps occurring with the onset of secularisation. As William V. Harris has observed:

> The epiphany dream can only have wide currency in a world in which it is taken for granted both that divine power takes a strong interest in charismatic individual humans, and that such a human is to be believed when he or she makes an unsupported claim about his/her inner experience.[62]

Such beliefs would persist more strongly in Muslim lands than in Europe and be contested at a later date (from the second half of the nineteenth century onwards). Despite contestation, they would continue to dominate in many areas into the twenty-first century.

Medieval Muslim authors were unacquainted with Homeric epic and would probably have been unimpressed by it, but because of the noted respect for Homer and his pervading influence among later Greeks they were the heirs to some of its key ideas about visionary contact with the divine. Thus Muslims would also come to fear the possibility that a dream figure might not be a genuine saint or prophet or other esteemed person and might bring a message to mislead the dreamer. The messenger would no longer be sent by Olympian Zeus; instead Satan would take over the role of the old deities in sending humans astray through false dream messengers and messages.

Muslim philosophers and dream interpreters would surely have been surprised and dismayed by Aristotle's rejection of the divine origin of apparently veridical dreams, but they remained blissfully unaware of his true opinions and clung to a very different image of Aristotle as a believer in God-sent dreams.[63] No doubt Muslim scholars would also have disagreed with Artemidorus' doubts regarding the cause of true dreams, had they been aware of his views. Nevertheless, his methods were to have a deep impact on their own practice. It is notable that most Muslim interpreters, with the striking exception of the philosopher Ibn Sina, did not follow Artemidorus in the organisation of their guides to dreams, but, like the 'early writers', placed matters relating to the divine at the beginning of their manuals. Nevertheless, they did delight in making creative linkages through wordplay and could appreciate the ingenuity of Artemidorus, while discarding what they could not believe.

When interpreting dreams of the Qur'an, Muslim authors employed some of the same practices utilised by the Jewish authors of the Talmudic dream book, for example with regard to the meanings ascribed to personalities of the Hebrew Bible recognised as prophets in the Islamic tradition. Muslim interpreters would also emulate the rabbinic method by explaining the meanings of dream images with reference to Qur'anic verses in place of biblical verses. The scholars of Islam were to share the same outlook on the potential power unleashed by the interpretation of God-sent dreams, which were understood as constituting a small fraction of prophecy; consequently, they also appreciated the need for the religiously educated scholar to assume the powerful role of one who interprets the divine messages of true dreams, since the outcome of the dream is directly affected by its interpretation and can have fatal results in the hands of the poorly qualified interpreter.

Despite sharing some of the same anxieties, it may be observed that early Muslims took a more positive view of dreams than that recorded among their Christian counterparts. Although Jews, Christians and Muslims all held the opinion that certain dreams were God-sent, Jews and Muslims were generally more inclined than the early Christians to acknowledge the possibility of veridical dreams as a major source of guidance for pious individuals.

While Muslims and Christians feared that dreams might have a devilish origin, the fear appears to have had a less negative impact on perceptions of dreams in the world of Islam. The Muslims inherited the view promoted by Tertullian, dividing dreams according to their origins from three sources: God, Satan and the soul, but attributed this opinion to the Prophet Muhammad. Like the Christians, they also supported the practice of strenuous prayer and fasting to promote the possibility of receiving true dreams. Furthermore, they developed a high regard for the waking vision.

Given the paucity and questionable reliability of sources, it is impossible to know with certainty whether, or to what extent, the earliest Muslim dream interpreters continued practices absorbed from pre-Islamic Arabian tradition. However, it seems credible that the interpretation of dreams had become separated from other forms of divination very early in the Islamic period and was elevated above them due to its close association with prophecy. As both Judaism and Christianity were already active in the Arabian Peninsula immediately prior to the rise of Islam, it is likely that they, rather than the Arab tribal traditions, were the major trajectories through which ancient traditions of dream interpretation were passed on to Muslim oneirocrits. This process was to be accelerated with the establishment of Islam in the lands adjacent to Arabia.

CHAPTER 2

THE PROPHET AS MODEL VISIONARY

The Prophet and the World of the Unseen

Medieval Muslim writers focus on the intrusion of the supernatural into the life of Muhammad as a feature to be treasured; it is a sign of his prophethood and intimately linked with his being chosen by God to convey the final divine words of revelation to humankind in the form of the Qur'an. Dreams and visions play a central role in their accounts as vehicles that connect the Prophet to that unseen, supernatural world known in Arabic as *al-ghayb*. He is regarded by these writers as the model for Muslims of the perfect dreamer and visionary as well as being the ideal, God-guided interpreter of his own and others' dreams. Dreams lie at the very foundations of Islam because Muhammad was related to have received his earliest revelations in dreams for a period of six months before his first great vision of the angel Gabriel commanding him to recite God's word. From that time in around 610 CE he would be the recipient of many dreaming and waking, visual and auditory experiences, in which the medieval authorities claim that he was opened to true perception of God's hidden world. Such a viewpoint is exemplified in the earliest full biography of Muhammad as God's Messenger by Ibn Ishaq (d. 767), as preserved in the revised edition of Ibn Hisham (d. 833).

Ibn Ishaq's narrative is full of stories of supernatural interventions in Muhammad's life and that of his family members and others who came into contact with him. However, for some modern Muslim biographers the irrational aspects of such a life are uncomfortable subject matter and they appear ill at ease in writing of them, preferring instead to concentrate on the account of the morally perfect man and social reformer. Muhammad Husayn Haykal's *The Life of Muhammad*, first published in 1935, is one of the best known of these works, emphasising the rationality of the Prophet and Islam and downplaying anything that is suggestive to him of superstitious, traditional stories.[1] Andrew Rippin aptly observes: 'Because of Haykal's sense of rationality, he sees fewer miracles playing a role in Muhammad's life but puts an emphasis on natural processes to explain some of them. The heavenly journey is taken as psychological for example.'[2]

Critical historians also frequently have problems with this type of material, as it is hard to reconcile with factual evidence. W. Montgomery Watt commented on the tale of a Christian monk who recognised the seal of prophethood between Muhammad's shoulders: 'This is only a story of course. It is based on primitive ideas. It is the kind of story one expects to find among people who look upon all writing as akin to magic.' However, while dismissing the historical reliability of the tale, Watt observes that 'it is significant because it expresses a popular Muslim view of Muhammad. He was a man who had been marked out from his youth, even from before his birth, by supernatural signs and qualities.'[3] More recently Fred Donner has noted of the traditional materials concerning Muhammad that they contain a great deal of 'dubious storytelling'. He notes the difficulties when many sources are not contemporaneous with the period of the Prophet, but are of a much later date, and he adds:

> There is also reason to suspect that some – perhaps many – of the incidents related in these sources are not reliable accounts of things that actually happened but rather are legends created by later generations of Muslims to affirm Muhammad's status as

prophet, to help establish precedents shaping the later Muslim community's ritual, social or legal practices, or simply to fill out poorly known chapters in the life of their founder, about whom, understandably, later Muslims increasingly wished to know everything.[4]

Donner, therefore, discards the traditional accounts of a legendary nature and considers only the more mundane aspects of the Prophet's life according to the classical sources, after which he explores the problems with the sources and the standard version of the biography.

Our concern here is with just those elements that Donner discards and that Watt would have identified as stories based on primitive ideas. More specifically, we are, of course, concerned directly with those narratives that appear to contain information about dreaming and visionary foreknowing. We are not so much interested in establishing the historical truth of these accounts as in seeking to understand their place in the development of thought about dreams and visions among medieval Muslims. In the process we ask to what extent the reports and comments mark a continuation of pre-Islamic thinking and practice or the introduction of new Islamic elements. What purpose might such narratives serve for the Muslim scholarly elite or the wider community? Do they have a central role to play in the promotion of the status of the Prophet Muhammad or in offering continuing guidance after his demise? We begin with the remarkable events surrounding his birth.

Signs Heralding the Prophet's Birth

In the pre-Islamic Near East it was not unusual to look for supernatural signs presaging the arrival of a person of great importance, one of the most famous being the star seen by the Magi in the East at the time of Jesus' birth.[5] Reports of waking and dreaming visions played a prominent role in drawing signs to public attention and Ibn Ishaq contributed to the recording of visions and extraordinary omens before the birth of Muhammad b. 'Abd Allah b. 'Abd al-Muttalib at Mecca in the Hijaz region of western Arabia.

The traditional date of Muhammad's birth is commonly given as 570 CE, 40 years before his call to prophethood. Mecca of this period was a significant trading post, an intermediary point between southern Arabia and Syria, even if the goods traded were not always of an exotic character.[6] It was also home to an important sanctuary for followers of Arab tribal religious traditions: at the heart of this sanctuary lay the Ka'ba, the cube-shaped building that constituted the house of Allah, although other lesser deities were also worshipped at Mecca. As Meccans travelled for trade in the region, it is not surprising that they also had contacts with Jewish and Christian communities in the Arabian Peninsula and the larger communities further afield in the Byzantine Empire. In addition, both Christian-ruled Abyssinia and Zoroastrian-dominated Persia under Sasanian rule had their own interests in Arabia. It is, therefore, to be expected that the visionary traditions of the various pre-Islamic religions of Arabia and the neighbouring regions fed into the accounts of dreams and visions popularly related over the two to three hundred years before they were recorded by Muslim writers in the forms that are extant today.

It remains a matter of conjecture as to the exact time at which the stories contained in Ibn Ishaq's narrative first began to circulate. What we have is a heavily edited early ninth-century version of a narrative from the mid-eighth century, relating purported events of the late sixth century.[7] According to Ibn Ishaq, 'Abd Allah b. 'Abd al-Muttalib was setting out to be married to Amina bint Wahb; his father was accompanying him. As they proceeded on their way, a woman accosted 'Abd Allah, claiming to have seen a light on his forehead. However, after he had consummated the marriage, the same woman saw him, but left him alone because the light had vanished.[8] Although it is not stated explicitly, the implication appears to be that 'Abd Allah had passed on the light to his son at the moment of Muhammad's conception. For many Muslims this light can be interpreted as the Divine Light that passed into the Prophet and thus ensured his immunity from all sin. Muhammad, destined to be God's Messenger, is shown through this narrative to be a pure vehicle for receiving God's guidance and communicating it to humankind, both through the revelation of the Qur'an and through his own God-guided actions and sayings.[9] In an alternative report the woman is described as seeing a 'white spot' between 'Abd Allah's eyes, a marking similar to the white blaze on a horse.[10] Whiteness is associated with goodness and purity, and therefore functions as a further assurance that the Prophet is pure from a pure lineage. The woman is said to have 'seen' the light or white spot, but it is not entirely clear how she saw either of them. The common assumption is that the tale concerns a literal sighting, but it could also be an alleged dream that is being recounted, since dreamers are regularly recorded as 'seeing' their dreams. It could also be a waking vision.

Other remarkable reports tell of the visionary experience of Muhammad's mother, Amina. Ibn Ishaq relates:

> People allege — and God knows best — that Amina bint Wahb, mother of the Messenger of God, used to tell how, when she was pregnant with the Messenger of God, she heard a voice saying to her: 'You are pregnant with the lord of this community. When he falls to earth, say "I seek refuge for him with the One from the evil of all who are envious; then call him Muhammad".'[11]

The report records an auditory experience, but it remains unstated whether Amina was asleep or awake. The voice bears a message that exalts the Prophet's status. Even before birth he is identified as 'the lord of this community'. Given that Ibn Ishaq was writing in Iraq in the mid-eighth century, he would have been living in an environment in which there was still a sizeable Christian population and the report of Amina's dream or vision may be seen as defensive of Islamic doctrine. It contrasts most obviously with Mary's vision of the angel before the birth of Jesus, as described in Luke's Gospel:

> 1:30 But the angel said to her, 'Do not be afraid, Mary; you have found favour with God. 31 You will conceive and give birth to a son, and you are to call him Jesus. 32 He will be great and will be called the Son of the Most High...[12]

The angel and the mysterious voice both give reassurance to Mary and Amina respectively that they are to give birth to sons of great importance and they are instructed as to their names. However, whereas Jesus is identified by the angel as 'the Son of the Most High', Amina is reminded of the absolute oneness of God, with whom she is to seek refuge on behalf of Muhammad. As God is the One, He does not have a son and hence the Christians' belief is rejected with echoes of Qur'an 112:

1 Say, 'He is God the One, 2 God the Eternal. 3 He fathered no one nor was He fathered. 4 No one is comparable to Him.'[13]

Ibn Ishaq then mentions that Amina had a remarkable, visual experience: 'And when she was pregnant with him, she saw a light coming out from her, by which she saw the palaces of Busra in Syria.'[14] The symbolism of the light emanating from the pregnant woman replicates much older accounts, or pictorial depictions, that presage the birth of a great man or, in its earliest occurrence, a god. In ancient Egyptian imagery the sky goddess Nut is portrayed with the sun rising from her womb. This is a literal representation of Nut's giving birth to 'the sun god Re, who passed below her arched body during the daylight hours, was swallowed by her at sunset, and passed through her body at night'.[15] However, the symbol of the sun rising from the pregnant woman continued to be applied to significant births. An important instance of a Roman dream narrative is recorded by Suetonius as having been dreamt by Octavius, father of the Emperor Augustus (31 BCE–14 CE) during the pregnancy of his wife, Atia. According to Suetonius, 'Octavius dreamt that the radiance of the sun rose from the uterus of Atia.'[16] As this brief dream account follows the claim that Augustus was thought to be the son of Apollo, the Greek sun god, the reader is expected to make the connection between Augustus and Apollo and to realise that the dream confirms the claim. Suetonius writes that he has made use of the work of an Egyptian scholar, Asclepiades, who wrote a work comparing various religions.[17] It has been suggested that this narrative was in circulation during the lifetime of Augustus and may have served as propaganda to enhance his position in the eastern part of the Roman Empire, especially Egypt.[18]

In the case of Amina, the image of the sun or the sun's radiance has been changed to that of an extraordinarily powerful light that illuminates the earth from Mecca in Arabia as far as Syria. No longer does it herald the birth of an Egyptian sun god or a Roman hero, the demi-god son of Apollo, but the birth of a man from the clan of Hashim in the Arab tribe of Quraysh. However, he is to be no ordinary man; he will be one in whom the Divine Light of the One God, Allah, radiates.

Looking out beyond the borders of Arabia to Sasanian Persia, the historian al-Tabari (d. 923) relates the troubled dreams of the ruler and the Zoroastrian high priest following the birth of Muhammad. He recounts that an earthquake struck the palace and the holy fire of the Zoroastrians was extinguished; 'and the high priest saw [in a dream] unbroken camels leading pure Arabian horses, which had crossed the Tigris and spread throughout his lands. When Chosroes awoke, he was alarmed by what he had dreamed.'[19] It is not clear that the content of the two dreams was identical, but that may well be the intention. Accounts of dreams experienced by more than one person are noted from the ancient Near East and classical antiquity.[20] The high priest and Chosroes, being males of high status, serve to confirm the likelihood of the dream's divine origin. Chosroes' behaviour in waking from the dream in a state of alarm also conforms to what might be expected of the dreamer from the dream reports of the ancient Near East; and the sudden awakening again asserts that it is a divinely sent dream. The symbolism is not hard to decipher; the reader can easily conclude that the camels and Arabian horses advancing beyond the River Tigris signify the forthcoming Muslim conquest of Sasanian Persia.

In the absence of historical knowledge, medieval writers added many fantastical stories to the record of events surrounding the birth of Muhammad.[21] In many cases their tales appear to be designed, as Donner suggests, 'to fill out poorly known chapters' in the Prophet's life, being eager also to satisfy a popular audience. One such tale concerns Muhammad's Bedouin wet-nurse, Halima, who is wandering in the wilderness and near to starvation when she dreams of an unidentified man, who takes her to a place where she drinks 'sweet, white water'.[22] The man advises her to travel to Mecca where she will find an abundance of food and he calls on God to fill her breasts with milk. His prayer is granted and Halima wakes to return to her people with her breasts overflowing with milk, the ideal wet-nurse for the perfect child.

The Call to Prophethood

According to Muslim tradition, Muhammad had reached the mature age of 40 before he began to receive the dramatic dreams and visions that marked the beginnings of prophethood. The early sources paint a picture of Muhammad as he sought isolation in the wild country around Mecca and spent time in a cave on Mount Hira' for spiritual retreat during the month of Ramadan. Ibn Sa'd (d. 845) identifies precisely the timing of the great vision that revealed the first verses of the Qur'an: 'The angel came down to the Messenger of God on Hira' on Monday 17 Ramadan. The Messenger of God was 40 years old at that time. It was Gabriel who brought him the revelation.'[23] Gabriel is mentioned here as the angelic messenger, although the Qur'an would make no mention of him until the period of the Prophet's residence in Medina. Ibn Sa'd comments on Muhammad's visionary experience: 'Revelation first came to the Messenger of God in the form of true visions; he never saw a vision but it came like the break of day.'[24] Influential sources such as Ibn Ishaq and al-Bukhari (d. 870) note that these 'true visions' were seen by the Prophet in his sleep.[25]

According to Ibn Ishaq, it was the custom of Muhammad's tribe, the Quraysh, to resort to Mount Hira' to perform acts of devotion and Muhammad used to participate in this practice for a month every year. He relates:

> It was the month of Ramadan when the Messenger of God went out to Hira' accompanied by his family and stayed there until it was the night on which God honoured him with his task as

Messenger and thus had mercy on his worshippers. Gabriel came to him with God's command. The Messenger of God said: 'While I was asleep, Gabriel came to me with a piece of brocade with writing on it. Then he said: "Read!"' [The Messenger] said: 'I said: "I cannot read." He then wrapped me in it until I thought I would die; then he released me.'[26]

The whole process was repeated until on the fourth and final occasion the angel commanded the Prophet to recite the opening verses of Qur'an 96:

1 Read! In the name of your Lord who created. 2 He created humankind from a clot of blood. 3 Read! Your Lord is the Most Generous, 4 who taught by the pen, 5 taught humankind what it did not know.

After obeying Gabriel's command to read aloud these divine words, according to Ibn Ishaq, the Prophet remarked that the angel left him and he continued:

'I woke up abruptly from my sleep and it was as though the words were written on my heart. Then I went out until I came to the middle of the mountain and I heard a voice from the sky saying: "Muhammad, you are the Messenger of God and I am Gabriel." I raised my head to look up at the sky and there was Gabriel in the form of a man planting his feet on the horizon, saying: "Muhammad, you are the Messenger of God and I am Gabriel."' He said: 'I stayed looking at him, neither advancing nor retreating. Then I began turning my face away from him to the far horizon.' [The Messenger] said: 'Even when I looked to the furthest point of the horizon, I saw him like that; and I remained standing, neither advancing nor retreating, until Khadija sent her messengers to search for me. They reached the highest part of Mecca and returned to her, while I was standing in that place; then [the angel] left me.'[27]

It is notable that Ibn Ishaq's narrative distinguishes very clearly between Muhammad's dream of the angel Gabriel and his waking vision of him. In the time-honoured manner of Near Eastern dreamers he awakens sharply from the dream and thus confirms its divine origin. However, he also moves out of the dream into an ecstatic visionary state, which is both aural and visual, because he both hears and sees the angelic messenger sent to him by God.

The Prophet's immediate reaction to the vision of the angel, as described by Ibn Ishaq, is not dissimilar to the accounts of Jewish and early Christian visionaries in the presence of angels; he is struck by both wonder and terror. When he returns to his wife Khadija, he calls on her to cover him, perhaps seeking protection from the power of the supernatural; he is utterly shaken by the dreaming and waking vision of Gabriel and fears for his state of mind, urgently asking his wife to help him make sense of what is happening to him. Is he possessed by the *jinn* or is he a poet who derives his inspiration from them? It is interesting that Ibn Ishaq does not present Muhammad as having the prophetic ability to recognise a true vision at this stage; he is still in preparation for prophethood.

Khadija is portrayed as the devoted wife, but it is also she who is the first to appreciate that the Prophet's dreaming and waking visions are being sent to him by God and she is convinced that God would not humiliate him in view of his exemplary character. She assures him that he is to be the prophet of his people. However, she does not rely on her insights alone, but consults her cousin, Waraqa, a convert to Christianity, who reinforces Khadija's interpretation of the visions' significance, that Muhammad is indeed the prophet of his people. Waraqa is noted as saying that the great *Namus* (perhaps derived from the Greek *nomos*, 'Law') that was given to Moses has also been given to Muhammad.[28] The effect is obviously to confirm the Prophet's status in a line of prophets, including Moses, but not yet to acknowledge that he is the final seal of prophethood. There is also a subsidiary message here regarding the interpretation of dreams and visions; it is that anyone, even a woman or a Christian, could be an interpreter of true messages from God.

Visions of the New Prophet

'O Messenger of God, how did you first know with absolute certainty that you were a prophet?' According to Tabari, this question was asked by Abu Dharr, one of the Prophet's Companions who was particularly known for his life of strict asceticism. Muhammad replied to him by recounting a remarkable incident that may be understood as a report of a miraculous event or a God-sent dream or vision. He told Abu Dharr that two angels had appeared to him while he was 'somewhere in the Valley of Mecca'.[29] They first weighed him against one man, then against ten, then a hundred, then a thousand. He outweighed all of them and one of the angels concluded that he would outweigh all his community. Following the weighing, one angel ordered the other to open Muhammad's breast. Tabari records:

> He opened my heart, and took out from it the pollution of Satan and the clot of blood, and threw them away. Then one said to the other, 'Wash his breast as you would a receptacle – or, wash his heart as you would a covering.' Then he summoned the *sakinah*, which looked like the face of a white cat, and it was placed in my heart. Then one of them said to the other, 'Sew up his breast.' So they sewed up my breast and placed the seal between my shoulders. No sooner had they done this than they turned away from me. While this was happening I was watching it as though I were a bystander.[30]

Tabari's narrative is one of the later, and fuller, versions of the story of the cleansing of the Prophet's breast. Ibn Ishaq had already recorded several versions. One notable variation is that the angels are not yet identified as such by Ibn Ishaq, but are described as 'two men dressed in white robes'. He first recalls Muhammad as saying, 'They laid me on my back and split open my belly and they looked for something there, but I don't know what it was.' He then offers a fuller version, in which the Prophet describes the men as bringing 'a golden bowl full of snow' with which they washed his heart and belly. It is clear by this point that it is Muhammad's heart that they are looking for and from which they take out a black blood clot and throw it away.³¹

There is evident development in the story as persons and objects are more fully identified and described. The robes and snow in Ibn Ishaq's narratives are all white and thus signify goodness and purity. However, the *sakinah*, which is 'like the face of a white cat', is a more sophisticated and consciously theological reference. The word appears in the Qur'an in the sense of a God-given state of peace and tranquillity, but, according to Tabari, the Prophet could actually see it as a physical presence. By contrast with the pure whiteness of the good elements, sin is linked to the blackness of the blood clot.

Various aspects of the story are disputed. One of these is the timing of this miraculous visionary event. It is commonly placed early in the Prophet's childhood, endorsing the view that Muhammad was rendered free of sin at a young age when the angels purified his heart. However, the cleansing has also been located as occurring at a time immediately before the Prophet's ascension to Heaven, the *mi'raj*. Tabari goes so far as to record the purification rites twice: firstly in childhood and then before the *mi'raj*.³² He remarks that the Meccans were accustomed to sleep beside the Ka'ba at Mecca, a practice that is likely to have been similar to that of incubation at temples in the ancient Near East and classical antiquity, the aim being to receive divine guidance through dreams.³³ Tabari writes that Gabriel, Michael and a third angel descended and performed the same action of opening Muhammad's breast.

> Then they brought water from Zamzam and washed away the doubt, or polytheism, or pre-Islamic beliefs, or error, which was in his breast. Then they brought a golden basin full of faith and wisdom, and his breast and belly were filled with faith and wisdom.³⁴

There is a certain contradiction between the two occasions of cleansing as described by Tabari. If there were indeed two cleansings, then the first would appear not to have had a permanent effect because pre-Islamic Arabian beliefs were allegedly still present in

Muhammad's adulthood. It has been argued that the story of the opening of Muhammad's breast does not properly belong with the story of the ascension and represents a later addition.[35] In that case, Tabari has simply made a mistake in reproducing the story here. However, it is also logical to repeat the rites of purification before the Prophet can be admitted to enter Heaven and encounter his Lord. This is not unusual in the initiation of significant figures across a variety of religious traditions. Dismemberment, including the tearing out of the heart, may be a step in the spiritual preparation of the individual to be purified.[36] In relation to the whole structure of symbolism in the particular case of the Prophet's ascension, the placing of his cleansing immediately before his ascent to Heaven makes good symbolic sense. Having been torn apart and internally purified, the new Prophet becomes a new man, ready to meet his Maker and be given a mission to his people.

According to Tabari's narration, the Prophet was taken up to Heaven directly from the Ka'ba following the cleansing and was asked whether his mission had yet begun. Gabriel affirmed that it had and led Muhammad up through the seven heavens to meetings with previous prophets, including Jesus, Moses and Abraham. The account at this point is somewhat mundane, giving only summary mention of these past prophets. Muhammad then arrived at Paradise 'and there before him was a river whiter than milk and sweeter than honey with pearly domes on either side of it'. He came finally to the Lote Tree of the Boundary and it was there that 'his Lord' drew near to him.[37]

This is a reference to a very early vision described at the opening of Qur'an 53:1–12, followed by a second vision at the heavenly Lote Tree, described in 53:13–17:

> 1 By the star when it sets, 2 your companion has not erred and he has not gone astray. 3 He does not speak out of fancy. 4 Indeed it is nothing but a revelation revealed. 5 One of mighty powers taught him, 6 one of great strength. He stood upright 7 on the highest horizon. 8 Then he drew near and descended 9 until he was two bows' lengths away or nearer.

10 He then revealed to his servant what he revealed. 11 The heart has not lied about what it saw. 12 Will you dispute with him about what he saw? 13 And he saw him on another occasion 14 at the Lote Tree of the Boundary 15 next to the Garden of the Refuge, 16 when the Lote Tree was mysteriously covered. 17 He gazed steadily without staring. 18 Surely he saw some of the greatest signs of his Lord.

According to Tabari, the Lote Tree was 'covered by the like of such jewels as pearls, rubies, chrysolites and colored pearls. God made revelation to his servant, caused him to understand and know, and prescribed for him fifty prayers (daily).'[38] The Prophet returned, passing on the way by Moses, who advised him to seek a reduction in the number of prayers because of the weakness of his community. Eventually God informed Muhammad as His Messenger that the Muslims were to pray just five times a day.

Tabari's report of Muhammad's ascension is simpler and more prosaic than some earlier, as well as later, reports. Its focus is on the initiation of the Prophet in his mission and his encounter with 'his Lord'. Hence the means of Muhammad's ascension, whether by a ladder or on a fabulous beast, is not noted and his meetings with earlier prophets are given scant attention.[39] It is left unclear as to whether the whole experience was a dream vision, since the angels came for Muhammad while he was sleeping by the Ka'ba. The reader may conclude either that it was indeed a dream or alternatively a physical event.

Tabari claimed that the ascension occurred 'when the Prophet became a prophet'.[40] Another miraculous visionary event then took place at a later date after his mission was becoming established in Mecca; this was the mysterious night journey, the *isra*.[41] However, there is disagreement in the early sources as to the timing. Ibn Ishaq places the Prophet's night journey before his ascension to heaven.[42] This was to become the most popular version of events, asserting that the Prophet first made his mysterious journey to Jerusalem and then ascended from there to Heaven. It thus parallels the ascension of Jesus from the holy city, where by the fourth century Jesus' footprint was being displayed to pilgrims visiting the Basilica of the Ascension.

However, the connection of Jerusalem to the Prophet's ascension is arguably no earlier than the reign of Caliph 'Abd al-Malik (685–705), when the caliph sought to promote the sacred status of Jerusalem.[43] The original form of the story appears to have involved the Prophet's ascension from Mecca and would, therefore, have been closer to the version still being relayed by Tabari.

One widely held view is that Qur'an 17 alludes to the *isra* in the first verse:

> Praise be to Him, who caused His servant to travel by night from the holy mosque to the farthest mosque, whose confines We have blessed so that We might show him some of Our signs. He is the One who hears, the One who sees.

The usual assumption has been that the 'holy mosque' referred to the mosque at Mecca and the 'farthest mosque' to the Masjid al-Aqsa at Jerusalem near to the Dome of the Rock. The Messenger of God was supposed to have been miraculously transported from Mecca to Jerusalem and back in a single night, a journey that would normally take a camel caravan 40 days to complete. However, some scholarly opinion has understood the 'farthest mosque' as referring to the celestial counterpart of the Meccan sanctuary rather than an earthly site. Another view has been that it refers to a place of worship a short distance from Mecca, to which the Prophet had travelled by night in a more mundane manner.[44]

The ninth-century biographer Ibn Sa'd produced a very short version of the *mi'raj* story, which is thought to be based on the oldest documents.[45] He then wrote a noticeably fuller account of the *isra*. With his usual precision he observes that the Prophet travelled by night from his house in Mecca to Jerusalem on 17 Rabi' al-Awwal, a year before the Prophet emigrated from Mecca to Medina. According to Ibn Sa'd's timing, this would place the event six months after the ascension. He records:

> The Messenger of God said: 'I was carried on a white animal that was a cross between a donkey and a mule and with wings

on her thighs, with which she drove her legs onward. When I approached to ride her, she shied, so Gabriel put his hand on her mane and said: "Are you not ashamed of what you are doing, Buraq? By God, no-one has ever ridden you before who was more highly honoured by God than Muhammad." She was so ashamed that she broke out in a sweat. Then she steadied herself for me to ride her.'[46]

It is no surprise that Buraq is mentioned as being a 'white animal', whiteness being associated with goodness. More surprising perhaps is the mention of her as a hybrid creature combining the characteristics of a mule and a donkey. It is worthy of note that she is neither an Arabian horse, who could have been a symbol of nobility, nor a camel, as might befit an Arabian prophet. It has been remarked that the early Muslims were not entirely convinced of the virtues of camels, which they sometimes declared to be 'born of the devils';[47] and they might, therefore, judge them to be unsuitable steeds for the Messenger of God. A donkey could have been seen as moulded too closely on the example of Jesus, whereas a donkey/mule hybrid was original and unique. She was then claimed as the mount of all the previous prophets, but none nobler than the Prophet Muhammad.

Ibn Sa'd describes how, on reaching Jerusalem, the Prophet tethered Buraq at the same place where his prophetic predecessors had tethered her. He especially notes the Prophets Abraham, Moses and Jesus, as well as the other prophets assembled there, but they have no imam to lead them in prayer; then Gabriel leads Muhammad forward to act as their imam, making the point that he is of higher rank than the prophets of the Jews and Christians and even superior to Abraham as the prophet of the pure, ancient religion.

However, Ibn Sa'd devotes more space to discussing the Meccans' reaction to the Prophet's account than he does to relating the miraculous journey to Jerusalem. The tribe of Quraysh are generally incredulous, but, in this version of the tale, Gabriel declares that the Prophet's close friend Abu Bakr pronounces his story to be true and so acquires the name *al-Siddiq*, the one who attests to the truth. A female relative reported that she had seen the Prophet praying the evening prayer before going to bed and that she had also seen him get up in the morning, suggesting that the *isra* may have been a dream vision. Ibn Sa'd insists that the night journey was a vision that the Prophet saw with his own eyes, but leaves it vague as to exactly how he saw it.[48]

The same uncertainty as to the nature of the Prophet's experience is evident in the narrative of Ibn Ishaq. He comments that he heard from her family 'that 'A'isha, the wife of the Prophet, used to say, "The Messenger of God remained in his place, but God transported his spirit by night."' Ibn Ishaq further remarked: 'I have been told that God's Messenger used to say, "My eyes sleep while my heart is awake." God knows best about what happened and how he saw what he saw. But, whether he was asleep or awake, all that was real and true.'[49]

Strong foreign influences have been detected in the stories of the night journey and ascension. Apocalyptic Jewish literature of the third century BCE to third century CE seems to have provided important models for the medieval Muslim accounts.[50] Thus the Prophet's ascension may be patterned on that of biblical figures such as Abraham and Moses. It has also been argued that the ascension of Jesus from Jerusalem offered a significant example for Muslim storytellers.[51] In addition, some Zoroastrian features have been noted.[52] However, the dream of ascension has also been located in a pre-Islamic Arabian setting, being remarked especially in relation to the visionary experience of the poet Zuhayr, who claimed that he ascended so high in his dream that he could touch the sky before falling to the earth.[53] These varied precedents would give rise to a considerable amount of speculation as to the major source or sources of inspiration for the stories concerning the Prophet.

The Prophetic Experience of Divine Revelation, Visions and Dreams

For the rest of his life Muhammad is recorded by Muslim sources as continuing to receive the Qur'anic revelation. Nile Green has observed that the Qur'an 'may be seen as a visionary text'.[54] However,

THE PROPHET AS MODEL VISIONARY

Muslim orthodoxy has been anxious to establish the Prophet's reception of the divine message as a very special type of visionary experience, distinct from other forms of vision and dreaming. According to a well-known report, the Prophet was asked how the revelation came to him. He replied that there were times when the angel took human form and spoke the words of revelation as a plain message; at other times the message came to him like a bell ringing in his ears and afterwards he was left with the knowledge of God's words. The revelatory experience could be painful and Muhammad was seen to perspire profusely even in bitterly cold weather.[55]

The Qur'an assured Muslims of the unique nature of the Prophet's visions that resulted in his passing on the divine message to humanity. These occasions of revelation were to be distinguished by the early Muslims from his other God-given visions, such as the *mi'raj* and *isra*, as well as yet other visions of Heaven and Hell; revelatory visions were also to be clearly marked out from God-sent dreams. The Qur'an uses three terms for good dreams: *ru'ya*, which occurs six times (12:5, 43, 100; 17:60; 37:105; and 48:27); *manam*, which is present in four places, twice with the meaning of sleep (30:23; 39:42) and twice with the meaning of dream (8:43; 37:102); and *bushra*, bearing the sense of good tidings, but also applied to a dream in 10:64. The word *hulm* is used in the plural form *ahlam* in the Qur'an and is associated with indecipherable, meaningless dreams (*adghath ahlam* in 12:44 and 21:5.)[56]

The Qur'an also endorses dream interpretation, for which the account of the Prophet Joseph (Yusuf) provides important examples. Although Joseph was to become the most famous of dream interpreters, it is his father the Prophet Jacob (Ya'qub) who first recognises the significance of Joseph's early dreaming. Joseph tells his father that he has seen 11 stars, the sun and the moon bowing down before him (Qur'an 12:3). Jacob then advises him not to tell the dream to his brothers in case they conspire to harm him (12:5). The implication is that this dream does not require much skilled interpretation for them to realise that they are the 11 stars and their father and mother the sun and moon. As a prophet, Jacob has insight into the future and tells Joseph that His Lord will choose him and will teach him to interpret dreams (12:6). This gift will be developed as he reaches maturity.

Jacob's prediction comes to pass when Joseph interprets the dreams of his fellow-prisoners in the Egyptian gaol (12:36–42). Finally, he is called upon to interpret Pharaoh's dreams of seven fat cows eaten by seven thin ones, seven green and seven withered ears of corn. With prophetic insight Joseph foresees the seven years of plenty followed by seven years of famine (12:43–9). The Qur'an thus assures the Prophet Joseph of a revered place in the Muslim tradition of dream interpretation. It also offers significant support for the practice of interpreting dreams (*ta'bir*) or oneirocriticism, helping this form of divination to gain the approval of religious scholars.

The Qur'an and Prophetic Dreams at Medina, 622–32 CE

The Qur'anic account of Joseph has been understood by Muslim tradition as a revelation sent down to comfort Muhammad in a time of increasing persecution. Thus it has been seen as an assurance that God did not abandon His prophets, although they faced opposition and difficulties. With God's support they would eventually succeed. The last period of the Prophet's residence at Mecca is traditionally presented as a painful and challenging episode in his personal life, as he suffered the deaths of his beloved wife Khadija and his uncle Abu Talib in quick succession around 619 CE. While Khadija's death brought a loss of emotional support, the death of Abu Talib had serious consequences for the continuity of Muhammad's mission in Mecca. Although not accepting the new faith, Abu Talib, as clan head of Banu Hashim, provided Muhammad with the protection of his clan; his successor was unwilling to do the same. Without clan protection the survival of the Prophet and his mission were both under threat, since the Meccan notables perceived the new message as a danger to the old religion and Muhammad as challenging the leadership of the tribal elders of Quraysh. The Prophet then began to look outside Mecca for a place that would offer a more welcoming environment for the reception of his preaching; he managed to negotiate a move for the Muslim believers to settle in the oasis town of Yathrib about 200 miles to the North. Yathrib was later to be known as 'the city of the Prophet', *madinat al-nabi*, which has become familiar as Medina. The move, known as the *hijra* or 'emigration', took place gradually and was completed when the Prophet and Abu Bakr al-Siddiq left their home city for a new life in Medina in July 622. The Prophet's *hijra* marked the beginning of the new Islamic calendar.

The Qur'an attests to particular dreams of the Prophet in the Medinan period of his mission. The first such dream occurred in the Islamic year 2/624 CE, when a small number of Muhammad's followers confronted a much larger contingent of Meccans at the battle of Badr. Before the battle the Prophet was said to have had a dream in which the Muslims appeared to be facing only a few of the enemy. God explains in Qur'an 8:43–4 that in the dream He had shown the Meccans to Muhammad as few in number because, if He had shown them to be the large force that they actually were, the Prophet and believers would have lost heart and succumbed to internal conflict. As it was, they held steadfast and defeated the much stronger body of unbelievers.

This dream narrative has been observed to be quite similar in nature to biblical passages in which 'God appears to the faithful in times of danger, violence, and despair to offer reassurance and heavenly comfort (e.g. Genesis 28; Matthew 1, 2; Acts 16, 27).'[57] However, it is also a case where God gives this 'comfort' by concealing the truth for the ultimate benefit of His worshippers. The occasion contrasts strikingly with the 'dire Dream' in Homer's *Iliad*, which Zeus sends to deceive Agamemnon with the expectation that it will be an easy task for the Greek army to capture Troy. While the Greek epic portrays the gods as prone to deceive human dreamers, often without regard for their welfare, the Qur'an presents Allah as caring for the believers and deceiving them for their own good. The Prophet's dream before Badr may be compared with Qur'an 37:102–7, which recalls Abraham's God-sent dream, in which he sees himself to be sacrificing his son. Abraham prepares to carry out what he believes to be a divine command, but finds that an animal has been substituted for his son and the dream was actually a test of his devotion to God. The deceptive dream has a beneficial outcome, although, unlike Muhammad's dream before Badr, the truth is *not* the exact opposite of what was seen in the dream. Muslim dream interpreters would take account of these Qur'anic paradigms in their analysis of their clients' dreams. The general conclusion is that a veridical dream from God does not necessarily come true in a literal fashion; its real meaning may be quite different or even the complete opposite of what is seen by the dreamer.

On the other hand, a dream may show literal reality, but not at the time when the dreamer expects it to come true. Al-Waqidi (d. 822), author of one of the earliest sources on the Prophet's life at Medina, records that, in the year 6 after the *hijra*/628 CE, Muhammad had a dream in which he and the believers were performing rites of pilgrimage at the Ka'ba in Mecca.[58] Muhammad understood the dream to have been sent to him by God and that it would, therefore, come true in the very near future. He told the Muslims, who were also convinced that such a dream would be fulfilled immediately. Consequently, they set out unarmed to accompany the Prophet to Mecca. However, the Meccans were not as yet ready to allow their enemy to enter the sanctuary. They halted the Muslims' advance at Hudaybiyya on the borders of the sacred territory. There the Prophet negotiated with the Meccan unbelievers and reached an agreement with them. The Muslims would not proceed any further, but would go back to Medina and would also halt their blockade of Mecca. In return, the Meccans would give them permission to perform the rites at the Ka'ba in the following year. Both sides also agreed to implement a ten-year truce, which was to become an important example for Muslims involved in future peace negotiations.

In the year 7/629 CE the Prophet and his followers returned to Mecca and, according to Muslim tradition, Qur'an 48:27 was revealed at that time:

> God has truly brought the dream of His Messenger to fulfilment: 'God willing, you will enter the Sacred Mosque safely, with your heads shaved and hair cut short, not fearful.'

He knew what you did not know and He has also assured you of imminent victory.

The Qur'anic verse testifies to the truth of the Prophet's dream, which some so-called 'hypocrites' in Medina had begun to doubt. However, it also shows that even God's Messenger did not have full knowledge of the dream; that power lay only with God. The 'victory' to which the Qur'an refers is the conquest of Mecca in 630 CE after Muhammad concluded that the Meccans had broken the truce agreed at Hudaybiyya. He, therefore, set out to liberate his home city from unbelief through a Muslim takeover that is said to have involved minimal loss of life.

The Prophet as Dream Interpreter

The Qur'an indicates that the Prophet received veridical dreams from God, but not that he was able to understand them until God had shown him the truth after the event. However, the traditional Muslim image of Muhammad is of a man who had much greater awareness of the meaning of his dreams and of the dreams of others. He thus becomes, with God's permission, a master of dream interpretation or *ta'bir*, further establishing the importance and respectability of an art that has already been approved by the Qur'an.

Two of the Prophet's many dreams provide noteworthy and well-known examples. They differ substantially in form and substance. The first dream concerns Muhammad's personal life, but also impinges on his public life, as the two could not easily be separated in view of his status as God's Messenger. The following report is allegedly related on the authority of 'A'isha, whom he later married:

> God's Messenger said: 'I saw you twice in my sleep; a man was carrying you in a silken cloth. He said: "This is your wife." Then he removed the covering and she was you. I said: "If this dream is from God, then it will come to pass."'[59]

The dream of 'A'isha is both visual and auditory, since a short dialogue takes place between the unknown man and the Prophet.

Unlike the dreams to which the Qur'an alludes, this narrative takes the form of the ancient epiphany or message dream, in which a deity or the deity's representative addresses the dreamer with a clear message. In this case, the unknown man seems to have been sent by God to inform Muhammad that he is to marry 'A'isha. The Prophet's response is notably cautious, showing some uncertainty as to the truth of the dream; he accepts only that the marriage 'will come to pass' if the dream is truly from God.

On a personal level, the dream can be seen as a reassuring message that God's Messenger will find happiness in marriage after the pain of losing Khadija. On a public level, it provides evidence that the Prophet did actually receive God-sent dreams that came true in his daily life because he did subsequently marry 'A'isha. The dream account clearly has the effect of enhancing not only the status of the Prophet, but also that of 'A'isha and, more indirectly, the status of her father, Abu Bakr, who would become the next head of the Muslim community after Muhammad's death. This dream is readily understandable and carries authority among those who believe in veridical dreaming and trust the dream's narrators.

By contrast, a dream experienced by the Prophet before the battle of Uhud in 625 CE is full of symbolism and required his own skilled interpretation. The outcome of the battle is variously assessed. At best it may be viewed as indecisive due to the Meccans' inability to drive home their advantage against the Muslims, whom they encountered on the mountain of Uhud outside Medina. At worst the battle was a defeat for the Muslim forces and a setback after their victory at Badr in the previous year. Ibn Ishaq provides the earliest report of a dream that the Prophet related publicly to the Muslims in Medina: 'I saw (in my dream) cattle, and I saw a notch in the tip of my sword. I saw that I put my hand in strong armour, which I interpreted as being Medina.'[60] In these simple statements the Prophet only gives the favourable interpretation of Medina's strength and his reliance on the city. The cattle and the notch on the sword are left unexplained, perhaps because they could only have unfavourable interpretations. By not interpreting dream images that signified misfortunes, the dream interpreter could hope to prevent an evil outcome. This concern with the dangers of interpreting ill omens lest they come true has ancient Near Eastern origins that were passed down through the Jewish rabbinic tradition and continued to influence Islamic thought. Of course, it is impossible to know whether Ibn Ishaq's report is of an actual dream that was dreamt and interpreted by the Prophet Muhammad. However, it does indicate the apparent continuation of certain attitudes to dream interpretation.

Nevertheless, subsequent chroniclers were less cautious than Ibn Ishaq in their attempts to inform their readers of the interpretation of the Prophet's symbolic dream. Ibn Hisham added that scholars had told him that the Prophet interpreted the cattle as symbolising some of his Companions who would be killed in the battle of Uhud, while the notch in his sword signified a man from his family who would be killed.[61] Following the battle, this man was easily identified as Hamza, an uncle of the Prophet who was noted for his reckless courage and who was martyred in the fighting. Waqidi offers an account with a more developed and different interpretation, in which the Prophet addresses the Muslims and they ask him to explain his dream. The Prophet first describes his night vision:

> 'I dreamed that I was wearing strong armour and I saw my sword broken at the tip. I saw cattle being slaughtered and I saw myself following a ram.' Then the people said: 'How did you interpret it, Messenger of God?' He said: 'The strong armour is Medina, so stay within it. My sword being broken at the tip signifies my being wounded. The slaughtered cattle are those of my companions who will be killed. As for my following a ram, a ram is the detachment of fighters we will kill, God willing.'[62]

Here the breaking of the Prophet's sword is interpreted as relating directly to his own injury sustained in the battle rather than referring to the killing of his uncle, although Waqidi does note this alternative interpretation.[63] The cattle in the dream are clearly described as 'slaughtered' and the additional symbol of the ram is introduced as an unusually good omen, indicating military success. This explanation of the ram is putting a positive spin on an otherwise inglorious result; the Meccans deceived the Muslim fighters by pretending to retreat so that the Muslims charged out to attack and claimed some of their opponents' lives before they were caught by the Meccan counter-attack. Waqidi, as a chronicler of the Prophet's campaigns, is arguably less concerned with the art of dream interpretation than he is with recounting the military aspects of Muhammad's life.

The Prophet has also been depicted as showing an active interest not only in his own dreams, but also in those of his Companions. He is said to have encouraged others to come to him with accounts of their dreams, asking them after the dawn prayer: 'Did any of you have a dream?'[64] In many cases the Prophet's interpretation of a dream could serve as advice to aid a believer in leading a more committed life as a Muslim. In certain cases it could be an instigator of change for the whole community. A famous example concerns the introduction of the call to prayer, the *adhan*. According to Ibn Ishaq, a man called 'Abd Allah b. Zayd approached the Prophet to tell him about his dream, in which a man in green clothing (the colour of Islam) passed by him, carrying a pair of wooden clappers, which were used by the Christians for announcing the prayer times.[65] The man asked 'Abd Allah if he wanted to buy the clappers and for what use. 'Abd Allah replied that he would use them to call the faithful to prayer. The man told him that there was a better way to summon them and taught 'Abd Allah the call to prayer.

When the Prophet heard about 'Abd Allah's dream, he declared it to be truly from God. From this time the human voice was employed in the chanting of the call to prayer. The Prophet's close friend 'Umar b. al-Khattab is reported to have come forward to claim that he had had exactly the same dream. The Prophet then praised God at this news.

As noted earlier, the sharing of a dream experience by two or more people continues an ancient belief in the validity of the shared dream. However, the form of the dream narration is relatively modern in its description of visual episodes, although it also contains stylised dialogue and a self-consciously innovatory Islamic element; it grants

The Prophet as Model Visionary

divine authority to a fundamental ritual of Islam. Yet not all early sources promote the reception of the distinctive Islamic call to prayer via a divinely inspired dream. There are suggestions that the original formula of the *adhan* was very much simpler than that quoted in the reported dream and may only have consisted of the words, 'Hasten to prayer' (*hayya 'ala 'l-salat*). A further report asserts that it was 'Umar who proposed the *adhan* without any mention of a dream.[66]

The Prophet's Legacy to Dreamers, Visionaries and Dream Interpreters

The importance attached to visionary experience in the Islamic world has its roots in the dreams and visions attributed to the Prophet and the first Muslims. Of course, critical historians cannot be satisfied as to the authenticity of the material and it is impossible to ascertain whether any dreams were ever really dreamt or visions seen. Similar records can be found in the pre-Islamic heritage of Arabia and the central lands of Islam and, all too often, the narratives serve similar purposes: to testify to divine support for rulers and religious leaders and to confirm the remarkable qualities associated with them. The ability to interpret dreams is notable among these qualities.

The similarities with pre-Islamic accounts highlight the essentially conservative Muslim approach to recording and interpreting dreams and visions, commonly as a method of foreknowing. Yet, despite the continuity with the old ways, it is clear that early Muslim writers were determined to put an Islamic stamp on ancient models. In doing so, they focused to a considerable extent on the Prophet's role in promoting the value of the God-sent messages that he received as a dreamer and visionary, at the same time establishing the importance of following his example in order to seek divine guidance after his death.

CHAPTER 3

SCHOLARS AND SAINTS IN THE PATH OF THE PROPHET

True and False Dreaming and the 'Speech of the Soul'

The eighth to ninth centuries CE mark the formative period of Muslims' thought on dreaming and other visionary experience, a period that is coterminous with the beginnings of the Islamic religious sciences. In this chapter we will look first at the work of those early scholars who collected reports (*hadith*s) relating to dreams, especially the traditional accounts concerning the sayings and actions of the Prophet. It was these *hadith* specialists who played a key role in supporting the Muslim public's belief in the significance of God-sent vision and gave rise to the study of dream interpretation (*taʿbir*) as an approved discipline among the religious sciences.

Reference is made to *hadith* collections, regarded as canonical by the Sunni Muslim majority and all of which contained sections devoted to the subject of dreams. The main focus is on the two most highly esteemed works of al-Bukhari (d. 870) and Muslim b. al-Hajjaj (d. 875), including only those *hadith*s that the compilers regarded as thoroughly trustworthy or 'sound'. However, note is also taken of those collections that were respected despite containing some reports that were considered to be less reliable. The number of *hadith*s concerning dreams varies markedly between these works; Abu Dawud (d. 889) only records nine, whereas Bukhari relates more than 60 and other canonical compilers between 25 and 38. Certain key *hadith*s that justify the importance of dreams are mentioned by more than one writer, although there may be minor differences and the names of those who narrated and passed down the same *hadith* may differ. The following is a typical example from the collection of Bukhari:

> Ahmad b. Yunus told us that Zuhayr said that Yahya Abu Sa'id said: I heard Abu Salama say, I heard Abu Qatada saying that the Prophet – peace be upon him – said: The true dream (*ru'ya*) is from God and the false dream (*hulm*) is from Satan.[1]

The same saying of the Prophet is remarked in several collections. However, Muslim, for example, has a slightly different list of names as later links in the chain of narrators, although he concludes with Abu Qatada reporting the Prophet's words, which he passed on to Abu Salama.[2] The first part of the *hadith* appears to be in conformity with a Qur'anic view of *ru'ya* as a good dream of divine origin, but the second part is less obviously in agreement with the Qur'an. *Hulm* has been noted as occurring in the plural form of *ahlam* in the Qur'an, where such dreams are understood to be indecipherable, confused dreams from an unidentified source rather than being identified as definitely of satanic origin. However, this twofold division between divine and devilish origins of dreams corresponds with a view that found expression among the Christians of late antiquity, namely that some dreams of the pious originated from God, while others (perhaps most dreams) came from Satan. Fear of being deluded by the devil seems to have exercised a powerful hold on the many Christians who accepted the notion that only a very few saintly persons would be granted God-sent dreams.[3]

Bukhari later includes a longer *hadith* of mixed content, which contains a comment by Muhammad b. Sirin (d. 728), the most famous of early Muslim dream interpreters. He observes: 'But I say this. He said: "And it used to be said that the dream is of three kinds: the speech of the soul, nightmares from Satan and good tidings (*bushra*) from God."'[4] Ibn Sirin's remarks appear to be presented as his own addition, in which he mentions one old-established view on the tripartite division of dreams, admitting the anonymous nature of the attribution by noting that 'it used to be said'. The comment is the Arabic equivalent of Tertullian's Latin pronouncement that dreams derive '*a deo, a daemonio, ab anima*' (from God, from the devil, from the soul), and thus this saying was already 400 years old before the time of the Prophet (and possibly older); as has been noted already, it was even then an effort to adapt the ancient Stoic view on the origin of dreams as being from the gods, demons or the soul, with the apparent aim of making it acceptable in a monotheistic environment.[5] The statement that dreams originated from three sources, including the human soul, was reproduced as a Prophetic *hadith* by other canonical *hadith* collectors rather than being presented as a comment by Ibn Sirin.[6] The idea that dreams originated either from God or from Satan was obviously inconsistent with the idea that they could also be the product of the human soul and that many dreams were actually of human origin. However, Muslim dream interpreters seemed ready to acknowledge both views on the origin of dreams without an obvious effort being made to prefer one over the other, especially since both were supported by Prophetic *hadith*s.

Although the above views on the origin of dreams had also been circulating in Christian circles, this does not necessarily indicate that Muslim transmitters of *hadith*s acquired such ideas from Christian sources. They may have done so, but it is also quite possible that, like the compilers of the rabbinic dream book of the Babylonian Talmud, they participated with the Christians and Jews in a common cultural milieu and thus inherited a great deal of shared opinion on the subject of dreams and other visionary experience. However, it is noticeable that Muslim scholars of the eighth to ninth centuries have more in common with the rabbis than with the Christian authorities in that they appear far more hopeful than the Christians that they can benefit from the reception of veridical divine messages through dreams and visions.

Dreams and Continuing Prophecy

The reception of the Qur'an via the Prophet was so central to the guidance of the first Muslims that its impending loss with the

Prophet's death had the potential to cause major disruption. According to Ibn Ishaq, when the Prophet passed away on 8 June 632, the believers were in a state of shock. 'Umar b. al-Khattab addressed them with great emotion, refusing to accept that Muhammad was really dead and asserting that he was only temporarily absent and would soon return.[7] Abu Bakr al-Siddiq then came forward in an effort to control the situation and confirm to the assembled Muslims the reality of the Prophet's death, saying, 'O people, those of you who were worshipping Muhammad, Muhammad has died, but those of you who were worshipping God, God is living and does not die.'[8] Abu Bakr's timely intervention stressed not only the need to come to terms with the death of the beloved Prophet, but also the need to preserve the essence of the faith: belief in the ever-living God and the requirement to worship only Him. During this critical time for the new faith Abu Bakr was to emerge as the first caliph of the Muslim community, God's vicegerent on earth (*khalifat Allah*). He was to head the incipient Islamic state from the summer of 632 until his death in 634. He was also to be regarded as a skilled interpreter of dreams.[9]

It is unknown at what point after the Prophet's death certain *hadith*s were circulated in a manner that seems to give assurance that dreams can have a positive role in guiding the Muslims after prophecy has come to an end. A famous Prophetic saying is told on the authority of Ibn al-Musayyab (d. 712), also known as a dream interpreter, citing his source as Abu Hurayra (d. *c*.678), who stated: 'I heard God's Messenger saying, "Nothing remains of Prophecy except for glad tidings." They said, "What are glad tidings?" He said, "The righteous dream."'[10] This is explained more fully as being 'the righteous dream which the Muslim sees or which is seen for him'.[11]

True dreams of pious believers thus began to be promoted as a minor form of prophecy. Among the most frequently cited *hadith*s supporting this viewpoint are those that claim that dreaming constitutes a small fraction of prophecy, usually a forty-sixth or a seventieth part.[12] One explanation of the portion as a forty-sixth is that the Prophet received revelation from God over a period of 23 years, of which the first six months (one forty-sixth of the total) consisted of God-sent dream visions. Other fractions are more obscure, but the format is strikingly similar to that of a Jewish saying in the rabbinic dream book contained in the Babylonian Talmud: 'A dream is one-sixtieth of prophecy.'[13]

It was reassuring for the emergent Muslim community to be told that they could still receive divine messages of guidance through dreams even after the Prophet's death. However, a key question remained. How could they know which dreams to believe? Presumably even pious Muslims would have some dreams that were of human origin, the 'speech of the soul', if not of satanic inspiration. One Prophetic *hadith* provides a partial answer by stating, 'When the end time draws near, the believer's dream will hardly ever be false.'[14] This saying would have more practical use in a context where people believed that the end of the world was approaching, as may well have been the case among Muhammad's immediate followers. Such an outlook of apocalypticism fits readily with a number of Qur'anic verses that describe the dramatic events of the Last Day and sometimes observe that they are imminent.[15] The above *hadith* may, therefore, have seemed particularly relevant in the earliest period of Islam.

As time wore on and the Hour did not arrive, further *hadith*s acquired increasingly important status. Among the most influential for confirming the truth of certain believers' dreams and visions were those that spoke of seeing the Prophet in sleep or perhaps even while awake. Bukhari records several very similar reports, including, 'Whoever has seen me in sleep will see me in wakefulness and Satan cannot take my shape.'[16] The *hadith* not only endorses the veridical nature of a dream vision of the Prophet, but also suggests that it is preliminary to seeing him in a waking vision. It appears also to imply that such a vision is in some way superior to the dream, as would come to be understood in Muslim pietistic circles. The assurance that Satan could not assume the dream form of the Prophet would also be of great importance in ensuring that the appearance of the Prophet was in itself a guarantee of visionary truth. The Prophet was dead, but his guiding presence would continue far into the future, bringing comfort, but also contention, as many Muslims, pious and impious, claimed to have seen him and heard him speak to them with both personal messages for their own spiritual benefit and messages for the community at large.

Anecdotes on the Interpretation of Symbolic Dreams

The *hadith*s discussed above all testify to the seriousness with which the Muslim community came to regard the process of dreaming. Further *hadith*s provide examples of dreams as experienced by the Prophet and the first generation of Muslims. Some are literal visual, and often aural, dreams, while others contain an enigmatic image (or images) that require interpretation; for example, a woman relates that she has seen in her dream that one of the Prophet's Companions has a flowing spring. The Prophet then interprets the spring as symbolising the man's good works. By the eighth century, in addition to the *hadith*s, many anecdotes were circulating recounting enigmatic dreams, whose meaning was not immediately obvious; the anecdotes focused on the interpretations given by dream interpreters. The names of two such interpreters have come down to us; they are Ibn al-Musayyab and Ibn Sirin, both of whom have been encountered as transmitters of *hadith*s concerning dreams. It is very unlikely that they compiled guides to symbolic dreams since they lived in Arabia of the seventh to early eighth centuries, a place and time in which the oral preservation of dream lore would be far more likely. In the case of Ibn Sirin, a number of dream manuals have been erroneously attributed to him and he has become highly regarded as the popular face of Muslim dream interpretation, but his status appears to have been inflated over time. However, the ninth-century chronicler Ibn Sa'd recorded a collection of 13 interpretations of dreams by Ibn al-Musayyab, collected by Waqidi.[17]

Ibn al-Musayyab, A Forgotten Interpreter of Dreams

Ibn al-Musayyab was noted as a *hadith* specialist and as an eminent religious jurist living in the Prophet's city of Medina, where he was born during the caliphate of 'Umar. In his youth he witnessed the tensions in the community that marked the latter part of the Rightly

Guided Caliphate in the time of Caliphs 'Uthman (644–56) and 'Ali (656–61), their assassinations and repeated states of civil war. He saw Medina cease to be the capital of the Islamic state, a role that was taken over by Damascus under the Umayyad dynasty (661–750). There was much pious criticism of the Umayyad rulers in the religious scholarly circles of Medina, as they were often viewed as resembling kings rather than caliphs. Since the scholars expected caliphs to act responsibly as religious heads of the Muslim community and God's vicegerents on earth, they saw the Umayyads as falling short of this ideal, living in decadence and entertaining worldly ambitions.

However, Ibn al-Musayyab appears to have supported the status quo, whatever the shortcomings of the Umayyads. When a rival to the rule of Caliph 'Abd al-Malik (685–705), 'Abd Allah b. al-Zubayr, attempted to set himself up as a caliph at Medina, Ibn al-Musayyab was pressured to take the oath of allegiance to this usurper, but he refused and was badly beaten for this refusal.[18] His loyalty to 'Abd al-Malik was further tested when, in 704, he was called upon to take the oath of allegiance to the caliph's two sons, Walid and Sulayman, with the aim of ensuring that both sons would succeed their father as caliphs, instead of the caliphate passing to Walid's sons and bypassing Sulayman. Ibn al-Musayyab again refused to take an oath of which he disapproved.[19] He declared that he would not swear allegiance to anyone else while Caliph 'Abd al-Malik was alive. The governor of Medina duly beat him, dressed him in rough clothing and sent him outside the city to a mountain pass where criminals were crucified. Ibn al-Musayyab thought that he was about to die, but he was brought back to Medina after his terrible ordeal. 'Abd al-Malik was reputedly very angry with his governor and told him that he should either have beheaded Ibn al-Musayyab or left him alone.[20] Walid succeeded his father as caliph in 705 and, in 710, passed by Medina on pilgrimage. The Prophet's Mosque was cleared of people for his visit, but Ibn al-Musayyab remained in his place, performing prayer. Caliph Walid reputedly went over to greet him and said: 'This is the last of the old school.'[21] In effect, he acknowledged the integrity and religious devotion of the old man belonging to only the second generation of Muslims. Ibn al-Musayyab died in 712, a year described as 'the year of the specialists in religious law (*fuqaha'*), [for] in it most of the Medinan *fuqaha'* died'.[22]

Piety, religious learning and moral integrity were all to be regarded as necessities for any Muslim dream interpreter. Ibn al-Musayyab is thus seen to fit all these requirements. His piety and moral integrity are illustrated above and he was noted for being learned concerning *hadith* and a transmitter of some of the best-known *hadith*s relating to dreams. He was also a revered religious jurist (*faqih*), who was said to have been knowledgeable about all the judgements made by the Prophet and the Rightly Guided Caliphs Abu Bakr and 'Umar and possibly also 'Uthman.[23] As an interpreter of dreams he was reputed to have acquired his knowledge from Asma', the daughter of Abu Bakr, who acquired her own knowledge from her father, who acquired his training from the Prophet.[24] It is interesting to note that the understanding of dreaming is passed on through a woman, Asma', who inherits her skill from the first caliph to be considered by the Sunni Muslim majority as rightly guided by God. Finally, the link to the Prophet is of critical importance in conveying the ability to know the truth hidden in the enigmatic messages of dreams. Ibn al-Musayyab's work in interpreting a dream has been described by John Lamoreaux as 'a charismatic act' and 'an instance of prophecy'.[25] He appears to possess the kind of intuitive knowledge of the significance of dreams that comes from an association with those who have been close to divine guidance.

The anecdotes preserved by Ibn Sa'd have a format similar to that of *hadith*s in that they open with a chain of transmitters of the dream narrative and its interpretation. The chain goes back to the person who was an eyewitness to the event and who describes the context and the telling of the dream before recording Ibn al-Musayyab's interpretation. There is no attempt to inform the reader of the meaning of particular dream images, but only of the overall meaning of the dream. In certain cases, the dream conveys a personal message to the dreamer, for example when a man tells Ibn al-Musayyab that he saw his teeth falling out in a dream and he buried them. The interpretation given is that, if this is a veridical dream, all his family will die and he will then bury them. The teeth are only the symbolic image and the dream is easily understood as soon as they are identified as representing family members. The identification of teeth as family is found in the *Oneirocritica* of Artemidorus, but this work is not known to have been available in Arabic by this time.[26] The idea is also present in Jewish tradition. It is unknown through what route this common interpretation of the dream had become established among the Arabs.

A few other anecdotes contain subject matter of a political character and could potentially have implications for public life of the day. One example is as follows:

> Muhammad b. 'Umar (al-Waqidi) told us: Musa b. Ya'qub told us on the authority of al-Walid b. 'Umar b. Musafi' al-'Amiri on the authority of 'Umar b. Habib b. Qulay', who said: 'I was sitting with Ibn al-Musayyab one day. I had been having a bad time and was burdened with debt, so I came to sit with Ibn al-Musayyab, not knowing what was going to happen to me. Then a man came up to him and said:
>
> "Abu Muhammad, I have had a dream."
>
> "What was it?" asked Ibn al-Musayyab.
>
> "I saw as though I took hold of 'Abd al-Malik b. Marwan and forced him to the ground, making him lie face down. Then I fastened four stakes in his back," the man said.
>
> "You didn't have this dream," replied Ibn al-Musayyab.
>
> "Yes, I really dreamt it," he said.
>
> "I will not interpret it for you unless you tell me the truth."
>
> "Ibn al-Zubayr dreamt it and he sent me to you," the man admitted.
>
> "If his dream is true, 'Abd al-Malik b. Marwan will kill him and four of his own offspring will all become caliphs", said Ibn al-Musayyab.'
>
> 'Umar b. Habib continued: 'Then I went to see 'Abd al-Malik b. Marwan in Damascus and told him of Sa'id b. al-Musayyab's interpretation. He was delighted and asked after Sa'id and I told

[the caliph] how he was. Then he ordered my debt to be paid off, and so I benefited from him.'[27]

The dream narrative and its interpretation fit with the image of Ibn al-Musayyab as supporting the caliphate of 'Abd al-Malik and refusing to pledge allegiance to Ibn al-Zubayr or even the caliph's own sons during his lifetime. The anecdote was clearly beneficial as political propaganda in support of the Marwanid line of Umayyad caliphs. It is unknown when, or by whom, the tale was put into circulation. Four sons of 'Abd al-Malik did indeed succeed their father as caliphs: Walid (705–15), Sulayman (715–17), Yazid II (720–4) and Hisham (724–43). It is entirely possible that the story was promoted at some point between 724 and the time when the Umayyad Caliphate came to an end in 750. This would, of course, place the circulation of the account after Ibn al-Musayyab's death. During that period the facts would have been known about the succession and it could have been politically desirable for Umayyad rulers to portray caliphs of their dynasty as foreseen in a God-sent, veridical dream that was interpreted by a reputable, pious scholar of Medina. However, it is also possible that some version of the account (perhaps including fewer sons) may be of earlier date, but impossible to trace back reliably to Ibn al-Musayyab. His interpretation is not explained, but may result from a practice of interpreting a dream as having a meaning that is the opposite of what appears to be the case. Thus, to an untrained eye, Ibn al-Zubayr would appear to vanquish 'Abd al-Malik by throwing him to the ground and driving stakes into his back. However, according to the dream interpreter, it is 'Abd al-Malik who is the victor. The wooden stakes that arise from his back may be analogous to the ancient images of trees or vines growing up from the body to show a line of future rulers. In any case, it is important that the dream is given a favourable interpretation for the Umayyad dynasty, since this is the way in which the dream can come into effect. Naturally the impact on the public would be more powerful if the dream narrative could be located as early as possible and ascribed to an important religious authority.

A further curious dream event is also given the interpretation that four sons of 'Abd al-Malik will succeed to the caliphate. On this occasion a man came to Ibn al-Musayyab and told him that he saw in his dream that 'Abd al-Malik was urinating four times in the *mihrab* of the Prophet's Mosque at Medina.[28] Taken literally, the dream would represent a scandalous taboo and could be potentially damaging to the Umayyads in the eyes of their critics. However, there was ancient Near Eastern authority for viewing taboo acts committed in dreams as good omens.[29] This seems to apply to this case, in which the urine can be equated with semen, a symbolic interpretation going back to ancient Egypt and Mesopotamia. The symbolism is left for the readers/audience to work out for themselves.

Ibn Sirin, Legendary Father of Muslim Dream Interpretation

Nevertheless, the anecdotes of Ibn al-Musayyab have been largely forgotten and it is Muhammad b. Sirin (d. 728) who is remembered as the key figure in disseminating early Muslim knowledge on the subject of dreams and their interpretation. He is said to have been born in 654, two years before the end of the caliphate of 'Uthman.[30] He came from humble origins, his father having been captured and enslaved during the Muslim conquest of Iraq, although later freed on the orders of Caliph 'Umar. His mother was a slave of Caliph Abu Bakr and highly valued by three of the Prophet's wives. Ibn Sirin allegedly fathered 30 children by one wife, but the only child to survive was his son 'Abd Allah. He earned his living as a cloth merchant, although his business appears to have been unsuccessful to judge by his constant state of debt. Despite being deaf, he was noted as a transmitter of *hadith*s, including some well-known ones relating to dreams. Of course, this is the traditional picture that has been preserved and it may be subject to inaccuracies. If Ibn Sirin were indeed deaf, it would have been extremely hard for him to transmit *hadith*s in an age where transmission depended heavily on oral communication.

Ibn Sa'd writes at some length about Ibn Sirin as a pious recorder of *hadith*s, but his biography is absent of any reference to him as an interpreter of dreams.[31] This is strange, as he is known to later

Muslim writers as the founding father of the Islamic science of oneirocriticism (ta'bir). Hundreds of anecdotes about his interpretations survive in Islamic literature, including dream manuals, and he also acquired a reputation as the author of some of these manuals. Has this later acclaim been misguided?

Modern scholarship has established that no currently known dream book was produced by Ibn Sirin, although several works have been published under his name and many more survive in manuscript form. The earliest of these works appears to have been compiled in the tenth century.[32] However, such was his high status as a dream interpreter that manuals were commonly catalogued as being authored by Ibn Sirin, even when their true authors' names were mentioned in the introductions of these books and even when they were written in languages other than Arabic, such as Persian, Turkish and Malay. To this day the most popular of these books are still available with Ibn Sirin's name on their title pages.

Accepting that it is very unlikely that Ibn Sirin wrote a dream book, is there any reliable evidence that he ever acted as a dream interpreter? This remains uncertain, although John Lamoreaux has observed that 'already within a generation of Ibn Sirin's death there was a massive body of lore in circulation concerning his interpretations of dreams'.[33] This was transmitted by his students and by his son, 'Abd Allah. By early in the eleventh century one author of a dream manual included in his book 'hundreds of traditions about dreams interpreted by Ibn Sirin'.[34] He had apparently gleaned these anecdotes from sources of the eighth and early ninth centuries that are not known to be extant. There is, therefore, a possibility that Ibn Sirin may have taken an interest in dreams and their interpretation and a slight possibility that he may have learned about oneirocriticism from Ibn al-Musayyab.[35]

However, it is impossible to know which of the many anecdotes about Ibn Sirin refer to an actual occasion on which he exhibited his skill as an interpreter of dreams. It is likely that much popular lore became attached to his name. For example, Ibn Qutayba (d. 889), author of the oldest extant Muslim dream book, told one story in which a man came to Ibn Sirin, asking him to interpret a dream experienced by someone else. In the dream the dreamer picked up some eggs and separated the yolks from the whites. He then took the whites for himself. Ibn Sirin demanded that the dreamer come to him in person before he interpreted the dream. The man then admitted that it was his own dream. Ibn Sirin then told him that he was a grave-digger, who robbed the dead of their shrouds, symbolised in the dream by the whites of the eggs. The man confessed his guilt and promised not to repeat his crimes. The same story with the same interpretation has been identified as occurring in the rabbinic dream book from the Babylonian Talmud.[36] How it came to the attention of Ibn Qutayba is not known, but it is reasonable to suppose that Ibn Sirin did not interpret such a dream. Perhaps it is more important to note the early Muslim interest in these enigmatic dreams, especially those with a moral message, such that hundreds of these narratives circulated and made Ibn Sirin into a popular household name.

Political and Moral Messages

By the ninth century, despite the popularity of enigmatic dream texts, moral messages were also conveyed through literal dreams. Sometimes the dream narratives include short visual episodes, for example when the dreamer sees the palaces of Paradise. However, the old style of the epiphany dream is the dominant form; in this case, the dreamer listens to a person from beyond this world as they deliver a message and often engage in a limited dialogue with the dreamer. Despite some fears that demons might impersonate the dead, dream communication with the dead appears to have been generally valued. The voices of the dead might speak of the terror of punishment after death or allude to the joys of Paradise; they might advise the dreamer to read the Qur'an or to seek death as a martyr. The dead were thought to have true knowledge that they wished to communicate to the living, as, according to Ibn Sirin, 'Whatever the deceased tells you in sleep is true/the truth (*haqq*), for he resides in the world of truth.'[37]

Although dreams of this type are recounted in a variety of literature, including historical and biographical works, the only full book to be dedicated to the subject is *Kitab al-manam* (the Book of the

Dream) by Ibn Abi al-Dunya (d. 894).[38] However, many of his dream anecdotes are also contained in the work of later Muslim scholars, such as al-Ghazali (d. 1111), Ibn Qayyim al-Jawziyya (d.1350) and al-Suyuti (d.1505). The following anecdote is indicative of Ibn Abi al-Dunya's approach to interaction between the living and the dead in his narratives. He tells of a man who dreams of his deceased friend and, in the course of conversation with him, the deceased informs him that he knows that his family's cat has died a few days ago and that his own daughter will die in six days' time. The dreamer then goes to check with the family of the dead friend and they tell him about the cat. He asks after the little girl and is told that she is playing. He goes to see her and finds that she has a fever. Six days later she dies.[39] The dream tale makes the point that the dead have knowledge of the future as well as the present and the past. The dead know but cannot act, while those who are alive act in ignorance. However, in this instance the living friend has knowledge that he has gained from the deceased and yet is still helpless to prevent the death of the little girl. The dream text appears to be making a case for predestination, asserting that fate cannot be changed even by those with true knowledge of what is to come. The story of the dream may be seen as challenging the proponents of free will in this period by means of a narrative that is not itself open to challenge because it originates in the 'world of truth'.

Thus a dream anecdote, which might seem to be of private and personal concern to the dreamer and his friend's family, acquires wider implications for the ninth-century reader. Numerous other anecdotes provide edifying messages to assure the reader that it is possible to attain a happy afterlife by means of prayer and the performance of religious duties and further meritorious deeds. In addition, Ibn Abi al-Dunya narrates tales of some 30 dreams about caliphs, the four Rightly Guided Caliphs (Abu Bakr, 'Umar, 'Uthman and 'Ali) and the virtuous Umayyad Caliph 'Umar b. 'Abd al-'Aziz ('Umar II), who are all held up to public view as models of righteousness.[40] The narratives bear both religious and political messages as they recount the state of the caliphs after their deaths and promote an image of them as ideal leaders of the Muslim community.

There is also evident a desire for reconciliation between Caliphs 'Uthman and 'Ali and between 'Ali and Mu'awiya, the reader being expected to be all too well aware of the tensions and tragic divisions that had caused hostility between the partisans of each caliph and his critics, leading ultimately to civil war that threatened to destroy the Islamic state. According to one of the anecdotes about Caliph 'Umar II (717–20), he dreamt of being in the company of the Prophet, Abu Bakr and 'Umar b. al-Khattab, when 'Ali and Mu'awiya joined them. 'Ali exclaimed: 'By the Lord of the Ka'ba, it was my destiny.' Mu'awiya, who was standing behind him, then declared: 'By the Lord of the Ka'ba, I have been forgiven.'[41] These cryptic remarks tell us that Caliph 'Ali does not reproach Mu'awiya for having set in chain the series of events that led to religious and political splits in the community, 'Ali's eventual assassination and Mu'awiya's accession to the caliphate. 'Ali understands his fate as predestined and not, therefore, to be blamed on his opponent. This anecdote is the only one that features Mu'awiya I (661–80), the first of the Umayyad caliphs. His declaration that God has forgiven him is very important in the effort to overcome the bitterness felt by many in the community towards the founder of the Umayyad Caliphate. Like the previous anecdote it makes the case for predestination.

A further 14 anecdotes discuss dreams that concern the Umayyad Caliph 'Umar II, supporting the traditional picture of him as the one virtuous Umayyad. They stress the caliph's high status in Heaven and the Prophet's love for him. One of the longer dream narratives is related by Fatima, daughter of Caliph 'Abd al-Malik and 'Umar's wife. She tells how she woke in the middle of the night and 'Umar told her that he had seen a remarkable vision. However, he refused to tell her about it until the next day after he had performed the dawn prayer and attended to his other duties. He then explained to his wife that he had been transported to Paradise in his dream, where he found himself on a broad green plain 'like a green carpet' and there before him was a white palace. A voice called first for Abu Bakr and afterwards for 'Umar b. al-Khattab and they entered the palace. The voice then summoned Caliphs 'Uthman and 'Ali and, after them, called on the dreaming caliph to enter.

They joined a gathering in which 'Jesus son of Mary' sat next to the Prophet; further to the Prophet's right sat Abu Bakr and on his left 'Umar b. al-Khattab. A voice called from behind a veil of light, commanding the dreaming Caliph 'Umar II to keep to his present course of action before giving him permission to leave the palace. Finally, he saw Caliphs 'Uthman and 'Ali coming out from the palace. He heard 'Uthman exclaiming, 'Praise be to God who has given me victory', whereas 'Ali was saying, 'Praise be to God who has forgiven my sin.'[42]

The dream narrative can be read as a piece of political propaganda promoting the position of the first two Rightly Guided caliphs, Abu Bakr and 'Umar b. al-Khattab, who are seated closest to the Prophets Muhammad and Jesus. Caliphs 'Uthman and 'Ali occupy a respected position, but their status is less exalted. Despite 'Uthman having been murdered, he is victorious after death. 'Ali is forgiven for his failure to pursue and prosecute the murderers of 'Uthman. As for the dreamer, Caliph 'Umar II, the one 'good' Umayyad, he is assured that he is on the right path and, as in other anecdotes, enjoys a high position that is comparable to that of the first two caliphs. The dream can also be read as one of reconciliation and forgiveness, delivering a message of hope for a better afterlife.

The Visionary Theory of a Muslim Philosopher

So far in this chapter we have been concerned with the developing Arabic tradition of anecdotal narratives relating to dreams, whether literal and clear or enigmatic and in need of interpretation. We have seen this anecdotal tradition being shaped by the efforts of religious scholars and noted how these scholars utilised dream narratives in order to endorse guidance through veridical dreams, to glorify the Prophet and caliphs as leaders of the Muslim community, but also to promote individual morality. However, such anecdotes provide limited insight into Islamic thought on the nature and process of dreaming and waking vision. That task was reserved for the Muslim philosophers, who were also frequently the scientists of their day and devoted to understanding and building on the Greek sciences rather than focusing on the Islamic religious sciences. Consequently, they were interested in seeking explanations of dreaming and visionary experience by drawing on thought which claimed to be that of Aristotle, but actually owed much to later Neo-Platonic views and to Neo-Platonist interaction with Aristotelian thought. The pioneering figure in creating an Arabic philosophy of dreams and visions was Ya'qub b. Ishaq al-Kindi (d. c.870).

Kindi is often described as the 'philosopher of the Arabs' because he was the only major Muslim philosopher of Arab descent. He was also the first significant contributor to the Islamic philosophical tradition. His family were not religious scholars but government officials, including in their number a governor of the important Arab city of Kufa in Iraq. Living under the 'Abbasid Caliphate that ruled from Baghdad after the fall of the Umayyads in 750, Kindi held the post of tutor to the son of Caliph al-Mu'tasim (833–42) and thus had access to court patronage. His interests extended widely beyond philosophy and he is noted as having written treatises for the caliph's son and other patrons on a range of subjects, including musical theory, alchemy, perfumes, types of swords and their manufacture, as well as the scientific study of weather.[43]

Kindi also produced a number of works on astrology, not all of which are extant, and was chiefly known in the medieval West as an astrologer due to Latin translations of his work.[44] The 'Abbasids had adopted the post of court astrologer from the Sasanian Persian Empire and consequently there was a degree of support for studying this form of divination; although some Muslim astronomers refused to acknowledge the scientific nature of astrology, others were ready to serve as astrologers to the caliph. While dream interpretation had widespread religious backing as a means of divination, astrology seems to have divided opinion. Kindi apparently assumed the role of a diviner in using astrology to answer questions put to him, for example declaring when would be the best time to embark on a journey, whereas his interest in dreaming appears theoretical and scientific rather than practical and divinatory in character. For a scholar concerned with the nature of dream vision, it is remarkable that Kindi also made a considerable contribution to the study of optics. He is recognised as having written ten treatises on this topic, of which four have been preserved, studying both geometrical and physiological aspects of vision.[45] One important work has survived only in Latin translation and is based on Euclid's *Optics*; its main contribution is in discovering 'that light proceeds in straight lines and in all directions'.[46]

As philosophers, Kindi and his associates played a significant part in developing a philosophical vocabulary in Arabic and in seeking to show that Greek thought could be applicable to the Muslims of their day and could actually serve to support an Islamic study of God and His creation. In his work entitled *On First Philosophy*, Kindi argued that metaphysics has God as its central concern, as He is the True One and the originator of all being, the source of oneness in all that He creates. It is notable that Kindi retained a firmly Qur'anic view of God as Creator of the world and that this view was in conflict with Aristotle's idea of God as the Unmoved First Mover.[47] Subsequent Muslim philosophers such as al-Farabi (d. 950) and Ibn Sina (known in the Latin West as Avicenna, d. 1037) would differ from Kindi in removing God from being the central focus of metaphysics and thus seek to avoid blurring the distinction between metaphysics and theology.

Despite deploying Aristotelian concepts, Kindi often drew on them 'to defend views and devise arguments that are not to be found in Aristotle'.[48] However, this approach does not appear to mark a conscious rejection of Aristotle, but an inadequate acquaintance with his thought. The problem was that Kindi's knowledge of Aristotle was filtered through the sieve of Neo-Platonism from the time of Plotinus (d. 270 CE) to the closing of the Platonic school at Athens in 529. A work that has been remarked as an important influence on early Islamic philosophy is the so-called *Theology of Aristotle*, which is actually an Arabic version of Plotinus' *Enneads*, Books 4 to 6. Kindi also seems to have been influenced by John Philoponus (d. sixth century CE) and his criticisms of Aristotle. As Ian Netton has observed, Aristotle was 'both revered *and* criticised in Alexandria before the Arab conquest'.[49] The problem was compounded by Kindi's unwillingness to recognise differences and disputes in the

Greek tradition and his readiness to view 'all of ancient thought as a single coherent system'.[50]

The same outlook affected Kindi's reception of Greek thought on the subject of dreaming. In common with other medieval Muslim and Jewish philosophers, Kindi did not have access to a reliable translation of Aristotle's *Parva Naturalia*, a collection of short treatises, which included his work *On Divination Through Sleep*.[51] Had he known Aristotle's true views on this topic, he would have been most surprised. As noted earlier, while Aristotle did not deny the existence of veridical dreams, he sought to explain them as phenomena of nature rather than as being sent by God. He concluded that the fulfilment of such dreams was usually a matter of coincidence, although in certain cases a dreamer might take some action as a result of a dream and thus bring it to pass. Another possibility was that dreams could be a subtle indication of a process that could not be felt while an individual was awake due to other distractions. This process could be an early sign of the development of an illness and thus the dream could aid medical diagnosis. Aristotle concluded that less intelligent minds were more susceptible to dreaming and that, if God had meant to guide humanity by sending veridical dreams, he would have sent the dream messages to the highly intelligent.[52]

Kindi believed that he was being faithful to the ideas of Aristotle when he embraced the view that veridical dreams were indeed sent by God. However, in a short treatise on the nature of sleep and dreaming, he shows that he was probably dependent on an Arabic rendering of Aristotle that was at least very liberal in its interpretation of the Greek text.[53] Effectively it was a version that was less markedly in conflict with Islamic thought, although it is uncertain whether this was part of the same version of *Parva Naturalia* that has survived in a seventeenth-century manuscript from the Raza Library, Rampur, India.[54] Kindi described how the vision that occurs in sleep does not happen through sense perception as in the case of everyday waking vision. Instead, the vision that the dreamer sees is produced by the 'form-creating' faculty of the imagination, which shows objects in 'their pure, noncorporeal forms'.[55] It is also possible to see visions through the force of the imagination while in the waking state and these visions are to be differentiated from the normal experience of sight.

The Visions of an Early Muslim Mystic

The formative period of the Sufi spiritual tradition corresponds roughly with the same period in the development of the Islamic religious sciences from around the late eighth to early tenth centuries. It is also of critical importance for the great significance becoming attached to all types of visionary experience as a means of drawing the individual closer to God. The earliest mention of the term *sufi* in a Muslim context has been traced to the second half of the eighth century. It is now usually accepted as denoting someone who wore wool in preference to linen or cotton garments, with the implication that such a person was renouncing worldly life.[56] This term had also been used in a Christian context to describe a group of sixth-century Nestorian Christian ascetics in central Iraq.[57] However, the link between the Christian and Muslim usage of the word *sufi* is unclear and open to debate.

It was not until the middle of the ninth century that the process of becoming a Sufi (*tasawwuf*) was starting to be seriously established, especially in the Baghdad circle around the great spiritual master al-Junayd (d. 910).[58] Here the emergent Sufis have been noted as 'a special sub- or even splinter group with much in common with the scholars but with an additional claim to the authority of direct contact with the divine realms'.[59] While they valued the same body of Islamic knowledge as the scholarly class in general, they also attached particular importance to direct personal knowledge, much of which they claimed to receive through deep reflection on their dreams and other forms of visionary experience. The early Sufis emphasised the need for a profound interiorisation of the Qur'anic revelation and sincere commitment to following in the way of the Prophet, especially with reference to imitating his virtuous qualities. As the Sufi tradition began to develop, its prominent figures came to regard their own revered masters as 'friends of God' (*awliya' Allah*), continuing in the same pious lifestyle as the first three generations of Muslims, the 'righteous predecessors' (*al-salaf al-salih*). Abu 'Abd al-Rahman al-Sulami (d. 1021), author of the earliest collection of Sufi biographies, *Tabaqat al-Sufiyya*, took such a view when he compiled his book covering the five generations of Sufis who followed the righteous predecessors.[60] This led him to begin with the earliest of the first generation in the late eighth century and conclude with the last of the fifth generation towards the end of the tenth century.[61]

Among the Sufis of the first generation, Sulami discussed the life of Abu Yazid (Persian Bayezid) al-Bistami (d. 875), although he was not the first to take an interest in this reclusive and severely ascetic mystic from Bistam (or Bastam) in northern Iran. Junayd was reputed to have commented on Bistami's visions and ecstatic sayings and a text has also survived that purports to be Junayd's account of Bistami's ascension through the seven heavens, although this is unlikely to be authentic and may be dated to a time after Junayd's death.[62] A tenth-century treatise that has been considered particularly important in preserving alleged sayings of Bistami is the work of Abu Nasr al-Sarraj (d. 988) and also contains what Sarraj regarded as Junayd's commentary on the sayings and his own discussion.[63] The usual difficulties are presented by later texts that may or may not contain genuine sayings or narratives of a little-known mystic from a remote location on the frontiers of Islam.

Ultimately, much about Bistami remains a mystery. Even the date of his death remains uncertain, as some reports mention his death as early as 848.[64] He became famous for his controversial, ecstatic sayings (*shatahat*), such as his exclamation 'Glory be to me! How great is my majesty!'. Remarks of this kind could only be applicable to God and appeared blasphemous when uttered by a human being. However, Bistami's defenders would claim that such utterances in a state of ecstasy were produced through the experience of extraordinary visions, in which Bistami saw himself transported into the presence of God. In that condition the mystic passed away from all consciousness of his own being and knew that only God truly existed and spoke through him.

Sarraj recorded a famous example of one of Bistami's visions, in which the mystic spoke as follows:

> 'As soon as I arrived at His Unicity, I became a bird whose body was of oneness and whose wings were of everlastingness. I continued to fly in the air of delightfulness for ten years until I reached an air that was like that a million times over. I continued to fly until I reached the plain of eternity and I saw there the tree of oneness.' Then he described its earth, roots, trunk, branches and fruit. He said, 'I looked and knew that this was all a deception.'[65]

Sarraj then related comments that he attributed to Junayd, explaining that arriving at 'His Unicity' refers to Bistami's first 'glimpse' of God's absolute oneness. Junayd interpreted his flight as a bird metaphorically, but concluded that Bistami had not actually reached the highest point of the mystic's visionary experience. Finally, Bistami's mention that he knew it was all a deception referred to his awareness that everything other than God is illusory and deceives humans into thinking that the world is real.[66]

The account of Bistami's ascension to heaven (*mi'raj*) provides an important model for Sufi narratives of ascension in imitation of the Prophet. It is a story that is repeated in several versions, but one of the oldest is the one dubiously attributed to Junayd. It occurs as a chapter in a larger work and differs in certain significant respects from the Prophet's ascension. In this version Bistami claimed that he was carried upwards from the first heaven by a green bird until he approached 'some legions of angels who were standing with their feet aflame amidst the stars, praising Allah morning and evening'. As he rose through the heavens, the angels constantly tempted Bistami to stay at their level by offering him dominion and all the pleasures of life in heavenly worlds pervaded by greenness and light. In the second heaven the angels took him to a river.

> Upon its banks were trees of light with numerous boughs hanging out into the air. Upon each bough was the nest of a

bird, that is, of one of the angels. And in every nest was an angel bowing down in prayer.

The equation of birds with angels is an interesting one and suggests that the 'green bird' may perhaps have been an angel and that Bistami in the previous narrative by Sarraj may have understood himself to have taken the form of an angel when he flew as a bird into the presence of God. In this *mi'raj* narrative Bistami related that, when God saw his sincerity in seeking only Him and rejecting all the temptations of the angels, He turned him into a gigantic bird. After flying across many kingdoms and seas, Bistami reached the throne of God and was brought near to Him until he melted 'like melting lead'.[67]

Truth and Falsehood in Reporting Dreams

In much of this chapter we have been occupied with the emergence of a Muslim anecdotal tradition regarding dreams and their interpretation. The roots of this tradition can be seen to lie in the reports of the eighth- and ninth-century chroniclers, an important role being played by authors such as Ibn Ishaq and Ibn Hisham, Waqidi and Ibn Sa'd. However, there is also an obvious parallelism between the relation of *hadith*s and anecdotal accounts of dreams, which is hardly surprising in view of the interest shown by *hadith* scholars in supporting the value of dreams as a form of divine guidance.[68] It has been noted that major collections of *hadith* contain sections of dream narratives so that there is some overlap between *hadith* and dream accounts. It appears that both types of report were subject to forgeries, necessitating the issuing of warnings to abusers in the same stark language. The inventors of *hadith*s were informed: 'He who lies in my name let him take his place in Hell'; the authors of false dream reports were cautioned: 'He who lies about his dream will have to tie a knot in a small barley corn on the day of judgement.'[69]

Faced with a mass of dubious material, *hadith* collectors made elaborate efforts to ascertain the reliability of the many sayings and accounts of the Prophet and first Muslims and thus ruled out a large number as inauthentic or of questionable origin. The degree to which they succeeded in their task remains constantly debated. However, the reports of dreams presented an arguably greater challenge, since they were recorded not only in *hadith*s, but also in a wider range of works from the formative period. There was furthermore no systematic method developed in order to assess the strength of dream narratives. The scholars of the eighth to ninth centuries are hardly to be blamed for their inability to pioneer such a method, given the age-old impossibility of knowing what any other person has really dreamt. In addition, they were confronted with the Prophetic assertion that the dreams of a pious Muslim have the capacity to contain a God-sent message. Therefore, it was always going to be a sensitive matter to query the truthfulness of the dream.

Some dream accounts appear to have 'the ring of truth' because they claim to have predicted future events that subsequently came to pass. According to their authors, they are a reliable way of foreknowing. Nevertheless, the authenticity of these accounts is open to question because they may have been composed at a later date after those events were known and, when they concern caliphs and other important figures, they function effectively as political propaganda. In such cases, 'the ring of truth' is definitely suspect. Many other dream reports are on the suspect list, including some that testify to the happy afterlife of those who have lived in accordance with the norms approved in Islamic morality and the wretchedness of those who have violated these norms. The work of Ibn Abi al-Dunya is replete with such dreams, containing much stylised and repetitive dialogue between the living and the dead. Yet, despite the doubts about a high proportion of dreams ever having occurred, there is a category of dreams that are almost certainly false, either in their entirety or in part; this category comprises of those dreams that have been related elsewhere in pre-Islamic records.

The stories of early Sufi visions, such as those told about Bistami, may be considered as an extension of the same anecdotal tradition, but complicated by the highly contentious nature of the vision and the caution against speaking of an experience so far beyond normal waking life. The philosopher Kindi apparently accepted the possibility of extraordinary waking visions and God-sent dreams, although he did so through the distorted version of Aristotle that was available to him. He emerges as the only writer discussed in this chapter to stand outside the Muslim anecdotal tradition of dreams and visions and to admit his debt to non-Muslim sources.

CHAPTER 4

THE DREAM MUST BE INTERPRETED

Guides to Symbolic Dreams

In the early Islamic period the greatest interpreters of dreams and visions were regarded as inspired by God. The Prophet Muhammad stands out as the foremost example of an inspirational interpreter and endowed with the highest level of religious authority. The community of Shi'i Muslims came to believe that their spiritual leaders, the imams, were also guided by God to receive similar inspirational insights into the true meaning of visionary experience.[1] For the emerging Sunni Muslim majority, the greatest authority on dreams after the death of the Prophet was Caliph Abu Bakr, followed by Caliphs 'Umar, 'Uthman and 'Ali, all being rightly guided by God. Abu Bakr was said to have passed on this inspired knowledge to his daughter Asma', who passed it on to Ibn al-Musayyab, who in his turn passed it on to Ibn Sirin. However, access to this remarkable insight became increasingly more restricted outside mystical circles and the claims of mystics to be in receipt of such knowledge through their dreams and visions became the subject of much debate.

By the ninth century most qualified dream interpreters were dependent on learning the science of oneirocriticism (*ta'bir*) from the body of knowledge that had built up in oral tradition and was beginning to be recorded in the form of handbooks by late in the eighth century. Interpreting a dream had become less of 'a charismatic act' and more a matter of mastering a deductive system in a manner not dissimilar from that of the ancient Egyptian and Mesopotamian oneirocrits, Artemidorus and the rabbinic authors of the Babylonian Talmudic dream book. On examining any one of the huge number of medieval Muslim guides to symbolic dreams, we are left with a strange sense of *déjà vu*, as so many features appear to be shared in common with the ancient masters of divination through dreams: the methodology employed by the interpreter, the format of the dream prediction and, not infrequently, similar meanings given to the dream images. Yet all these layers of regional dream culture are overlaid with an Islamic outlook. The many gods have been replaced by Allah, His angels and prophets, the Qur'an and other significant symbols of Islam. It may be questioned how deeply the Islamic ethos has been absorbed by the Muslim compilers of these dream books. For some authors it is obviously of the utmost importance that they conform to Islamic standards, while for others there appears to be less concern about the huge debt to the pre-Islamic past.[2]

The oldest dream manual to be composed in Arabic is thought to be the work of Kirmani, who lived under the 'Abbasid Caliphs al-Mahdi (775–85) and Harun al-Rashid (786–809).[3] Anecdotes describe him as deciphering the enigmatic dreams of these caliphs. Kirmani's dream book is not currently known to be extant, despite its immense popularity as a source for the compilers of dream manuals. Where did he gain his own knowledge of symbolic dreams? Fellow oneirocrits reported that Kirmani had received his talent as an interpreter of dreams through visionary contact with the Prophet Joseph, after which he found himself endowed with a full knowledge of dream symbolism. In addition, he studied writings attributed to the Prophets Abraham and Daniel as well as anecdotes concerning Ibn al-Musayyab and Ibn Sirin.[4] These reports suggest that Kirmani straddled the borderline between inspirational and deductive dream interpretation, whereas subsequent writers of guides to symbolic dreams were more evidently deductive in their approach.

Ibn Qutayba (d. 889) is the earliest of such writers to produce a guide that has survived (in two manuscripts at Ankara and

Jerusalem), although there have been debates as to the work's authenticity.[5] In its fullest version the book is divided fairly evenly between an introduction and a list of symbolic images seen in dreams together with their meanings. The introduction includes an explanation of the nine different methods to be employed in interpreting dreams, followed by a collection of about a hundred anecdotes, mainly concerning the interpretations of Ibn Sirin as well as some advice on correct conduct for the dreamer and dream interpreter. Ibn Qutayba particularly stresses the need for honesty and carefulness in both relating and interpreting the dream. It is, therefore, not surprising that he remarks on the high standards required of the interpreter and observes the necessity of being 'a scholar of Qur'ān and *ḥadīth* in order to interpret dreams according to their ideas, to be acquainted with Arab proverbs and rare verses of poetry, to have a knowledge of Arabic etymology and of current colloquial speech'. He adds that the interpreter must also have literary skills and be 'gentle, sagacious, endowed with a capacity to judge the countenance of the people, their character-features, their rank and state, to have a knowledge of analogy and an acquaintance with the principles of oneiromancy'.[6] Ibn Qutayba's comments confirm that by his time, if not earlier, the deductive study of enigmatic dreams was becoming established among the Islamic sciences.

Ibn Qutayba certainly emphasises the importance of adhering to Arab and Islamic tradition, although his methodology owes much to the ancient arts of dream interpretation known in the region.[7] He describes the following methods for the interpreter to put into practice. The first of these methods is called 'interpretation through names'. In this case, the interpreter proceeds by seeking to find a relationship between someone's name and another word having similar pronunciation. For example, if the dreamer's name or the name of someone seen in the dream is al-Fadl, then the dream is a good omen because it signifies the 'granting of benefit' (*ifḍāl*). In the same way, if the person's name is Rashid, the dream is a sign of 'guidance' (*irshād*) whereas a person called Salim is a prediction of 'safety' (*salāma*). The second method is 'interpretation via the meaning', in which the interpreter examines the characteristics of the objects seen in the dream in order to determine the dream's meaning.[8] Ibn Qutayba notes that this is the most common method in use. Later authors explain the practice more fully. Various species of flora and fauna are usually interpreted as representing different types of humans. Thus a palm tree is understood to represent an Arab because the palm grows in Arab lands. In the case of birds, a peacock signifies a non-Arab because it lives in foreign countries and an ostrich means an Arab because it is a bird known among the Arabs. A bird's actions may also point to the actions of a human, e.g. a bird flying indicating someone who will travel just as the bird travels.[9] The interpretation here is similar to one given by Artemidorus with regard to the dream of having a bird's head, indicating that the dreamer will travel from his or her homeland.[10]

Other methods depend on discovering a link between a dream image and a mention in a Qur'anic verse, *hadith*, proverb or some lines of Arabic poetry. One example is a dream of eggs, which are interpreted as relating to women because in Qur'an 37:49 chaste women in Paradise are compared to 'hidden eggs'. Dreams of ravens are viewed as an ill omen owing to a saying of the Prophet that the raven is 'a profligate man'.[11] While such references imply a firm Islamic basis for the interpretations, even these methods and, at times, the content have pre-Islamic origins. Both Artemidorus and the Talmudic dream book had asserted the profligate nature of the raven. The rabbis also attempted to make dream interpretation acceptably Jewish by reference to biblical verses. Thus Ibn Qutayba and subsequent Muslim oneirocrits sought to adopt much older interpretative practice and render it in harmony with their own religious beliefs.

A further method involves 'interpretation through the opposite and inverted'. The meaning of a dream can be the opposite of what is apparent. For example, weeping can be a sign of happiness and laughter can predict sorrow. The dream image can also be interpreted metaphorically so that a dream of plague can signify war; and the image can be inverted so that a dream of war indicates plague. A related practice is that of 'interpretation through increase and decrease'. Using this technique, the dream interpreter recognises that weeping can mean happiness, but, if there is weeping and also screaming, it means a disaster. The meaning can vary when different features of the dream image are varied by adding or taking away certain characteristics. Thus mice of the same colour represent women, but, if some of the mice are black and some white, they indicate nights and days.[12] This recognition that variations in the image point to variations in its meaning appears to date back to ancient Mesopotamia.

Ibn Qutayba holds that the meaning of dreams is affected by the time of day or the season of the year. The most potent dreams are those experienced in the day and in the spring and summer, while winter is a time when dreams are most likely to be deceitful.[13] Again, this represents a very ancient belief in the region, as exemplified in the daytime dream of the fifteenth-century BCE Pharaoh Thutmose IV, who slept in the shadow of the Sphinx and dreamt that he was destined to rule the whole of Egypt. The timing in the middle of the day is suggestive that this is a true dream of great power.

Finally, the interpretation of the dream is affected by the dreamer's status, including occupation, rank and religion; it would be especially important to know whether the dreamer was pious or impious. The good have better and truer dreams than the wicked, another idea already encountered in ancient Egypt and Mesopotamia. Hence Ibn Qutayba observes the need for the dream interpreter to be able 'to judge the countenance of the people, their character-features, their rank and state' because the same dream will have a different meaning depending on these factors. Some later compilers of dream manuals divide dreams into further categories in order to determine who is most likely to receive veridical dreams. Abu Ahmad Khalaf b. Ahmad al-Sijistani (d. 1008), ruler of Sijistan (on the borders of Iran and south-western Afghanistan), drew up a list of as many as 14 classes of dreamers, ranked according to the probable truth of their dreams. On the highest level were the Muslim religious scholars, whereas slaves, women, the young and the poor were considered less likely to be open to divine messages contained in their dreams.[14] The philosopher Ibn Sina (Avicenna, d. 1037) was even more inclined to limit the possibility of true dreams to a favoured élite; in his view, only 'kings and sages' were noted for the veracity of their dreams.[15]

It is remarkable that, despite some differences of opinion on certain aspects of dreaming, the methodology of Muslim dream interpretation altered very little over many centuries. Guides to enigmatic dreams highlight the essentially conservative nature of the tradition from the ninth-century work of Ibn Qutayba to the seventeenth-century key to dreams of 'Abd al-Ghani al-Nabulusi.[16]

The second part of Ibn Qutayba's dream book contains the list of symbolic images and their meanings. In later works many compilers would make this section into the major portion of their work. However, most of them would follow Ibn Qutayba's basic design. His opening chapters consist of religious topics, including God, His angels, prophets and the Qur'an. In this respect, Ibn Qutayba and the majority of Muslim writers differ from Artemidorus, who places humans first and breaks with the older practice of giving priority of treatment to the divine. Ibn Sina stands alone in following Artemidorus closely in his organisation of the topics. After the religious imagery, Ibn Qutayba deals with major natural features of the universe, such as the sun, moon and planets before he turns his attention to a range of animal and plant life and a variety of miscellaneous objects, for which he found no space elsewhere. John Lamoreaux has observed that Kirmani appears to be Ibn Qutayba's main source for these images, as he is the only author to be mentioned by name.[17]

Despite Ibn Qutayba's carefulness in presenting his methodology, he shows little concern to explain how he has deduced the significance of each object seen in dreaming. Sometimes he baldly states that an image equates to such-and-such a meaning, e.g. that 'the planet Venus is the king's wife'.[18] Elsewhere he adopts the pattern of the ancient omen texts, each omen taking the form of a conditional sentence: 'If he sees (or does) such-and-such in his dream, such-and-such will happen.' Alternatively, he writes: 'Whoever sees (or does) this, then such-and-such will occur.' Sometimes Ibn Qutayba adduces a Qur'anic verse, *hadith*, proverb or poetic extract by way of illustration, but it is left to the reader to work out their connection to the dream's interpretation.

Greek Legacies

In 1959 Toufic Fahd made an important discovery among the manuscripts of Istanbul University. It was a unique copy of Artemidorus' *Oneirocritica*, as translated into Arabic by the Nestorian Christian physician Hunayn b. Ishaq (d. 873 or 877).[19] Hunayn served as chief physician at the 'Abbasid court in Baghdad and is known principally as a translator of Greek medical and scientific texts. Despite some questioning as to Hunayn's authorship of the Arabic version of Artemidorus, it seems likely that he was indeed the translator.[20] Although Books 4 and 5 of the *Oneirocritica* are missing, Fahd's find aroused the interest of Hellenistic specialists because the manuscript is earlier in date than the extant Greek manuscripts of Artemidorus' work and scholars hoped that the Arabic translation would help to answer queries concerning the original Greek text.

However, although Hunayn took pains to translate literally whenever he could, he encountered certain problems. Artemidorus lived in a world where the deities of ancient Greece were still worshipped and respected. Hunayn obviously did not live in such a world. Not only was he a Christian, but his master, the 'Abbasid caliph, was a Muslim. He already had enemies among other Nestorian Christians, who were jealous of his position at court and who, at some point, schemed successfully to have him thrown into prison. Whatever Hunayn's personal feelings (and they are unknown), he could not afford to offend fellow monotheists of his day. The *Oneirocritica* is full of references to the Greek gods and matters relating to their worship. Therefore, Hunayn took the logical step of adapting Artemidorus' dream manual. As Lamoreaux remarks: 'While Hunayn does not go so far as to make Artemidorus into a Christian, he does convert him into what might be termed a generic monotheist, one whose views would be intelligible and acceptable to most of Hunayn's potential readers, whether Muslim, Christian or Jewish.'[21]

Since the Greek gods were anathema to Hunayn and his contemporaries, he generally proclaims them to be angels and occasionally even demotes them to human status. He replaces the gods of Olympus with the 'angels of Heaven'. Elsewhere he writes of 'God and the angels'.[22] Named deities become angels of the same name, for example when he observes: 'The angel called Apollo portends well for singers because this angel is the angel of all speech and singing.'[23] If the readers were puzzled on hearing of previously unknown angels with strange Greek names, they may have been even more confused on learning of angels with names in the feminine, e.g. Athena and Aphrodite. Hunayn cannot condone the existence of female angels. He seeks to resolve this difficulty by further adapting Artemidorus' words. Where Artemidorus had written that gods seen in a dream resemble rulers, the male gods indicating male rulers and the female ones female rulers, Hunayn reflects that angels bearing masculine names resemble male rulers and those with feminine names female rulers. As angels have no gender, it becomes a linguistic issue. It also means that the angels cannot be related to one another in the manner of the Greek gods and Hunayn must cut out the many references to deities who are father and son, brother and sister etc.[24]

Unfortunately for Hunayn, the ancient Greek dreamers appeared to act in some very odd ways when dealing with 'angels'. When Artemidorus describes them as placing wreaths of flowers and branches around the statues of the Greek gods and states that these plants are sacred to particular gods and 'prescribed by law', Hunayn is confronted by a real problem.[25] Such behaviour is distinctly strange and inappropriate. Hunayn changes it to make the dreamer place 'a garland of flowers on one of the statues of the angels' and adds that, if 'that garland was in accordance with the Sunna', then it would be a good omen.[26] While a Christian might conceivably make a statue of an angel, such an act would be censured by Muslims. It would be impossible to make a garland for such a statue 'in accordance with the Sunna' and it is evidently a peculiar, as well as shocking, way to behave.

Hunayn's sanitised *Oneirocritica* does not seem to have had an immediate impact on Muslim compilers of dream manuals. Instead, its effects were felt gradually, especially in literary and philosophical circles, about a century or more after Hunayn undertook the translation. Before the late tenth century oneirocrits were primarily religious scholars and do not appear to have been aware of non-Islamic influences on their craft, which they were anxious to present as a wholly Islamic system of divination. Ibn Qutayba is representative of this line of thought. Although some of his interpretations could also be found in the *Oneirocritica*, he never mentions Artemidorus. M. J. Kister speculates that

> these interpretations of dreams might have been already current in 'Irāq in the first centuries of Islam and might have lost their foreign character; they were probably absorbed at a very early period into the lore of Muslim oneiromancy.[27]

While this early absorption is highly probable, it is also quite likely that these interpretations originated in a common body of regional dream lore that was drawn upon by Artemidorus, the authors of the Babylonian Talmudic dream book and early Muslim writers on dream interpretation. When Muslim authors begin to cite the authority of Artemidorus, they make no mention of angels with the names of Greek deities or the curious acts of Greek dreamers in relation to these angels. It is by no means certain that they have read Hunayn's adapted text. If they have read it, they have ignored any of its subject matter that they may have found to be obviously incompatible with their views or simply irrelevant. However, it is also possible that they have accessed Hunayn's Artemidorus indirectly through extracts contained in works no longer extant and whose authors may already have edited out references that they considered undesirable for Muslims' consumption.

Even Ibn Sina, who is highly unusual in declaring his preference for the Greek approach to dream interpretation over that of the Arabs, nevertheless ignores any mention of the 'angels' Apollo and Athena. Such references are no doubt among the 'superstitions and unnecessary material' that he has 'cast away', according to his own statement of his method.[28] Indeed he overcomes a number of problems by simply cutting out Artemidorus' numerous examples. Otherwise, he acknowledges that he follows Artemidorus closely in his list of dream symbols and their meanings, beginning with human birth and proceeding through all the parts of the body. He then deals with topics that have some connection with humans before listing those without a human association. Sometimes he adds a traditional Muslim interpretation to the one provided by Artemidorus, but without much apparent respect for the Muslim viewpoint and little conviction as to its reliability.[29]

Not surprisingly, Ibn Sina is not known to have had any imitators among the Muslim composers of dream manuals. No others were ready to pronounce Artemidorus to be superior in his interpretations to those of their own religion. When they do refer to Artemidorus' work, it is as an additional source and commonly after they have outlined views that they claim to have inherited from Muslim tradition. Representative of such an approach is that of Abu Sa'd al-Dinawari (late tenth to early eleventh century), who composed a dream manual on a massive scale for the 'Abbasid Caliph al-Qadir (991–1031).[30] Dinawari was a government official and worked for some time in Nishapur in northern Iran. He may also have attended the court of Sijistan in the Afghan border area and met its prince and oneirocrit, Abu Ahmad al-Sijistani, who died in 1008, the same year in which Dinawari completed his vast book. He was noted as a skilled writer in Arabic rhymed prose and verse and also produced a literary treatise in Persian on the remarkable qualities of stones, a work containing many anecdotes.

Dinawari is notably more eclectic than Ibn Sina in the range of authorities to whom he refers. In his theoretical introduction he juxtaposes allegedly Muslim thought on the nature of dreaming and ideas drawn from Artemidorus and he adds shorter references to Aristotle, Daniel the prophet and other more obscure figures. His object is apparently to gather all the information accessible to him without too much regard for his sources' Islamic credentials and without any attempt to achieve consistency or argue in favour of a particular line of thought. While Toufic Fahd was ready to declare Dinawari's dream book to be 'an excellent synthesis of everything that was known on the subject at the time',[31] Lamoreaux was less than convinced. He remarks:

> For all its apparent erudition, Dinawari's introduction does not rise above being a relatively undigested compilation of disparate materials. The diverse traditions and opinions that he cites are seldom linked together by the author's own narration; instead, they stand next to one another in relative isolation. It is left to the reader to draw out their implications or resolve their contradictions.[32]

Dinawari's 'cut and paste' method is evident from the beginning of the introduction, in which he offers the following definitions of the nature of sleep:

> The Muslims say: If the blood and phlegm are unpolluted and the humours are balanced and purified, the person falls asleep quickly. If they are unbalanced and impure, he remains sleepless.[33]

> Aristotle says: If a man uses and exhausts his senses, his bond will weaken and loosen, so that he will barely (be able to) sense anything but will rest and sleep. This is because the senses are sustained by the spirit; when they are exhausted the spirit will long for rest.[34]

Dinawari is content here to relay what he has culled from his sources without any effort to pass judgement on them. It is interesting that the Muslims' explanation of sleep is not grounded in a religious, or indeed specifically Islamic, outlook, but draws on the Hellenistic medical theory of Galen (d. c.200). Galen asserted the need for a balance of the four humours in the human body (blood, phlegm, yellow bile and black bile) in order to maintain good health. This idea had been so fully absorbed into Muslim medical thought by the late tenth century that Dinawari was not even aware of the Greek origin of the concept that balance and purity of the humours were necessary to promote adequate sleep.³⁵ Ironically, it is Aristotle who identifies the role of the spirit in seeking rest, whereas the Muslims are concerned only with bodily functions. Dinawari's quotation from Aristotle is close to the Arabic version of *Parva Naturalia* (noted as being familiar to Kindi). The surviving manuscript of this work, MS Rampur 1752, reads: 'When a man uses his senses and then tires them out, they will become weak, because when you use sense-perception heavily, a (certain) bond will be loosened, so that you will barely (be able to) perceive anything (any more).'³⁶ Dinawari adapts the passage to be more explanatory, but sheds no more light on the meaning of the mysterious 'bond'.

For his typology of dreams Dinawari resorts to both Muslim traditions and Artemidorus, first declaring that there is a certain basic agreement between Muslim and Greek dream interpreters; they all acknowledge the existence of both true and false dreams. He then lists Qur'anic verses and Prophetic *hadith*s demonstrating that literal, epiphany dreams are a part of prophecy. There follow quotations from Hunayn's version of Artemidorus on distinguishing true from false dreams; those beings who speak the truth in dreams include angels because they are incapable of lying and also the dead because they have nothing to gain in this world by lying.³⁷

Dinawari proceeds with the same disjointed mode of presentation in the main part of his work, in which he records the meanings of lists of images seen in symbolic dreams. In discussing images intimately connected with religion, such as dream visions of the prophets, he is content to note Muslim views, often adding to them the views of Christians and Jews. He does find a modest place for Hunayn's angels,³⁸ but his debt to Artemidorus becomes more evident in the long section on matters relating to the human body.³⁹ For example, with regard to a dream concerning birth, he first mentions Muslim and Christian interpretations before presenting a long passage attributed to Artemidorus and a single line on the authority of a Zoroastrian dream interpreter, Jahmasb, to whom he frequently alludes in his manual.⁴⁰ Sometimes he illustrates the significance of an image with one or more anecdotes, in which both Ibn Sirin and Artemidorus figure prominently.

Other Muslim dream interpreters are less willing than Ibn Sina and Dinawari to acknowledge their debt to pre-Islamic Greeks and other non-Muslim sources. Instead of referring to Aristotle and Artemidorus, they may allude to 'a certain one of the ancients'[41] or even 'one learned in this art'.[42] They may also offer interpretations culled from Artemidorus without reference to any source whatsoever.

Later Developments in Classic Dream Manuals

By the eleventh century the Muslim tradition of dream interpretation had passed through the key stages in its development. The essential features were already established by the time of Ibn Qutayba, to be augmented by the Greek influences imbibed by men such as Dinawari and Ibn Sina and absorbed more discreetly by many later authors. Although some compilers were more concerned than others to maintain an Islamic ethos throughout their work, there is very little variation in the basic meanings assigned to dream images. As observed already with regard to the methodology of oneirocriticism, a strong element of homogeneity persisted over many centuries and across broad areas of the Islamic world.[43] Muslim dream interpreters were interested in preserving a reliable record of the tradition that had been handed down to them by their predecessors. They would have considered it most improper to express fresh ideas, since such a course of action would be likely to distance them from the truth that had already been accessed from the world of the unseen.

Three dream manuals were widely circulated from the second half of the nineteenth century due to regular printing; they are the works of Dari, Ibn Shahin and Nabulusi. For many Muslim readers, they came to represent the Muslims' contribution to dream interpretation, whereas some important early works were ignored because they remained inaccessible, being available only in manuscript form. The earliest of these three dream books is often popularly and falsely still attributed to Ibn Sirin, but was actually compiled by the elusive figure of Abu 'Ali al-Dari, about whom nothing appears to be known beyond his authorship of this treatise at some point between the eleventh and early thirteenth centuries.[44] Dari's book was first printed in Egypt in 1867 and has undergone numerous reprints. It is, in effect, an abridgement of a well-known dream manual by a Sufi from Nishapur in northern Iran, Abu Saʻd al-Waʻiz al-Kharkushi (d. c.1015). Kharkushi, in his turn, had abridged the massive work of Dinawari without any acknowledgement.[45] He seems to have been noted for his piety and asceticism, travelled widely in the Middle East and generously donated his money to community projects, such as the building of mosques, a hospital and a school. Although much of his book consists of formalistic lists of images and their meanings, he also includes a number of anecdotes, including accounts of the Prophet's and Ibn Sirin's interpretation of dreams. He also embellishes his manual with tales of Sufis' dreams, narrated to him by his teachers; these dreams were not enigmatic dreams requiring interpretation, but manifested in the ancient style of epiphany dreams, in which the Sufi might see God and hear His voice telling him of his rewards in the afterlife for virtuous acts on earth. Dari copied some of these dreams, but it is clear that, while they are representative of oneiric material in Sufi writings, they are not directly related to the interpretation of dreams, but are concerned to demonstrate the high spiritual state of the saint.

Ibn Shahin (d. 1468) is known as the author of two dream treatises, only one of which has survived in many manuscripts and in printed form from the late nineteenth century onwards.[46] His full name was Ghars al-Din Khalil b. Shahin al-Zahiri. Born in either Cairo or Jerusalem, he had a successful administrative career under the Sultans Barsbay (1422–37) and Jaqmaq (1438–53) in Egypt and Syria. The sources of his popular extant manual included Kharkushi and Dari, but he modelled the first 50 chapters of his book on a late fourteenth-century work by Abu ʻAbd Allah al-Salimi, a book considered by the major North African historian Ibn Khaldun (d. 1406) to be one of the most useful dream manuals available in his time.[47] He then added a further 30 chapters. Among the material that he treats more extensively than early authors are the topics of violence and torture, to which he devotes four chapters. This is likely to be a reflection of social conditions in late medieval Egypt.

The last compiler of a famous dream manual was 'Abd al-Ghani al-Nabulusi (d. 1731), one of the most distinguished Sufi scholars of the Ottoman Empire.[48] He lived to the age of 90 in his home city of Damascus, apart from times spent in travel in Syria, Egypt and Arabia and a short visit in his youth to Istanbul. In addition to teaching his many students and acting as a spiritual guide to his Sufi disciples, he was a prolific author and had written 140 books and shorter treatises by the time he was in his early fifties; he may have composed as many as 250 in his lifetime. The subjects ranged from interpretation of the Qur'an to scholarly studies of *hadith*s and Islamic jurisprudence, travel accounts, religious poetry and even a highly controversial record of his mystical experience in conversation with God.

Most of Nabulusi's writings are little read today and many survive only in manuscript or have been lost, but his dream manual, completed in 1685, has remained very popular since its first printing in Cairo in 1858. A main reason for its popularity is owing to its organisation. Entries are arranged in alphabetical order in the manner of a modern encyclopaedia, as Nabulusi set out to make his manual attractive for the general public to consult. He writes: 'I wanted to compile a book on this subject that would be organised according to the letters of the alphabet in order to make it easy for everyone to have ready access to it.'[49] He had already seen such an encyclopaedic key to dreams compiled by a thirteenth-century scholar, Ibn Ghannam (d. 1275 or 1294), but observed that it was brief in its treatment of the topics.[50] Ibn Ghannam's work is believed to be the earliest to take this form, but it was superseded by Nabulusi's fuller treatment, which otherwise differs little in content from previous oneirocritic writings. Certainly it was to prove more convenient for the 'do-it-yourself' interpreter of dreams, since it was simpler to look up individual images than to hunt through a series of chapters whose general structure had changed little from the time of Ibn Qutayba: chapters on God, prophets, angels and religious topics, matters relating to humans, animals, birds etc. The advantages of a user-friendly format are obvious. However, there is a risk that the process of divining the message in a veridical dream may become devalued when God and religious symbols are placed next to mundane ones. For example, the interpretation for 'angel' is immediately preceded by the one for 'tongs' or 'pincers' and discussion of the dream vision of Muhammad is followed by the image of 'a camel-borne litter'.[51]

A Zoological Encyclopaedia of Dream Signs

Nabulusi mentions his debt to Ibn Ghannam, but not to a less conventional encyclopaedia. Kamal al-din al-Damiri (d. 1405) was noted as a religious scholar and ascetic Sufi, who was respected by contemporaries for his knowledge of the Islamic sciences and revered for his saintly miracles. However, he achieved greater renown in Muslim lands for his zoological encyclopaedia, *Hayat al-Hayawan* ('The Life of Animals'), which he completed in 1371–2.[52]

Damiri made no claims to any scientific training that would have prepared him to write on his chosen subject. He was not a medieval zoologist. A few of the creatures he discussed were purely legendary, such as the *nasnas*, literally a semi-human animal resembling a person who had been cut in half so as to have only one arm and one leg, half a head with one eye and half a torso.[53] Damiri included 1,069 entries in his encyclopaedia of animals and birds, although some appear more than once under different names.

Apart from descriptions of the domestic animals and wildlife, their habitat and behaviour, Damiri remarks on many medicinal uses for their body parts. Other sections in the entries usually comprise of philological observations on the names of the various animals, birds and insects as well as proverbs concerning them. However, a number of the entries contain matter of particular interest to religious scholars: *hadith*s relevant to the animal under discussion, juristic views on the legality of consuming its meat and, finally, a section on the meaning of seeing the creature in a dream.[54] In the case of the *nasnas*, Damiri concludes that it signifies 'a man without much intelligence, who destroys himself and commits an act which lowers him in people's esteem'.[55] The same interpretations are to be found in the manuals of Dari and Nabulusi.[56]

Despite his status as a religious scholar, Damiri has no evident qualms about citing non-Muslim authorities alongside Muslim ones. He relates anecdotes concerning Ibn Sirin, but also refers frequently to Artemidorus and even occasionally to Jahmasb, the Zoroastrian interpreter of dreams cited by Dinawari. It is probable that Damiri derived his information on Artemidorus and Jahmasb from Dinawari, whom he readily acknowledges as a source. He is happy to draw on literary, historical and geographical writings in addition to scholarship in the Islamic sciences and the Muslim tradition of dream manuals.

Religious Symbolism in Damiri's 'Life of Animals'

Dreams of animals, birds and insects do not, at first sight, have obvious religious significance as do the dream visions of God, prophets, angels, the Qur'an or rituals of prayer and pilgrimage that are discussed in the standard dream manuals. Nevertheless, while many images refer to the staples of everyday life (riches and poverty, marriage and divorce, power and weakness), other seemingly mundane symbols do, in fact, relate to religion and morality. Animals and birds, insects and spiders, all commonly represent the character and behaviour of certain humans, as might be expected in fables and allegorical tales. They may stand for pious ascetics or irreligious oppressors. Sometimes the symbols may signify situations and states, such as piety or heresy, renunciation of the world or covetousness of worldly goods, that the dreamer or others are destined to experience in the future.

Interpretation through the Qur'an and Hadith are methods favoured by Damiri. For example, in seeking meanings for the vision of camels seen in a dream, Damiri relates their appearance to several verses of the Qur'an. If the dreamer sees that he owns camels, he observes that he 'will obtain a reward and security in his religion'. He adds that 'this is regarded as being due to God's saying, "Do you not behold how the camels are created?" (Qur'an 88:17).'[57] Similarly, when discussing the meanings of visions of cattle, he notes that cattle signify years, a common view in Muslim dream manuals, derived from Joseph's interpretation of Pharaoh's dream of seven fat cattle followed by seven lean ones as meaning that there would be seven years of plenty followed by seven years of famine (Qur'an 12:47–8). However, Damiri expands on the interpretation, remarking that this will be the case if the cattle are white or black. Black is commonly thought to augur something bad whereas white indicates the good, perhaps suggesting here that the white cattle would portend the years of plenty and black would be a sign of the ensuing famine. He then continues his interpretation with reference to a *hadith*:

> If they are yellow or red and they butt the trees with their horns and uproot them or cause buildings to collapse, then it means that seditions will occur in the place that they [the cattle] enter, due to the Prophet's saying, 'There will be seditions at the end of time like the horns and eyes of cattle'.[58]

Damiri makes use of several of the methods that were already clearly documented by Ibn Qutayba in the ninth century. He employs 'interpretation through names', noting supposed etymological links, for example, that 'the pigeon (*hamam*) on the sick man's head signifies that death is his fate (*himam*)'.[59] He draws on poetry and proverbs as well as 'interpretation through the opposite and inverted'; thus he remarks that, 'if the domestic ass becomes a wild one in the dream, it is a sign of harm and evil, but, if the wild ass in the dream becomes domesticated, it is a sign of benefit and wellbeing'.[60]

However, the method observed by Ibn Qutayba to be the most common, 'interpretation via the meaning', is also most commonly used by Damiri and yields a number of cases of religious symbolism. Damiri looks especially at the characteristics associated in popular culture with the creature seen in the dream. In his entry on the starling, he writes: 'The starling indicates frequent travelling by land and sea. Sometimes it indicates a traveller who travels extensively, such as the trickster who doesn't settle in a place.'[61] The association with travelling or a traveller appears to be the most basic meaning given to the dream of the starling, supposedly because starlings are noted for travelling long distances. This interpretation may date back to Kirmani in the late eighth century and possibly earlier.[62] Damiri expands on the basic concept to include the possibility that the dream image might relate to types of people who travel widely, hence the trickster. He also recalls the part played by the starling in sacred history; it was said to have considered all food and drink to be forbidden when Adam was expelled from Paradise and would only take food to Adam after God forgave him. Consequently, the starling could symbolise *halal* food. It could also represent the pious ascetic, who is scrupulous about what he eats and drinks and undergoes the extremes of fasting. Damiri also notes an alternative meaning for the dream of the starling, saying that it can sometimes show a mixture of good and evil 'or a man who is neither wealthy nor poor, neither noble nor humble'.[63] The idea of the mixing of different characteristics may be due to the variegated plumage of the starling. Damiri, in common with other interpreters, does not spell out the reasoning behind the various interpretations. It is left to the reader to make the necessary connections, but in many cases the original basis for a particular meaning being assigned to the starling is obscure, as it is with numerous other dream images.

The Problem with Dream Books

Dream manuals were intended to ease the task of deductive dream interpretation for those who were not inspired interpreters of dreams, offering lists of potential meanings for any object seen in a dream. Until the thirteenth century the normal format was to group similar images together in a chapter, for example a chapter on domesticated animals. This continued to be the most popular arrangement after that time and there was a high degree of conformity in structure among the majority of manuals. This meant that the would-be oneirocrit could expect to find the required section in approximately the same part of most manuals, discounting that of Ibn Sina. However, it would often be necessary to wade through pages of entries before finding a specified image and not all manuals would contain all the same images. Therefore, while it might be very easy to find information on dreams of lions, it could be much harder to find an interpretation for a weasel or a dolphin. From the later thirteenth century onwards encyclopaedias, whether devoted wholly or only partially to dream interpretation, were intended to make the task of consultation easier, but they remained less common than the manuals laid out in the traditional manner.

Encyclopaedic keys to dreams did help to establish quickly which dream symbols were discussed by their compilers. However, they did not enable the general reader to dispense with the services of a professional dream interpreter. The reader could be baffled by the wide variety of meanings listed under one entry. The case of the starling illustrates the difficulty. How do you know when seeing a starling in a dream predicts an encounter with a pious ascetic or a trickster? When does it represent *halal* food or the mixing of something with its opposite? Ibn Shahin adds yet further meanings for the starling: an infidel or a liar. He also observes that many starlings represent a group of people who are irreligious and irresponsible.[64] It is not clear why this should be the case. In pre-modern Muslim society the danger of an unqualified person making the interpretation was obvious because the dream was expected to come true according to the interpretation given to it, a view shared by Jewish dream interpreters. The interpreter bore a heavy responsibility to read the signs correctly because a bad interpretation could lead directly to the ruin or even the death of the dreamer or others. The dream manual might be considered a valuable tool in the hands of the trained scholar, but a dangerous one in the wrong hands.

CHAPTER 5

MUSLIMS DREAMING OF CHRISTIANS, CHRISTIANS DREAMING OF MUSLIMS

Muslim and Christian Dream Guides

In 1966 Toufic Fahd published his major study of Arab divination, including a lengthy section on divination through predictive dreams. In a bibliographic survey he managed to identify a total of 158 dream manuals in Arabic and more than 20 further manuals in Persian and Turkish.[1] The earliest of these manuals were from the eleventh century, while the majority were late medieval in origin. However, by 2002 John Lamoreaux had uncovered the existence of about 60 more manuals composed in the first 450 years of Muslim rule and remarked that they were similar in number to the Qur'anic commentaries composed in the same period.[2] The subject was clearly attractive to a wide range of educated authors, including religious scholars and Sufis, historians, philosophers and men of letters.

While these efforts at dream interpretation received support and approval from some Muslim rulers and many Muslim scholars, it appears to have been far harder for Christian dream interpreters in the Byzantine Empire to gain a favourable reception for their work in official and church circles. There was obvious dislike of dream interpretation and other forms of divination among the Christians of late antiquity; the practice was widely regarded as, at best, idle superstition and, at worst, 'devilish magic'.[3] However, from the ninth century onwards, a two-way traffic in material culture and ideas was slowly developing between the Christians and Muslims of the Byzantine and 'Abbasid states, and hence there grew up a limited readiness to share thought about divination through dreams.[4] This was probably also affected by the personal interest in divination of Emperor Leo VI (886–912), in whose reign dream interpretation was officially 'removed from the list of evil practices'.[5] Nevertheless, the few Christian dream manuals to emerge are notable for their anonymity, the authors apparently not wishing to attract too much notice from the authorities, whatever uncertain degree of popularity may have been enjoyed by dream interpreters. It can be observed that in the medieval West the same perplexing ambiguity is evident in attitudes towards the interpretation of dreams.[6] However, many more divinatory texts appear to have existed than in Byzantine lands and they survived in Latin and in a variety of European languages, including Middle English, Middle High German, Old French, Welsh and Irish.[7]

This chapter explores some medieval Muslims' views of Christians and Christianity as apparent in their discussion of the significance of dreaming about the other faith and its members. Given the great popularity of dream manuals and the importance attached to dreams among many Muslims, this divinatory dream literature seems to be a major, but little-studied, vehicle for the transmission of ideas concerning Christians in pre-modern Muslim societies. We have chosen to focus on extracts from the vast compilation of Dinawari because it was a work of ground-breaking importance for medieval Muslim scholarship and was utilised extensively by subsequent writers. On the Christian side, the chapter examines attitudes to Muslims and other faiths as they emerge in an anonymous Christian dream manual known as the *Oneirocriticon* of Pseudo-Achmet, a Byzantine Greek work of uncertain date.

Christians and Christianity in Dinawari's Book of Dreams

Dinawari concludes the introduction to his monumental work with a list of the names of Muslim and non-Muslim dream interpreters.

The list is culled from a lost tenth-century book by al-Hasan al-Khallal, which had supposedly included biographies of 7,500 interpreters of dreams. In the tenth category on his list Dinawari mentions Christian interpreters by name: Hunayn b. Ishaq the Translator, Abu Mukhallad and Rabban al-Tabari.[8] Abu Mukhallad is possibly to be identified as a member of a well-known family of Nestorian Christian physicians, who were resident in Baghdad, in which case he would have been a contemporary of Dinawari.[9] Rabban al-Tabari may well be 'Ali b. Sahl Rabban al-Tabari, court physician to Caliph al-Mutawakkil (847–61) and author of one of the earliest general works on medicine in Arabic. Although he has sometimes been thought to be of Jewish origin, it is more likely that he was a Christian from Tabaristan, the name 'Rabban' being Syriac for 'our master'; he may subsequently have converted to Islam.[10] In the main body of his work Dinawari includes a number of interpretations of dreams that he attributes to Christians. For example, in discussing the significance of dreaming of a lion, he writes: 'The Christians say, "If someone dreams that he eats the meat of the lion, he will hear evil speech slandering him".'[11]

In the eighth chapter of his great dream manual Dinawari deals with the subject of religions and religious duties. The bulk of the chapter, the first 63 sections, is concerned largely with Islamic objects, persons and activities seen in the dream, e.g. a mosque, Qur'an reciters or a Sufi gathering. However, some later sections concern dreams relating to other faiths. Only three religions are mentioned by name: Zoroastrianism, Judaism and Christianity. Sometimes the same or a similar interpretation is applied to all three. More commonly, the interpretation differs depending on which faith is associated with the dream object, person or activity. Adherents of any other faith are referred to more vaguely as worshippers of stars, trees and idols and there are also mentions of 'unbelievers' (*kuffar*).

In the seventy-fourth section Dinawari gives his basic interpretation of the significance of dreaming of a Christian: 'The Muslims have said, "The dream of the Christian (*al-nasrani*) means victory (*nasr*)".' The attempt to establish an etymological link, often false, between a dream image and its meaning has been noted as one of the classic methods in Muslim dream interpretation. After this example of false etymology in interpreting the dream image of the Christian, Dinawari continues with an interpretation of the dream of a Christian priest as 'an enemy whose evil is protected against'.[12] All those in equivalent religious roles in other faiths are judged to be enemies to Muslims, but it is only the Christian priests who are depicted as enemies who are effectively unable to harm Muslims. This may be linked to their status as non-combatants in warfare.

Elsewhere Dinawari discusses the significance of Muslims' dreams of Christians in different circumstances or of religious symbols associated with Christianity. Among dreams of the dead he gives an interpretation that is applicable in the case of seeing a dead Christian, Jew or Zoroastrian sitting 'on a throne, wearing green robes and a crown, with a bracelet on his arm, rings on his fingers or emerald sandals on his feet'. According to Dinawari's prediction, 'he will rise to high position and acquire power subsequently, obtain good fortune, happiness and power in this world to the same degree that he [the dreamer] saw him to be handsome and powerful in the dream'.[13] The throne, crown and adornments are obvious indications of rank. The colour green symbolises righteousness and piety in Islam and, according to the Qur'an (18:31; 36:80; 76:21), green robes are to be worn by the virtuous in Paradise. Among precious stones the emerald is also associated with righteousness, and emerald sandals would indicate a journey for the sake of religion.[14] This might be a spiritual, rather than physical, journey as in the Sufi mystic's journeying towards God. Had the dead person seen in the dream been a Muslim, the interpretation might have been related to the afterlife. However, Dinawari cannot make such a prediction with regard to the vision of a non-Muslim in a Muslim's dream. Consequently, the most favourable outcome must be connected with success in this world, earthly happiness and power.

In considering dreams of objects symbolic of Christianity, Dinawari offers various interpretations dependent on whether the dreamer is Muslim or Christian and often dependent on the dreamer's actions or other variants. For example, he offers the following explanation with reference to Muslims dreaming of churches:

If someone dreams of a church in his house, his speech will resemble the speech of Christians, and, similarly, if he dreams that his house becomes a church. If he dreams that it changes into a church, he will rebel against his leader. If he dreams that he is in a church, he will become a Christian. If he dreams that he is passing through a church, he will adopt an innovation (*bid'a*).[15]

It is hardly surprising that a Muslim who dreams of a church suggests to the oneirocrit someone whose commitment to Islam is questionable and who may be drifting towards heresy or be disloyal in worldly matters. For the Christian who dreams of a church, Dinawari offers both positive and negative predictions reported by Christian dream interpreters:

The Christians have said: 'If someone dreams that he goes to an altar and does repairs to it and mends it for some reason, he will do good and people will praise him. If he dreams that he destroys it, he will commit an act that will split a community or he will leave his religion.'[16]

While not interpreting Muslims' dreams of Christians and Christianity in a particularly black light, Dinawari frequently understands them in terms of the adoption of heretical beliefs and practices or the pursuit of innovation, as in the above case of a Muslim dreaming of passing through a church. However, Dinawari's predictions look decidedly moderate and restrained by contrast with some later medieval views. The popular work of Dari, falsely attributed to Ibn Sirin but compiled at an uncertain date before 1237, borrows from Dinawari, but shows a far greater degree of negativity towards Christianity. For Dari, the church seen in a dream symbolises, among other ill omens, a graveyard, brothel, tavern, place of unbelief and heresy, even hell itself.[17] It is possible that the experience of the Crusades may account for the more aggressively negative interpretation, perhaps as a response to popular demand for a darker depiction of the other faith than in the early eleventh century.

Dreams of metamorphosis, in which the dreamer changes to become someone or something seen in a dream, are a popular subject for discussion in the dream manuals. For Dinawari, when a Muslim dreams of changing into a Christian or a monk, it means that he will become a heretic. When he metamorphoses into an archbishop, it indicates that he will summon others to heresy. However, such interpretations assume that the Muslim dreamer does not object to the metamorphosis. If he dislikes the situation, the interpretation will be different. For example, if the Muslim dreams that 'he is called a Christian, dislikes it and wears fine white robes, he will flee from something in fear'. The white robes are a clear sign of his Muslim status and rejection of the other religion. Similarly, if he dreams of being called an archbishop but dislikes it, he will be accused of innovating or telling lies, but will actually be innocent. In all these cases the innovation or heresy is alluded to in vague terms. [18]

However, there are also cases where the performance of certain practices associated with Christianity and Judaism is interpreted with reference to Muslim heretical beliefs. Dinawari views a Muslim's dream of reciting the Torah without knowing it as a prediction that he will follow the Qadari theological position in support of human free will, and a recitation of the New Testament is seen as an indication that he will favour the belief of the Jabriyya in predestination.[19] Had the dreamer known the Jewish and Christian scriptures and recited them, the prediction would probably have been that he would become a Jew or a Christian. It is likely here that the scriptures of earlier faiths are understood to symbolise earlier Muslim doctrines that have been superseded by the new Sunni 'orthodoxy' supported by Dinawari's patron, the Caliph al-Qadir, just as the previous revelations of holy books were regarded as having been superseded by the Qur'an.

Pseudo-Achmet, a Christian Dream Interpreter

While little is known of Dinawari's life, the life of his Christian counterpart identified only as Pseudo-Achmet, author of a Byzantine Greek *Oneirocriticon*, is totally unknown. This was not always apparent, but, at present, we are more aware of what we do not know. At the end of the nineteenth and early in the twentieth century scholarly investigators believed that they knew the author's identity.[20] He was Achmet, son of Sereim, a Greek Christian despite his Muslim name, associated with the court of Caliph al-Ma'mun in ninth-century Baghdad. However, not everyone was convinced. As early as 1856, N. Bland had reached the conclusion that the unknown author had attempted to pass off his work as that of the most famous Arab authority on dreams, Muhammad b. Sirin.[21] It was not hard to detect Ibn Sirin's name even in its corrupted form. Achmet is a Greek rendering of the Turkish Ahmet and Arabic Ahmad, a name also given to the Prophet Muhammad, derived from the same radical letters, ḥ-m-d. It does not appear unusual for the letters n and m to be confused in Greek manuscripts, hence 'Sirin' becoming 'Sereim'.[22] However, certain anomalies in the text indicated that this dream manual was not the work of Ibn Sirin translated into Greek. Ibn Sirin could not have been active at the court of al-Ma'mun because he had died more than 80 years before al-Ma'mun's accession to the caliphate. The book's Christian nature was also obvious and made it impossible for it to be the work of the Muslim oneirocrit.

In 1925 an edition of the Greek text was published,[23] but it would be more than 60 years later before the *Oneirocriticon* was made accessible to a wider readership through translations into German and English.[24] Recent studies have concluded that the manual's compiler never made any claim to be Achmet, son of Sereim (Muhammad b. Sirin), but presented himself only as a dream interpreter working for his 'master' (*despotes*), a term generally used in this period for the Byzantine emperor, although it could be used for other figures in authority including princes and bishops.[25] The name Achmet may have become attached to the work as a result of a copyist's misunderstanding. Attempts to date the composition of the *Oneirocriticon* have assigned it to a period between 843 and *c*.1075.[26]

Pseudo-Achmet begins his dream book by noting with admiration the accuracy achieved by the Indians, Persians and ancient Egyptians in the matter of dream interpretation. Therefore, he claims to have drawn on these sources and organises the discussion of each dream symbol according to its interpretation by each of these peoples, for example. 'From the speech of the Indians on different faiths [. . .] From the speech of the Persians on faith [. . .] From the speech of the Egyptians on faith.'[27] In some cases he combines the interpretations of Persians and Egyptians on one symbol, for example on 'fire', and occasionally those of Indians, Persians and Egyptians, for example on 'pepper and mustard'. In his opening account of the value of divination through dreams he refers by name to Syrbacham, dream interpreter of the king of India, who expresses a distinctly Christian viewpoint:

> Very great wisdom is the gift of divination and the interpretation and decipherment of dreams that God has proclaimed to all: for it is written in the Holy Gospels: 'To the one who loves Me, My Father and I will come and tarry with him.' This is fulfilled through dreams. A witness of this is Joseph, who was entrusted with Mary, the mother of the Light, because he was so told in a dream.[28]

Throughout the work it is the interpretations ascribed to Indians that reflect Christian thinking. Baram is then introduced as dream interpreter of the king of Persia and presents the case for the benefits of his art as against the pains of astrology. Finally, Tarphan, the Egyptian Pharaoh's dream interpreter, notes that it was his master's great love of the gods that caused him to have significant dreams that would be fulfilled.[29]

However, it is evident that Pseudo-Achmet does not actually draw on the above sources, although their mention serves to give the work an exotic touch and air of erudition. It has been suggested that the name of the alleged Indian dream interpreter, Syrbacham, may be a corruption of Sanskrit *sri Brahmanah*, 'the reverend Brahman', borrowed perhaps from an Arabic source.[30] Nevertheless, there is very little Indian about this Byzantine dream book and the word 'Indian' was used vaguely, from the fourth century onwards, to refer to Eastern peoples, including Christians in the East.[31] At first glance the account of the symbolism of the elephant might appear to be an Indian topic, but the interpretation of the elephant as 'a very great and rich man' is common in Arabic dream manuals, as is the interpretation provided in Pseudo-Achmet, allegedly from the Persians and ancient Egyptians, of the elephant as 'an exalted, very rich foreign ruler'.[32]

Likewise, there is no reason to conclude that genuine Persian and ancient Egyptian dream knowledge lies at the root of interpretations ascribed to Persians and Egyptians, although in a few places Persian and Egyptian religion and customs are mentioned. The name Baram for the Persian dream interpreter is a corruption of Bahram, an authentic Persian name, and there is some information on Zoroastrianism, such as might have been gleaned from Muslim writers who were familiar with some Zoroastrian practices.[33] However, ancient Egypt was less familiar territory for both Byzantine Christians and Arab Muslims and this is reflected in the vague and erroneous information about Egyptian religion provided in Pseudo-Achmet's *Oneirocriticon*. The name Tarphan for the Egyptian dream interpreter is obscure. The representation of the Pharaoh as someone who has veridical, predictive dreams fits with the picture of the Pharaoh in the Joseph stories of Genesis and the Qur'an. There is no suggestion of familiarity with Hellenistic or earlier sources on Egypt.

So, if the *Oneirocriticon*'s sources are not Indian, Persian or ancient Egyptian, what are they? Two contemporary scholars have offered competing views. Steven Oberhelman surmises that the compiler of the *Oneirocriticon* made use of the original second-century Greek text of Artemidorus and also of Arabic Islamic and Byzantine Greek sources.[34] He stresses that Achmet drew directly on Artemidorus due to the very large number of 'exact correspondences'.[35] He also notes a number of references to the earlier Byzantine dream books of Astrampsychus and Daniel in the Indian sections of the book.[36] Maria Mavroudi is dubious about any use of the Greek Artemidorus. She observes that, although Oberhelman counted 124 instances of 'specific agreement' between the two texts, the wording is entirely different and that such a difference would be highly unlikely if the Byzantine compiler had actually used the original Greek text of Artemidorus.[37] After a close examination of 15 of the 124 cases of agreement, she was convinced that Pseudo-Achmet drew on Hunayn b. Ishaq's adapted Arabic version of Artemidorus.[38]

There is little doubt that Arabic dream books provide the principal basis for the dream interpretations found in the *Oneirocriticon*. John Lamoreaux has remarked that the sequence of dream symbols bears a close similarity to that in the early Islamic sources and that some parts of the work 'are a very nearly literal version of what is found in the early Muslim dream manuals'.[39] There are also 13 anecdotes scattered through Pseudo-Achmet's text relating to Muslims' dreams, of which about half have been identified in Arabic works.[40] However, although many parallels and similarities can be detected, it has not been possible to locate with any certainty the Islamic sources of the *Oneirocriticon* or to establish to what extent its author may have adapted and Christianised the material himself or possibly made some use of previous Christians' efforts in this direction.

Muslims in Pseudo-Achmet's Book of Dreams

The *Oneirocriticon* is not only a much shorter work than Dinawari's vast dream book. It is also much less well organised. In places the contents appear to be jumbled, giving the impression that the compiler has adopted a cut-and-paste technique in his use of Arabic sources, which have been inconsistently Christianised. The sections that are most consciously concerned with religious matters come early in the book and imitate early Muslim dream manuals in this respect. They share some topics in common, such as the resurrection of the dead, paradise, hell and angels; however, in the *Oneirocriticon* there is a primary interest in dream symbols familiar from the Byzantine writer's own faith, including Jesus Christ, apostles, patriarchs, bishops and monks.[41] The author gives only brief coverage to Christians' dreams of matters relating to other faiths. There is hardly any interpretation of their dreams about Muslims in general and none about their dreams of Muslim symbols, such as mosques, imams or Islamic ritual. This may seem strange in view of Pseudo-Achmet's heavy reliance on Muslim dream books, and it contrasts strikingly with Dinawari's readiness to discuss Muslims' dreams of the Bible and Christian priests, monks and churches.

In the Indian section representing a Christian viewpoint on different faiths, Pseudo-Achmet opens with interpretations of dreams about conversion to another faith.[42] Effectively, these dreams fall into the common category of dreams about metamorphosis. The author considers the possibility of a Christian dreaming of conversion to only three named faiths: Judaism, Islam and Zoroastrianism. Remarkably, it is Islam that receives only the briefest of mentions. Pseudo-Achmet writes:

> If a Christian dreams that he became a Jew, he was not perfect, but instead untrustworthy and blasphemous, and he will come into perdition; if the dreamer is a king, he will forcibly thrust heresy onto his subjects; if a commoner, he will of his own accord give false witness; if a woman, she will be treacherous to her husband; if a slave, he will plot against his master. If someone dreams of becoming a Mohammedan, the same interpretations apply. If someone dreams that he was a magus, he will be a lover of riches and wealth; for magians are worldly minded and think nothing of the retribution in the hereafter.[43]

It is noticeable that the fullest treatment is given to the dream of converting to Judaism, interpreted in wholly negative terms regardless of the dreamer's identity and status. It is also evident that, as in the case of Dinawari's predictions, the dream is not taken literally, for the dreamer is not expected to become a Jew. Instead, it symbolises moral lapses. The king's dream, understood as meaning that he will force his subjects into heresy, reflects a possible greater concern with heretics than with apostates renouncing Christianity in favour of another faith. In this respect, it echoes the concern of Muslim dream manuals, including that of Dinawari. The interpretation of the same event in the dreams of women and slaves is provided solely with reference to their relationship with the head of the household, who stands in the place of God; for the woman, this is her husband and, for the slave, his/her master. Their treachery is deemed equivalent to that of the free male dreamer who is disloyal to God through his moral imperfections.

Why does the *Oneirocriticon* offer no separate, different interpretation for the dream of converting to Islam, 'becoming a Mohammedan'? While Dinawari devotes approximately equal coverage to Muslims' dreams of Jews and Christians and notes some distinctive and some shared interpretations, it is notable that the Christian compiler appears to transfer an entrenched anti-Semitic judgement to his interpretation of Muslims in dreams without any attempt at differentiation between Muslims and Jews. One explanation for this approach could be the greater familiarity with Jews on the part of Pseudo-Achmet and his readers, whereas Muslims represented the unknown, but supposedly similar, enemies of the Byzantine Christians. Zoroastrians, referred to as 'magians' ('magus' in the singular here), are also negatively viewed as loving riches and caring only for this world rather than the afterlife. Considering that they proved no threat and would also have been quite unfamiliar to the Byzantine readership, why then did Pseudo-Achmet assign a unique interpretation to Christians' dreams of them? The answer probably lies in his sources and this may offer a further explanation for the fuller treatment of dreams of Jews. Interpretations for dreams of both Jews and Zoroastrians were to be encountered in Arabic dream books and could be adopted wholesale or adapted to suit the Christian author and his target audience. Obviously Muslim dream interpreters would not produce negative interpretations of dreaming of their co-religionists. Therefore, Pseudo-Achmet would be faced with a simple choice. Either he had to read Muslim writers' disparaging interpretations of Christians in dreams, which he would have found distressing, and then adapt these interpretations in order to apply them to Muslims, or he had to equate Muslims with members of a faith that was held to be reprehensible in Byzantine Christian eyes. He chose the second option, deciding to treat a dream of becoming a Muslim as having exactly the same significance as a dream of becoming a Jew. His third option would have been to create an entirely new interpretation specific to Muslims. If he believed in divination through dreams, he would have recognised the problems with inventing such an interpretation himself and taken what was for him the more acceptable and easier decision. Thus Pseudo-Achmet's inability to offer much interpretation of Christians' dreams of Muslims may be explained, at least partially, by the lack of a Christian oneirocritic tradition that could have provided a view of Islam and Muslims to satisfy a Byzantine Christian readership. The Arabic Islamic tradition of dream interpretation clearly could not meet such a need. In addition, Pseudo-Achmet may have assumed that his fellow Christians were too unfamiliar with Islamic beliefs to dream very much about metamorphosis into a Muslim.

It is in the anecdotal material that some dreams about Muslims are recorded, but these are Muslims' dreams of Muslims and not examples of Christians' dreams of Muslims. They are presented as cases in which the famous dream interpreter 'Sereim' (Ibn Sirin) made successful analyses of selected predictive dreams and, usually, they serve to illustrate a basic interpretation, for example in a short account that aims to elucidate the symbolism of hair seen in a dream; the story shows that hair growth indicates an increase in wealth, whereas hair loss signifies financial loss.[44]

Occasionally Pseudo-Achmet presents dreams of an allegedly historical character, notably one that claims to offer Sereim's interpretation of a dream dreamt by Caliph al-Ma'mun, despite the fact that the historical Ibn Sirin had died long before al-Ma'mun's reign. The dream narrative tells how the caliph urinated on the walls of the four corners of the Ka'ba in Mecca. He was then distressed by his apparent major sin in violating the holiest sanctuary of Islam. However, the dream event was interpreted as a good omen because the urination was understood as the act of begetting progeny, four sons to succeed their father as caliphs. The dream is evidently an adaptation of an anecdote found in Arabic sources and noted in Chapter 3 in the form given by Ibn Sa'd, in which Ibn al-Musayyab acts as the interpreter of the dream and 'Abd al-Malik (685–705) is the dreaming caliph.[45] Ibn Sa'd's account is probably the oldest version of the story, although an alternative version gives 'Abd al-Malik's father, Marwan I (684–85), as the dreamer. In the Arabic accounts the caliph is said to dream of urinating in the prayer niche of the Prophet's Mosque at Medina or in the niche of an unspecified mosque.[46] The connection of the dream with the Medinan location and with 'Abd al-Malik makes the best historical sense because that caliph's four sons (al-Walid, Sulayman, Yazid II and Hisham) all succeeded to the caliphate and it would be significant for them to stand in the Prophet's Mosque to lead the Islamic community in prayer following the example of the Prophet. Therefore, the dream of the Medinan prayer niche fits the context better than a dream of any random mosque or even of the Ka'ba. A remarkably similar prediction occurs in the Assyrian Dream Book, which states, 'If (in his dream) he urinates [...] on a wall and over [...]: he will h[ave] sons.'[47] Presumably the symbolism of urination against a wall and its interpretation as a sign of male heirs then entered the common stock of regional dream knowledge.

The Byzantine compiler of the *Oneirocriticon* offers a version of the dream and its interpretation that has been adapted to suit his readership. The only caliph to appear in his dream book is al-Ma'mun and the only Muslim dream interpreter is intended to be Ibn Sirin, while the only familiar Islamic holy site is at Mecca. By telling such an anecdote Pseudo-Achmet was apparently seeking to capture the imagination of his Christian audience with a strange tale of the exotic East. At the same time he or his sources passed on such tales in a form that preserved only names of personalities and places more likely to be known to Byzantine readers.

Dreams of Heresy and Fear of the Unknown

Not unexpectedly, dream images relating to Christians and Christianity are often interpreted in medieval Muslims' dream books as indicating moral defects and undesirable outcomes. Such dreams are commonly seen to predict heresy. Dinawari's work is no exception in this respect and would be an important source of reference for many later authors. Christians in general, monks and priests, the gospels, churches and monasteries may all have offered the dream interpreter easily recognisable signs indicating a lapse in faith and drift into heretical beliefs and practices, the unacceptable face of innovation. It is possible that the focus on Christian symbols masks a greater concern with the enforcement of Sunni 'orthodoxy' rather than a fear of the other faith. It is likely to be a true reflection of the anxiety felt in 'Abbasid official circles and among certain religious scholars, who perceived a need for a defence against the threat from fellow Muslims. The dream book image of the Christian as heretic was one that could serve to unify Muslims of the caliphate in their rejection of supposedly dangerous deviance.

Dinawari's interpretations were, however, not all negative because he was willing to record Christian dream interpreters' views without criticism and admit that Christians' own dreams of their faith might signal a good outcome. However, later Muslim authors usually drew on his unfavourable interpretations, commonly endorsing views of the heretical Christian and sometimes adding more derogatory comments. Sadly, Dinawari's positive use of Christian oneirocriticism was largely ignored.

Muslims of the 'Abbasid Caliphate had some general familiarity with Christians under their rule, whereas, for Christians of the Byzantine Empire, Muslims were largely unknown. A dream interpreter such as Pseudo-Achmet was caught between the necessity for dependence on Islamic sources and the need to present a picture of Muslims that would satisfy his Christian readership of the time, inevitably a picture that could not readily be culled from those Arabic sources. He could not paint too favourable a portrait of the other, yet he required one that could cater for his readers' taste for remarkable tales.

Byzantine dream interpretation was a limited exercise, fraught with difficulties and dangers for the interpreters owing to frequent disapproval of their art by the authorities. Hence it was a marginalised pursuit that might demand a cloak of anonymity, as in the case of the compiler termed Pseudo-Achmet here. The lack of sustained official and known public support also led to a restricted influence of ideas and attitudes transmitted to later generations through Byzantine Christian thought on dreams. By contrast, the Muslim interpreters of dreams, including Dinawari, had a considerable continuing impact on popular images of Christians in the Islamic Middle East for centuries, via later dream books reproducing the views of the 'Abbasid age and still in popular circulation into the twenty-first century.

CHAPTER 6

'AND IF A WOMAN DREAMS'

Gender, Vision and Power

It does not take long to realise that, among the thousands upon thousands of dreams and visions narrated and discussed in Muslim writings, the overwhelming majority are the dreams and visions of men. Among the minority that deal with women's visionary experience, it is not unusual to discover that an author's underlying interest is in the relevance of the event to men's affairs. The woman glimpses the unseen world as the mother, sister, wife, daughter, wet-nurse or slave of a significant male. We have already noted the visions of the Prophet's mother, Amina, preceding his birth. When dream manuals consider the meaning of a woman's dream, the oneirocrits commonly give predictions of marriage, divorce or childbirth. More rarely, female Sufi mystics have access to visionary encounters that elevate them to a status as major actors in their own right and their remarkable mode of 'seeing' mirrors that of their male counterparts and allows a wider range of outcomes for them.

Nevertheless, it is male authors and compilers who control the main output of dream texts, normally including those that feature women. Whether as religious scholars, Sufis or men of letters, they have the education and social position to decide the value of women's experiences and how they are to be presented. They can determine what is appropriate for women generally and for particular women, recognising some as exceptional figures of righteousness and open to the reception of supernatural contacts, while consigning others to routine domestic occupations or disapproved licentiousness. In this chapter we will be examining some of the efforts by male *hadith* specialists, biographers, historians and compilers of dream manuals, as they considered the significance of women's dreams and visions. Were their narratives and assessments, especially of dreams, utilised as one tool among many intended to keep women in clearly defined spaces within medieval Muslim society and remind their male readers that women had no place in the public sphere? On the other hand, were they perhaps no more than a natural representation of the everyday life of their time, in which the limitations of women's roles were acknowledged, alongside those of poor and vulnerable free males and slaves? Finally, was this male understanding of women's 'seeing' essentially a Muslim creation or was it to some degree a reflection of older regional norms and, in the dream manuals, a legacy from Artemidorus?

Women Dreamers, Seventh to Ninth Centuries

'Atika's Dream

In late February 624, shortly before the battle of Badr, the Prophet's paternal aunt 'Atika is said to have been terrified by a powerful and disturbing dream. The oldest extant account of this dream is by Ibn Ishaq in his eighth-century biography of the Prophet, but there is some speculation that it may have been put into circulation by professional story-tellers at an earlier date.[1] It was subsequently recounted by Waqidi and Tabari with some embellishments. Of course, there is the usual impossibility of knowing whether such a dream was ever dreamt and considerable doubts as to whether the tale has 'the ring of truth'. According to the dramatic and somewhat improbable reports, 'Atika related her dream to al-'Abbas, her brother, in a state of alarm.

According to Tabari's history, 'Atika told her brother that she was afraid because her dream might 'portend evil and affliction for your people' and, therefore, she asked him to keep it to himself.[2] She then described the dream to him:

I saw a rider coming up on his camel. He halted in the valley and shouted at the top of his voice, 'Hasten to your deaths, you people of treachery, in three days' time!' I saw the people gathering round him, then he went into the mosque with the people following him. While they were round him, his camel climbed on top of the Ka'bah with him on its back. Then he shouted three times at the top of his voice as he had before, 'Hasten to your deaths, you people of treachery, in three days' time!' Then his camel mounted to the summit of the mount of Abu Qubays with him on its back and he shouted the same thing. Then he picked up a boulder and sent it rolling down the mountain. When it reached the bottom it shattered into fragments, and a piece of it went into every house and settlement in Mecca.[3]

Al-'Abbas, in his turn, urged his sister not to tell anyone else. However, he did mention the dream to a friend, who told his father. The story then circulated among the tribe of Quraysh until it reached the ears of Abu Jahl, one of the Prophet's harshest critics. He taunted al-'Abbas and his brothers, asking them if it was not enough that the men of their family claimed to be prophets without the women also claiming prophecy. He issued a final warning:

We shall be watching over you for these three days, and if what she says comes true, then so be it; but if the three days go by and nothing of this comes about, we will put it in writing that your family are the greatest liars among the Arabs.[4]

Al-'Abbas flatly denied his sister's dream, but soon found himself in trouble with the women of his family because he had failed to stand up to Abu Jahl. However, on the third day after 'Atika's strange visionary experience a man arrived in a terrible state. He had cut off his camel's nose, turned his saddle back to front and ripped his shirt. He stood on the camel and shouted to the people that the Prophet and his followers were preparing to seize a large caravan of goods in transit to Mecca. The Meccans, led by Abu Jahl, set out to defend their property, but encountered the Muslims at Badr and suffered their first serious defeat. Abu Jahl was among the dead. 'Atika's veridical dream had been fulfilled.

The dream report has a sense of drama that is comparable to the ancient Mesopotamian nightmare of Dumuzi (see Chapter 1). Yet, in this case, the roles of dreamer and listener are reversed between the siblings. Dumuzi related his dream to his sister, whereas 'Atika related hers to her brother. Dumuzi's sister was skilled as an interpreter of dreams and aware of the dangers of mentioning such a terrible dream, although she relented and deciphered it for her brother with fatal consequences. Al-'Abbas is presented as lacking such insight; although he cautioned 'Atika not to mention it, he foolishly spoke about the dream himself, thus unleashing its power to come true in the most harmful manner. Accounts of the dream reached the malicious Abu Jahl and other Meccans, who did not care for the wellbeing of 'Atika or her family. The narrative further reinforces the idea that it is dangerous to tell a dream, especially an evil one, to those who bear ill will towards the dreamer. The threefold repetition of the dream's message, as in ancient Mesopotamia, asserts the truth of the predicted events and the message has even greater force because it is stated that the deaths of the Prophet's Meccan enemies will take place 'in three days' time'.

'Atika's dream has also been observed to contain characteristics similar to a biblical dream reported in Judges 7:13–14, in which, on the eve of battle, a Midianite dreams of the victory of Gideon over the forces of Midian.[5] Both dreams announce the imminent defeat of the dreamers' peoples. In both accounts the symbolic image of defeat and its effect on the vanquished is an object that rolls downhill from a great height and impacts the place where they are staying: in Judges the symbol is a barley loaf, which strikes the camp of Midian and in 'Atika's dream it is a boulder, which breaks in pieces and strikes every house in Mecca, bringing death to the inhabitants. In both dreams God has already promised victory to the opponents of the Midianites and the Meccans (to Gideon in Judges 7:7 and to the Prophet in Qur'an 8:7–12).

Despite the ancient Near Eastern qualities of the dream narrative, it is nevertheless a Muslim imagining of a non-Muslim's dream. As such, it is assumed to be a divine sign that God is with the Muslims and will overcome their enemies. It is a dream designed to strike terror into the Meccans as opponents of the Prophet and the new religion of Islam. It is also told as a visual and auditory episodic dream with minimal, and fairly obvious, symbolism so that it is readily understood without the need for a divinely inspired interpreter or one with advanced training to comprehend God's signs. This would be seen as necessary since neither the Prophet nor any other of his gifted Companions is recorded as present in Mecca. Yet the vehicle for reception of this veridical dream is alleged to be a close female relative of the Prophet, a situation that provides the narrator with an opportunity to portray Abu Jahl as deriding the Prophet's family, including its women.

Two Hadiths on Women's Symbolic Dreams

*Hadith*s concerning women's dreams are remarkably rare. Most *hadith*s on the subject of dreaming provide general information on dreams, while others tell of the Prophet's dreams and his interpretation of them or of other men's dreams. Occasionally women are mentioned as transmitters of such *hadith*s or appear as actors in the narratives. However, in the following two cases women are reported as experiencing dreams of a simple, symbolic nature.

Of all the many dream accounts compiled by Bukhari only one testifies to a woman's dream. It is in a short section headed 'Dreams of Women', but containing only two traditions, of which only one recalls a dream. The first report is transmitted on the authority of a woman and concerns another woman called Umm al-'Ala', one of the Medinan supporters of the Prophet. According to this *hadith*, the emigrant Muslims from Mecca were allotted places to stay in the homes of their Medinan hosts and 'Uthman b. Maz'un was assigned to the house of Umm al-'Ala'. Unfortunately, he became ill and died. After his death Umm al-'Ala' was full of praise for him and declared that God had honoured him. When word of this came to the Prophet, he questioned her and told her that even he had no idea how he, as God's Messenger, would be treated after death. Consequently, Umm al-'Ala' realised that it was inappropriate for her to speak of God honouring 'Uthman, since she could not possibly know if that had happened.[6] The implications of the *hadith* are evident; if the Prophet himself cannot know someone's fate in the afterlife, it is unreasonable for anyone else to presume that they have such knowledge and the point is made all the stronger by linking the story to an ignorant woman. It served as a cautionary tale for those who would too eagerly declare other Muslims to be martyrs. However, it is not concerned with dreaming.

However, the following *hadith* does contain a dream report and supports 'Uthman b. Maz'un's high status after death. It also shows that even an ignorant woman can be granted a veridical dream. In this case, the same woman recounts her vision briefly: 'I slept and saw a spring flowing for 'Uthman. I then informed God's Messenger and he said: "That [spring represents] his good works".'[7] It is a very simple, visual dream, comprising of only one symbol, which the Prophet interprets through his divine inspiration.

A further tradition concerning a woman's dream is recorded in the collection of Ibn Maja. He narrates how Umm al-Fadl came to see the Prophet and told him: 'God's Messenger, I saw as though one of your limbs was in my house.' He replied: 'You have had a good vision. Fatima will give birth to a son and you will suckle him.'[8] Ibn Maja observes that Umm al-Fadl became wet-nurse to Husayn, the son of Fatima and grandson of the Prophet. However, he does not seem quite sure about the identity of the child and adds that it may have been Husayn's brother, Hasan. The symbolism of the limb as representing a family member is simple, but the Prophet demonstrates his insight into the future by stating that his daughter Fatima will bear a son and this woman will be the nurse. Nevertheless, Ibn Maja notes that the Prophet was not entirely satisfied with Umm al-Fadl because she struck the child when he soiled the house. The *hadith* illustrates the Prophet's kindness and concern for his grandson, but also emphasises that even an imperfect woman could have a significant and truthful dream.

Dreams of Virtuous and Sinful Women

The moralising ninth-century anecdotes of Ibn Abi al-Dunya include a few that relate to literal dreams experienced by women, although the majority of such dreams are the dreams of men. It is not evident from these narratives that righteous women are expected to be the only ones to have veridical dreams. According to Ibn Abi al-Dunya, true dreams are seen by both virtuous and sinful women and by those whose moral qualities are unclear. Women dreamers may be vehicles for imparting important guidance for the Muslim community, but they may also receive guidance themselves.

Since the author is very concerned to provide news of the afterlife for those who are still alive, the reward earned by the virtuous dead is a prominent theme. Many anecdotes observe that the deceased reap the benefits of a life spent in reciting the Qur'an and being meticulous in the performance of religious duties. These duties include undertaking the armed jihad as fighters for God's cause and being martyred as a result of such dedicated service. Two anecdotes record women's dreams of male martyrs.[9] In one account a woman came to the Prophet and told him that she had dreamt of entering Paradise and seeing there 12 people, whose names she listed for him, (although the names are not given in the text). As it happened, the Prophet had sent out fighters to take part in an expedition. Shortly after the woman told him of her dream, a messenger arrived and informed the Prophet that the men she had seen in her dream had been killed by the enemy. Through the true dream the Prophet had already received the news of their martyrdom.[10] It may be inferred that the woman in the report was virtuous because she said to the Prophet that she dreamt of sitting down at a banquet in Paradise with the martyred men and he believed her story. Nevertheless, the woman's character is peripheral to the anecdote, which makes the point that a dream can offer reliable information from 'the world of truth' more quickly and accurately than news that is available by everyday means in the visible world.

In another account Ibn Abi al-Dunya reports that a woman had a dream of her father, who had passed away as a result of a stomach complaint some time before. The man told his daughter that he was actually a martyr, but that he was not on the same level as those martyrs who had been killed fighting for God's sake; he did not merit being married to the beautiful, black-eyed houris of Paradise.[11] The dream is marked as a veridical one because the words of deceased parents are thought to be truthful when they appear in the dreams of their sons and daughters. The woman functions as the bearer of truth from her father, but her gender and moral qualities are not central to the tale.

In a further anecdote a woman's piety appears to be relevant to her dream vision. This unnamed woman was resident in Mecca and, before she fell asleep, she was reciting the Qur'an. The narrator reports: 'She saw in her sleep as though servant girls were standing around the Ka'ba, carrying sweet basil in their hands and wearing clothes dyed with safflower.'[12] The scene suggested that someone was getting married, but then the narrator realised that the dream's true meaning was that a certain 'Abd al-'Aziz b. Rawad had passed away. The wedding was not a wedding in this world. The dream of these events at Islam's holiest site and including the imagery of marriage may have seemed more credible when experienced by a pious Muslim woman.

By contrast, a sinful woman was recorded as receiving a very different message in her dream. This woman is also unnamed. She arrogantly declared: 'By God, I have never been guilty of *shirk* [associating another being with God], never committed adultery, never killed my child and never made false accusations directly or indirectly, so God will not punish me at all.'[13] The narrator describes how she went to bed and was visited in her sleep by a mysterious person, perhaps an angel, who rammed her body with a smouldering staff and urged her to seek refuge in her house from the fire. It is implied that the fire is indeed the fire of Hell. The woman protested that she had never committed any of the major sins that she had mentioned earlier. However, the person in the dream was not persuaded of her claims to be innocent of sin and told her: 'You exaggerate, harm your near neighbour and talk about people behind their backs.'[14] Again he urged her to take shelter from the fire until she exclaimed that she repented and her family found her still proclaiming her repentance when she awoke. Like many other anecdotes in Ibn Abi al-Dunya's dream book, this tale contains a moral lesson. It is not only necessary to avoid committing major sins in order to avoid the fires of Hell. There is a risk of being condemned to a wretched afterlife even if one only commits common minor sins. The narrator does not expressly state that these sins are especially common among women, but it may be read as hinting that this is the case. The putative angel, who warns the woman of the need to repent, plays a similar role to that played by angels in early Christian dream accounts, where they may act as terrifying and threatening agents of warning and punishment. The sinful woman is not exempt from having a veridical dream, but it is not a very pleasant or encouraging one.

Visionary Female Mystics, Late Eighth to Early Tenth Centuries

Rabi'a of Basra (d. 801)

Very little is known of the earliest female mystics of Islam, including the most famous of such women, Rabi'a of Basra (d. 801), also known as Rabi'a al-'Adawiyya. Early sources make only brief mention of her, although many stories have survived and spread her fame in and beyond Sufi circles so that she came to be admired as the ideal embodiment of the devoted Muslim woman. According to a number of anecdotes, many of which have been preserved in a twelfth-century Persian work of hagiography by Farid al-din 'Attar, Rabi'a was the fourth daughter of poor parents, sold into slavery and later freed by a master who witnessed her extraordinary piety.[15] She was said to have remained unmarried, declaring that she had no time for a husband in a life dedicated to the pure and selfless love of God. Various prayers and short verses were popularly attributed to her and she was credited with witty and pithy responses in dialogue with others, including some well-known religious figures. The historicity of all these tales is extremely dubious and it is unlikely that any more can be said of her than that she appears to have existed as a pious woman in Basra in the latter part of the eighth century.[16]

Nevertheless, Rabi'a became an important personality for the Sufi tradition, and in popular Muslim piety, because she was held up as a memorable example of the ideal lover of God, regardless of gender.

'Attar makes the point that gender is indeed of no significance for the Sufi devotee:

> If anyone asks why her memorial is placed among the ranks of men, we reply that the chief of the prophets – peace and blessing upon him – declares: *God does not regard your forms*. It is not a matter of form, but of right intention [...] When a woman is a man on the path of the lord Most High, she cannot be called woman.[17]

Consequently, 'Attar's edifying anecdotes are equally relevant to women and men. Since the mystic has no separate existence from the deity and there is no longer any 'you and I', all outer bodily appearances no longer matter. Nevertheless, 'Attar's last statement implies that the woman achieves a higher status than that of a mere woman by becoming a man on God's path. The male is clearly regarded as superior to the female.

'Attar was writing approximately four centuries after the lifetime of Rabi'a and the lack of sufficient earlier information makes it impossible to know whether he was reproducing narratives about her that had been in circulation over a long or short period or whether he was inventing stories that could serve as moral lessons in a manner similar to those collected by Ibn Abi al-Dunya. Apart from anecdotes that recount Rabi'a's admirable virtues and deep insight, there are several occasions on which 'Attar mentions dreams of the Prophet or waking visionary experience, which usually has a significant aural element, as Rabi'a hears a mysterious voice that seems intended to be understood as the voice of God.

According to 'Attar, Rabi'a's parents already had three daughters, a heavy burden for a poor family. Her name means the 'fourth'. Her father slept in a state of grief, not knowing how he could provide for his family and not liking to ask for help from anyone. In his sleep the Prophet came to him in a dream and reassured him that his daughter would be 'a noble lady' and would intercede for 70,000 of the Muslim community.[18] The Prophet also commanded him to go to the emir of Basra and deliver a message on his behalf, saying that the emir should give 400 gold dinars to atone for the number of times he had invoked the Prophet's blessings. Rabi'a's father then wrote down the dream and took it for someone to give to the emir. The emir was so grateful to learn that the Prophet had remembered him that he gave the 400 dinars to Rabi'a's father and thus alleviated some of the pressures on her family. As recorded in a famous *hadith*, a dream of the Prophet cannot be false and, therefore, the dream anecdote lends support to the belief in Rabi'a's high spiritual status and the care taken of her and her family by God's Messenger himself. This dream is presented as an old-style epiphany dream, a form repeated in another account that tells of the Prophet's dream appearance to Rabi'a, when he asked her: 'Rabi'a, do you love me?' She replied: 'O Prophet of God, who is there that doesn't love you? But love of the real has so pervaded me that there is no place in my heart for love or hatred of another.'[19] The 'real' here signifies God as the only Absolute Reality in existence, a frequent Sufi term used with reference to the deity. The dream reinforces a view of Rabi'a as being so focused on total love of God that she has no love available for any other being, even the Prophet. She was said to have shut herself up in her house and refused to come out even to look at the beauty of springtime, remarking that she was occupied with looking on the Creator and not on the creation.[20]

After Rabi'a's parents died, writes 'Attar, there was a severe famine in Basra and she was separated from her sisters and enslaved. In an attempt to escape from her slavery she ran off, but fell down in the street and broke her hand. She called upon God, not in order to complain or receive any help, but in her desire to know if He was pleased with her. It was then that she heard a voice telling her not to be sad because 'a grandeur' would be hers 'such that the closest of the heavenly company' to God, i.e. the prophets and saints, would be proud of her.[21] This type of conversation with God, assuring the Sufi saint of a high spiritual station, is not uncommon in biographies and autobiographies of Sufis and may also feature in separate collections of conversations between God and the mystic. On another occasion 'Attar relates that Rabi'a had been fasting and keeping vigil for seven days and nights until she became desperately hungry and wanted to break her fast. However, she suffered a series of mishaps; someone brought her food, but the cat managed to spill it and her water jug broke when she was about to drink from it. She protested to God. Then she heard His voice warning her that, if He gave her all the happiness in the world, He would take away the grief of her longing for him. The warning was to remind her that she should only desire what God desired.[22] Such correctional teaching is also frequent in Sufi dreams and visions and it can serve, in addition, as a means of educating those reading or listening to the tales.

Finally, an example of this kind of dream, allegedly experienced by Rabi'a, is recorded in a much later hagiographical account of Sufi lives by 'Abd al-Ra'uf al-Munawi (d. 1621).[23] Munawi included a number of women among the Sufi saints in his collection and did not apparently see a need to discuss the issue of gender.[24] He describes how Rabi'a fell asleep just before dawn, a time that has traditionally been considered particularly conducive to the reception of true dreams. She also praised God in her prayers before sleeping, which would render her more likely to be guided by Him in her dream. She recalled seeing in her dream vision a tall and beautiful tree with 'three kinds of fruit' growing on it, 'unlike any of this world's fruits, the size of a maiden's breast: one white, one red, and one yellow, shining like moons or suns against the green background of the tree'. When she asked about the tree, a voice told her that it grew as a result of her prayers. Then she saw that there was some golden fruit on the ground and remarked that it would be better if it were on the tree with the other fruit. The voice replied: 'This fruit was on the tree, but during your prayer of praise, you thought about whether the dough was rising, and [at that moment] it fell.'[25] Thus even the purest and most devoted lover of God could be in need of moral correction through dreams and waking visions.

The Wife of al-Hakim al-Tirmidhi
(Ninth–Early Tenth Centuries)

By contrast with the accounts of Rabi'a, which are widely separated from her in time and written by men of later ages, al-Hakim al-Tirmidhi (d. between 905 and 910) composed a far more personal record of his wife's extraordinary dreams and visions. Tirmidhi came from Tirmidh situated on the River Oxus (Amu Daria) in a remote region of Central Asia and he has become known especially for his seminal thought on the nature of sainthood and the doctrine of the 'seal of the saints' (*khatm al-awliya'*), the one in whom sainthood is perfected, a concept that became famously linked to the major Sufi master Ibn 'Arabi (d. 1240).[26] He stressed the important role of dreams in communication between God and those that he brings near to Him, the saints.[27] Tirmidhi was the author of a spiritual autobiography, possibly the earliest by a Muslim writer. In this work he focused on the inner life of the mystic, but told of his unnamed wife's dreams and visions in addition to his own and he also related occasional dreams of other acquaintances.

Tirmidhi's wife is a major actor in his account. He presents her as a channel of communication between the supernatural world and himself, dreaming of matters that relate to his own spiritual station, development and role. However, he also writes of his wife's dreams and waking visions that concern her personal development and mystical experience. He clearly values her spiritual state very highly and considers it important enough for her to merit treatment as a significant mystic. At a time of civil strife in the area when Tirmidhi had been suffering from enemies in neighbouring towns slandering and persecuting him, his wife dreamt that she saw someone with curly hair and white clothes walking through the air above the path. He called out to her, asking her where her husband was and she said that he had gone out. Then the visionary figure told her that she should inform Tirmidhi that 'the prince' commanded him 'to act justly'.[28] The figure in the air is probably an angel, since a figure with this appearance identifies himself as such in a later dream, while the prince is understood to be God. This dream seems to occur early in the process of Tirmidhi's wife dreaming on his behalf.

Tirmidhi relates that his wife continued to receive visions concerning him and observes that they always took place just before dawn, a particularly meaningful time of day to have veridical dreams. They required no interpretation because they were clear, literal dreams, containing both visual and auditory elements. In one of these dreams the wife was sitting with her two sisters by a large pool of pure water and there were bunches of white grapes floating on the surface, which they picked up and ate. They were wondering who had sent them the grapes, when a white-clothed being came and instructed Tirmidhi's wife concerning her husband's recitation of Qur'anic verses. He told her that he was one of the angels who travel the earth and dwell in Jerusalem. He held fresh green myrtle in his right hand and sweet basil in his left and explained to her that the angels place the basil on the hearts of the sincere (*al-sadiqun*) and the myrtle on the hearts of the righteous (*al-siddiqun*). The angel then gave Tirmidhi's wife a message for her husband, saying that she should ask him: "'Don't you wish that you could have these two?" And he pointed to the myrtle and the herbs.'[29] He then commanded her: "'Tell him: Purify your house!" I said: "I have small children, and I cannot keep my house completely pure." He said: "I don't mean from urine. What I mean is this" – and he pointed to his tongue.'[30] The house here is used in a metaphorical sense to apply to the soul. It is used in the same way in an autobiographical dream narrative by the littérateur Abu Hayyan al-Tawhidi (d. 1023), whom an unspecified person commands to 'improve' his house.[31] However, Tirmidhi's wife first understands the command literally and requires an explanation. The angel gives her a piece of the myrtle, indicating that she has achieved righteousness and is thus on a higher level than those who are described simply as 'sincere' worshippers. She is assured that she and her husband are at the same spiritual stage and that the angel will give him the myrtle and sweet basil that he is holding. When she asks the angel why he does not make this announcement in front of her sisters, he replies: 'They are not like you and they are not your equal.'[32] This is the point at which Tirmidhi first makes it clear that his wife is more than a messenger and not only a vehicle for alluding to the significance of his own spiritual position.

At the end of his autobiography Tirmidhi concludes not with his own mystical experiences but with those of his wife. These remarkable visions occurred over three days, beginning when she was sitting outside in the garden. She felt as though her chest was full up to her throat, heat was spreading through her body and her heart was burning. Wherever she looked she saw the world with fresh eyes and it was as if all of creation was filled with beauty and she experienced intense joy. On the third day she reached the highest point of her mystical awareness and 'the knowledge of the names of God was revealed to her. Each day new names opened up to her, and the glowing light was upon her heart, and the inward meaning of the names was revealed to her.'[33] After ten days she came to tell her husband that she had received revelation of God's one hundredth name. Tirmidhi's reasons for choosing to end his autobiography with his wife's visions are unknown, but it provides a rare and personal insight into the place of dreams and visions in the development of a Muslim mystical couple and one that does not privilege the male over the female.

Dream Manuals and Women's Dreams

The picture of women's dreams that we glimpse in the classic dream manuals differs markedly from the record of the dreams and visions ascribed to female mystics and even some of the other women named in early Muslim anecdotes. John Lamoreaux remarks: 'All Muslim dream manuals are in accord that there is no person who is not able to receive divinely sent dreams. It matters not whether one is a North African shoemaker, an Afghani holy warrior, or a menstruating woman.'[34] Nevertheless, the 'menstruating woman' appears rather low on the list of those considered likely to be the recipients of true dreams and dream manuals seem to be written largely with the Muslim male dreamer in mind.

Sijistani, in the introduction to his manual, ranks dreamers in a hierarchy of 'fourteen grades' according to their propensity for having veridical dreams.[35] While male dreamers are given more prominence in his list, he notes that veiled women are more able to experience meaningful dreams than the unveiled. Personal spirituality is regarded as an important factor in enabling contact with the divine. Hence Sijistani would presumably have expected women such as Rabi'a and Tirmidhi's wife to be open to God-sent vision. However, he and the other medieval oneirocrits do not give much space to the meanings of dreams that may be seen by women. Among the symbolic images that may be seen in sleep, many images are judged to have no special relevance for women. Sometimes towards the end of an entry the author writes: 'And if a woman dreams...' and then discloses the particular meaning of that image for a female dreamer. In such cases, the woman's dreams 'appear to relate primarily to household matters such as marital or domestic affairs, physical looks, pregnancy, and birth of children'.[36] Such dreams are far removed from the lofty, spiritual visions of the mystics, but they are also clearly separated from mundane dreams of matters understood to be the affairs of men.

Since the surviving dream manuals are all the work of men and men, such as Ibn al-Musayyab and Ibn Sirin, are the named interpreters of dreams in anecdotal narratives, it is hardly surprising that most attention in the manuals is devoted to males and particularly to free, adult, Muslim males. The dreams of male and female slaves and children are given minimal mention because they are classed alongside the dreams of free women as being of less consequence for Muslim society than the dreams of men, particularly élite men. It is arguable that the dreams of women, slaves and children might not be discussed at all, if they were not recognised as impacting the lives of the dominant males within the family.

Was there any pre-modern tradition of women acting as interpreters of dreams? Lamoreaux is one who has raised the question and asked if there were 'perhaps even distinctively female modes of dream interpretation', but he has found no evidence to support or refute the possibility.[37] Despite the recognised importance of women as dream interpreters in the ancient Near East,[38] they appear to have been marginalised in such roles in medieval Muslim society. While many male interpreters are known by name, it is very rare for any woman to be acknowledged in this way. The case of Asma', the daughter of Caliph Abu Bakr, is an exceptional and very early case of a reported female interpreter of dreams. Otherwise, the occasional allusion to an unnamed 'female interpreter' or 'female scholar' is recorded in the ever popular work of Dari (Pseudo-Ibn Sirin). Illiteracy obviously imposed severe limitations on the extent to which medieval Muslim women could be regarded as authorities in what was seen as a branch of the religious sciences. However, it has been suggested that they may have acted informally as interpreters within an oral tradition catering to their families and other women in a similar manner to that observed as operating in modern Egypt.[39] The practical difficulty is that this remains speculation in the absence of documentary evidence and, even if such a tradition were proved to exist, it would be impossible to know whether it differed substantially from the male interpretative tradition without the reliable preservation of many women's interpretations of dreams. At the present we are left with the work of male scholars and littérateurs, some of whose views are considered here.

Dinawari, Dari and Nabulusi on Women's Dreams

Dinawari's vast dream manual has already been noted for its extensive influence on the genre. It is, therefore, to be expected that two of the most widely circulated of the pre-modern dream books, those of Dari and Nabulusi, often present interpretations identical or very similar to those of Dinawari concerning the meanings attached to women's dreams. The three oneirocrits thus bear witness to some of the most popular ideas on the subject among Muslims of the eleventh to seventeenth centuries; these ideas have continued to enjoy popularity among a modern readership due to the regular printings and extensive sales of the works by Dari and Nabulusi. Consequently, this combination of dream books is of value in identifying some common male interpretations of Muslim women's dreams.

Although Dinawari's book enjoys few readers today, it is relatively more helpful than the other two manuals in locating the origins of certain views that gained widespread acceptance, although references usually remain too vague to be readily traced. In the long section on the meanings of dreams about various parts of the human body and biological processes, such as childbirth, Dinawari follows his usual procedure of citing a variety of sources for particular interpretations: the Muslims, the Christians, the Jews, the Indians, the Zoroastrian sage Jahmasb, philosophers and, of course, Artemidorus.[40] Generally, references to Artemidorus are more easily identified than in the case of other sources and the debt to Artemidorus is particularly evident when Dinawari considers the significance of women's dreams.

One example concerns the normally male attribute of a beard seen in dreaming. Before citing Artemidorus, Dinawari offers several interpretations of dreams about a woman growing a beard. Without naming his source, he first remarks that, if a man dreams of a bearded woman, it may be a positive sign that he or his son will acquire wealth;[41] presumably this is because the woman represents one of his possessions and the growth of a beard indicates the growth of something else belonging to him, i.e. income. However, it can also predict the sickness of the man's wife. It is likely that this negative prediction is given because it is considered unnatural for a woman to have a beard and, when a dreamer sees something unnatural, it frequently portends a bad outcome such as sickness and death. It can also be a sign that the woman will never have children, apparently because the beard is associated with males and males cannot bear children. If the woman has a son, he will be the master of the house and enjoy a good reputation. The more positive outcome seems to be due to the connection of the beard with the woman's son rather than the woman herself. Dinawari does not actually spell out the reasons behind the interpretations and it is left to the reader to work out the rationale.

Dinawari then cites Artemidorus for further meanings.[42] He remarks that the significance of a woman dreaming that she has a beard will vary depending on whether she is married or a widow. If she is married, it predicts that her husband will be separated from her. If she is pregnant, she will bear a son and see him attain maturity. If she is involved in a lawsuit, she will have nothing to fear because she will receive the respect given to men. However, if the woman is a widow, possessing a beard is a sign that she will remarry. Dari and Nabulusi reproduce all the above interpretations relating to the bearded woman, but, like Dinawari, without offering explanations.[43] For the reasoning behind the interpretations ascribed to Artemidorus it is necessary to look to Artemidorus himself. His argument in the case of the widow is that she will marry a man who has so much sympathy for her that 'their faces will seem to merge into one'.

Hence she will appear to acquire his beard. As for the married woman, she 'will lose her husband and will manage her household alone, being, in truth, both wife and husband at the same time'. If she was pregnant and saw her son as an adult, she would then gain a beard.[44] The woman involved in the lawsuit would be respected because she had a man's attributes.

In all the interpretations derived from Artemidorus it is notable that a woman can acquire honour and status through becoming more like a man, as symbolised by the beard, or by having male children. Such an outlook fits with the views of the Muslim oneirocrits and there is, therefore, no need to censor or reject the Greek understanding. Nevertheless, it is only Dinawari who admits that he has culled this information from Artemidorus, whereas Dari and Nabulusi ignore the non-Muslim origin of the material. Dinawari's interpretations from unnamed sources appear to be even more focused on male superiority and dominance within society, since positive associations are made between the dream image of the bearded woman and the male acquisition of wealth and a good position. The growth of a beard is seen as contrary to nature for the woman and generally indicates misfortune for her, sickness and infertility.

By contrast with the masculine symbol of the beard, the breast might be expected to offer more favourable interpretative possibilities concerning the woman. In some circumstances it does, but not always. Dinawari discusses the dream image of the breast with reference to Muslim tradition and then to Artemidorus.[45] He introduces his subject by citing the Muslim opinion that the breast represents a man's wife and his daughter; the beauty of the breast symbolises their beauty and its imperfection symbolises their imperfection. The focus is on the image as it affects the man rather than the woman in her own right and the interpretation that follows is highly negative towards the woman. Dinawari reports the Muslim view that, if a man dreams of 'a woman hanging by her breasts, she will commit adultery and bear a son by someone other than her husband'.[46] This interpretation is based on a saying attributed to the Prophet on the occasion of his ascension to Heaven, when he was shown a vision of Hell with an adulterous woman hanging by her breasts.

Dinawari then cites Artemidorus, offering several examples of interpretations that are more directly concerned with the effects on the situation of the female and in which references to the husband or other males are noticeably absent.[47] He follows Artemidorus closely in considering different outcomes depending on the age and circumstances of the women and girls involved. Both Artemidorus and Dinawari remark that, if a young woman dreams that she has milk in her breasts, it means that she will become pregnant and give birth to a child; the meaning in this case is obvious. If a rich woman has the same dream, she will incur expenses and become impoverished, apparently because the milk represents wealth that is leaving the woman. The dream is interpreted differently for the virgin; it is a sign of marriage, since the girl would be unable to have milk in her breasts until after she had sexual intercourse with a man, as explained by Artemidorus and copied by Dinawari. However, if a little girl has this dream, it predicts her death. Artemidorus explains: 'For all things, with few exceptions, that are out of season are bad.'[48] The idea of a right and wrong timing for a dream affects both Greek and Muslim dream interpretation, but Dinawari and his imitators do not see fit to mention it. Perhaps this is simply a mark of casualness in their use of ancient sources or they may assume that their readers are sufficiently familiar with the concept to work it out without their aid.

Since the Muslim oneirocrits culled the lists of interpretations from different cultural contexts, there are obvious inconsistencies. These inconsistencies pose the same problems for the interpretation of women's dreams as they pose for dream interpretation in general. While the dream interpreters recognised the need to differentiate between people of various ethnic, religious, cultural and class backgrounds, their manuals remain theoretical and it is impossible to know how or whether they managed to reconcile the information and apply it to actual women's dreams. Some of the manuals contain anecdotes, including ones that are applicable to both named and unnamed women's dreams. However, it is unlikely that they tell us anything reliable about dreams that were really dreamt and interpreted. In effect, they are diverting stories from a range of

Muslim and non-Muslim sources, whether intended purely for entertainment or for moral edification. This impression is confirmed by the appearance of some of the same tales in other works of Islamic literature. For example, both Ibn Qutayba and Dinawari repeat the story already noted among the dream narratives of Ibn Abi al-Dunya, in which a virtuous woman dreamt of a wedding in the vicinity of the Ka'ba and discovered that it indicated the death of a pious Muslim rather than an earthly wedding.[49]

Women's 'Seeing' Through the Eyes of Men

This selection of women's dreams and visions has been excerpted from a variety of genres, but it is noticeable that the anecdotal form links all these male-authored texts. In some cases anecdotes incorporate archaic elements that remain meaningful for medieval Muslim readers, as observed in Tabari's account of the dream of 'Atika, which reproduces ancient Near Eastern ideas about the dream, but nevertheless offers a Muslim slant on salvation history. In the eyes of men the female dreamers often, but not always, appear imperfect and ignorant, but are not exempt from receiving true information through dreams. However, sometimes gender does not seem to be of particular significance in the narrative and a male protagonist could have served equally well in the account. The female mystics, Rabi'a and Tirmidhi's wife, stand out as being exceptionally honoured and admired, but their status as women is of little consequence. Rabi'a is even explicitly described as becoming a man on the path to God and, therefore, not properly a woman at all.

The texts generally indicate an acceptance of women's position as being inferior to that of men, unless they are marked out by an outstanding degree of spirituality that allows them to be treated as honorary men. The compilers of the dream manuals are arguably the most restrictive in confining female dreamers to dreams of domestic matters that exclude them from the public sphere. It could be argued that this is simply a realistic representation of the lives of medieval Muslim women and that similar limitations applied to other vulnerable members of society, such as poor men, slaves and children, whose situations rendered it unsuitable to interpret their dreams as indicating that they would rule or attain important posts in the state. In places the manuals do contain some misogynistic views, but they are also the product of a highly conservative tradition that is concerned with preserving inherited lore with minimal personal judgement. The dream interpreters seldom express their own opinions and may be seen to reflect notions accepted in the society of their day and often including much older regional thought on the subject of women's dreams.

CHAPTER 7

ENVISIONING GOD AND HIS PROPHET

Dreams and Visions on the Journey to God

While any pious Muslim might hope to receive divine messages through the medium of dreams, for Sufi spiritual wayfarers both dreams and waking visions were of utmost importance in their pursuit of guidance on the journey to God. These experiences were thought to offer insight into the benefits of particular religious duties and behaviour, correct the seeker's faults and give assurance of forgiveness for sins. Biographical and autobiographical accounts of Sufis' dreams and visions could also serve to promote an individual's status among disciples and the masses. Understandably, special value became attached to visionary encounters with God and His prophets, especially the Prophet Muhammad.

This chapter examines a small selection of the many Sufi reports of 'sightings' of God and the Prophet from the twelfth century onwards and observes changes in the phenomenon since that time, concluding with a study of visions in fifteenth- to nineteenth-century Africa. At times these narratives of visionary events led to popular acclaim and approval for the protagonist and resulted in endorsement as a saint. On other occasions they led to controversy, as in the case of the Andalusian mystic Ibn 'Arabi, who has divided Muslim opinion over the centuries since his death in thirteenth-century Damascus. It was also possible for the aspiring Sufi to relate remarkable meetings with the Prophet and yet to be ignored, a notable example being that of Muhammad al-Zawawi, a fifteenth-century North African. It is quite likely that there were many such instances, but it is rarer to learn about those who were not believed than about those who had their saintly visions confirmed by an admiring following.

Visualising God through the Heart

Medieval Muslim theologians were deeply divided as to whether it would ever be possible to see God with one's own eyes.[1] The majority of Sunni scholars came to the view that only believers would be able to see God in the afterlife; unbelievers would be unable to see Him. However, in this life some argued that only Prophet Muhammad had been granted a vision of God on the occasion of his ascension to Heaven. Most of the Shi'a and some other theologians denied the possibility of seeing God even in the afterlife. According to the dream manuals, ordinary believers were considered capable of seeing a dream image of God or hearing His voice in their dreams, although it did not always mean that they had found favour with God, since certain dreams could signify the opposite. Apart from prophets and Shi'i imams, it was Sufi mystics who most frequently laid claim to experiencing visions of God through the heart, but not through the sense perception of the eyes.

Some of the most remarkable accounts of visionary encounters with God occur in the work of the Iranian mystic Ruzbihan Baqli (d. 1209). They support the idea that God has selected Ruzbihan for sainthood and spiritual authority in the world. Thus, in an early narrative, he writes:

> I saw God on the roof of my house, with the qualities of might, majesty, and eternity. I saw as it were the world entire, a resplendent light, manifold and great. And he called me from the midst of the light, in the Persian tongue, seventy times: 'Ruzbihan, I have chosen you for sainthood (*wilaya*) and selected you for love.'[2]

Since it would be common to sleep on the roof of a traditional Middle Eastern house, it is not clear whether Ruzbihan is actually describing a dream or possibly a vision in a state between sleeping and waking. This extraordinary epiphany has both visual and auditory elements; it is also intensely personal, expressed in the language of Sufis' 'intimate conversations' or 'communion' with God (*munajat*).[3] While such communion could take the form of heartfelt, personal prayer, it could also be expressed in more controversial forms of dialogue between God and the mystic or divine monologue, as often emerges from Ruzbihan's outpourings.

On another occasion Ruzbihan speaks of seeing the prophets and the first four caliphs of Islam, together with all the angels. He sees God showering them all with roses and pearls, before He tells the assembled company that He has chosen Ruzbihan for sainthood and declares: 'I have placed in him the receptacles of my knowledge and my secret.'[4] After pronouncing that He has preserved Ruzbihan from any disobedience to Him, God is described as announcing:

> He is my vicegerent (*khalifa*) in this world and all worlds; I love whosoever loves him, and I hate whosoever hates him. None disobeys my judgements, and none rejects my order, for I am 'one who acts when he wishes'.[5]

Ruzbihan frequently writes in his visionary diary that God has chosen him for an exalted role to act as vicegerent over the created world, a role once entrusted to Adam and of greater scope than the caliphate entrusted to the successors of the Prophet.

The visions distance Ruzbihan from making extravagant and unsupported claims to spiritual supremacy, but, at the same time, they do underpin the idea that Ruzbihan is the beloved of God and, in the manner of the Shi'i imams, is preserved by Him from committing any sin. For those who believed in such visionary encounters, the effect is to be reassured of God's loving care for His lovers, the mystics, and to confirm that His chosen saints have an important, cosmic role to play in the world. For critics it is a dangerous mark of delusion and inappropriate for any human being to lay claim to this experience.

In the Islamic West a near contemporary of Ruzbihan was the famous and influential Sufi shaykh Ibn 'Arabi (d. 1240), who was born in the Spanish town of Murcia and brought up in the great city of Seville where his father was employed in the service of the sultan.[6] He travelled extensively in North Africa and in the eastern Arab world, spending time in the holy city of Mecca and ending his days in Damascus. His life, like that of Ruzbihan, was filled with visions, including the vision of God. Later in his life he recalled how in his young manhood he experienced a period when, in common with many other mystics, he felt abandoned by God. However, this sense of abandonment left him because he was granted a vision of God, in which he heard God reciting to him a Qur'anic verse (Qur'an 7:57) that gave him assurance of God's mercy.[7]

Ibn 'Arabi refers to his own visionary experience on a number of occasions in his monumental *al-Futuhat al-Makkiyya* (Meccan Illuminations), which he claimed to have composed under divine inspiration, completing the first draft in December 1231 at Damascus and finishing the second in 1238 not long before his death at the age of 75. Among his other writings he also produced a short work entitled *Kitab al-Mubashshirat* (The Book of Visions), in which he told his readers of some of his own visions in the hope that they might prove useful to them. One spectacular experience that he records in this collection is of uncertain date, but appears to derive from his time in Seville as a young man. It concerns a dramatic vision of the end of the world and the Resurrection, when Ibn 'Arabi observes:

> I saw in a vision that the Resurrection had taken place. People were rushing forward: some were clothed, others naked; some were walking on their legs, others on their faces.
>
> Then God came, 'in the darkness of thick clouds accompanied by angels' (Qur'an 2:210), seated on His Throne which was being carried by angels. They placed the throne to

my right. While all this was happening I experienced no fear or anxiety or fright.[8]

According to the account that follows, God then touched the visionary with His palm and Ibn 'Arabi boldly addressed His Lord, first remarking that human rulers make demands on their subjects because they are poor, whereas God is rich. What then has God to gain by making demands of His creation? Ibn 'Arabi continues:

> He [God] smiled and replied: 'What do you want?' I answered: 'Authorise me to go to Paradise [i.e. directly and without rendering accounts]'. He gave me His authorisation.
> Then I saw my sister Umm Sa'd. I said to Him: 'And my sister Umm Sa'd!' He replied: 'Take her with you'. Then I saw my sister Umm 'Ala'. I said to Him: 'And her as well?' He replied: 'Her as well!' I said to Him: 'And my wife Umm 'Abd al-Rahman?'[9]

Ibn 'Arabi claims that God gave permission also for his wife and for another lady of his acquaintance, until he asked for all his friends and relations to be allowed to enter Paradise without rendering accounts, as well as any others for whom God chose to give permission. In the end he says: 'I [only] took with me everyone who fell within my gaze (God alone can count them): *those whom I knew and those whom I did not know*. I made them go in front of me, keeping behind them so as to prevent them becoming lost on the way.'[10] The named persons for whom Ibn 'Arabi intercedes in this vision are all women and this fits with his perception that women are capable of reaching the highest levels of spirituality. Holy women are known to have played an important role in providing him with spiritual guidance at an early age during his time in Seville. They included Fatima bint Ibn al-Muthanna, an elderly lady living in extreme poverty, and Shams Umm al-Fuqara', whom he encountered at Marchena of the Olives, a citadel outside Seville. He recollects of Shams: 'She usually concealed her spiritual state, although she would often reveal something of it to me in secret because she knew of my own attainment, which gladdened me.'[11]

The effect of this early vision of the Resurrection was apparently to offer reassurance to Ibn 'Arabi of God's favour towards him and to foretell that he would be granted a high spiritual state. However, it does not appear to have made him complacent, since much later in his life during a stay in Mecca he had a dream vision that showed him encountering God on the Last Day. Far from being confident that he would enter Paradise, Ibn 'Arabi was in a state of fear, thinking that God would punish him for neglecting to give sufficient guidance to his disciples. He had been thinking of abandoning the effort to serve as a spiritual guide to others and to concentrate instead on his own attempt to journey to God. But God gave him comfort and reassurance that he was only being asked to advise his followers. The dream gave him the strength to return to his task and help others on their spiritual journey.

Conscious of the risks of being accused of heresy if such intimate conversations with God were made public, some later Sufis restricted information to a small circle of their most trusted peers and disciples. For example, Nabulusi, the author of the famous dream manual and a dedicated follower of Ibn 'Arabi, composed an account of his communion with God during a seven-year retreat in his house in Damascus from 1680 to 1687.[12] He seems to have been fearful that the work might be used by his enemies to attack the audacity of his ecstatic claims to intimacy with the Divine Being. Some of his intoxicated statements appear especially bold, but at the same time are also less vivid than those of Ruzbihan and Ibn 'Arabi and are sometimes couched in more obscure language. Nabulusi declares, like Ruzbihan, that God has decreed him to be His 'secret'. Daringly he asserts: 'God appeared to me in my form and He said, "I am Absolute unrestricted Being and you are my restricted form".' Later he exclaims: 'Then he called out to me from my own calling out and He revealed His essence (*dhat*) and my essence to me and I heard but one voice talking and I witnessed one ecstatic being.'[13] Such extravagant claims seem far removed from the modest conservatism of his dream manual and would have been extremely dangerous for him if seen by some of his harsher critics in Damascus. Both he and Ibn 'Arabi, whom he looked upon as his spiritual father, were subjected to fierce attacks at the time, spearheaded by Turkish jurists of the Kadizadeli movement that had spread to Syria from Istanbul and threatened those Sufis of whom the group disapproved.[14]

Marcia Hermansen has remarked on the increasing intellectualisation of visions among the mystics of pre-modern South Asia in the seventeenth and eighteenth centuries, with regard to a range of subjects and not only the vision of God. She observes that there is a move away 'from the more intuitive, stream of consciousness mode of visionary experience of the classical Sufi tradition to one more closely associated with cognitive strategies'. The intuitive type of vision is well represented in the visionary diary of Ruzbihan Baqli and a number of visions of Ibn 'Arabi, where the vision seems to be experienced 'without deliberate forethought', whereas the visions of some later scholarly mystics 'reflect a process of judgment resulting from cognitive processes'.[15] Hermansen focuses on the cognitive approach to problem-solving through visions in the writings of Shah Wali Allah of Delhi (d. 1762), the Indian scholarly reformer.

Seeing the Prophet in Dreams and Visions

Despite the great importance attached to seeing the Prophet in dreams and waking visionary encounters, the phenomenon appears to have been relatively rare in the late medieval period. However, by the late eighteenth to early nineteenth centuries, visions of the Prophet were far more widely attested and had become an accepted rite of passage for aspirants to sainthood.[16] The belief that Satan could not assume the shape of the Prophet in a dream was famously endorsed in a Prophetic *hadith* and lent support to the view that such visionary encounters must necessarily be true. Hence visions of the Prophet could be cited to lay claim to the highest ranks of sainthood and even the status of the Mahdi, who would usher in an age of justice before the end of the world. Controversially, they could be used to introduce new prayers or even implement laws that were not established in the sharia, despite the criticisms of religious scholars. The scholarly

Envisioning God and His Prophet

suspicions of abuses are often understandable, not least because of concerns that accounts of the Prophet speaking in dreams and visions might undermine the careful study of *hadith*s and the image of the Prophet painstakingly built up through historical scholarship.

That image was already being thoroughly transformed by the time of Ibn 'Arabi. Even by the ninth century, if not earlier, the very human person of the Prophet was being re-evaluated as the idea emerged of the Muhammadan Light, according to which the Prophet had existed from pre-eternity in the form of light derived from the Light of God.[17] In this form he predated even Adam and his light passed into the souls of the prophets and, according to the Shi'a, into their imams. However, it was with Ibn 'Arabi that the perception of the Prophet in his cosmic role became fully developed so that the human seventh-century prophet receded into the background. Ibn 'Arabi is probably the first to speak of the Prophet as also being the Perfect Human Being (*al-insan al-kamil*), who manifests the beautiful qualities of God to the utmost degree in creation. Although other created beings can manifest aspects of the Divine, it is the Perfect Human Being in whom all God's Names are present and who serves as a mirror to display them in the fullest form. Therefore, Ibn 'Arabi encouraged others to seek out visions of the Prophet, whether in sleep or wakefulness, in order to look at him as at a mirror and perceive the Attributes of God.[18]

With regard to his personal visionary experience, Ibn 'Arabi recalls on various occasions his encounters with the souls of the prophets. In a highly significant vision at Cordoba in 1190, he tells of seeing a gathering of all the prophets.[19] On a second occasion he claims to have witnessed not only the prophets but also all the believers who had ever been in existence or who would come into existence before the end of the world. He then learned that every saint is at the foot of a prophet. Yet questions have remained as to the reason behind the visionary gathering. Was this mystery handed down in secret by Ibn 'Arabi's disciples? It has been observed that there is a belief among his followers that the prophets gathered in order 'to congratulate him on being nominated the "Seal of Sainthood", the supreme heir to the Seal of the prophets'.[20] This is a tenuous claim at best, but it is only one of the occasions on which Ibn 'Arabi's supporters would claim visionary endorsement of his role as the Seal of Muhammadan Sainthood, the one who most fully and perfectly manifested the Prophet's quality as saint or 'friend of God' (*wali Allah*). It was a claim that would be bitterly contested and denounced by a number of later medieval scholars from the time of Qutb al-Din al-Qastallani (d. 1287), author of a polemical biography of Ibn 'Arabi.[21] Yet opposition to the great Sufi master most famously crystallised around the devastating attacks of the eminent jurist Ibn Taymiyya (d. 1328), who has been described as 'the most implacable and consequential opponent of Ibn 'Arabi and his followers'.[22] Opponents would be concerned that Ibn 'Arabi's claim to such an exalted state of sainthood endangered the position of the Prophet Muhammad and weakened the role of legislative prophecy.

In his youth Ibn 'Arabi attached great importance to visionary contacts with all the prophets, but especially with Jesus, whom he considered as his first spiritual teacher, and, subsequently, Moses and Muhammad. Under the guidance of the three prophets he was drawn to the Sufi way to God, but it was the Prophet Muhammad who urged him to follow in his path at a time when he admitted to having been ignorant of Islamic learning. In his *Book of Visions* he recounts how he saw himself being surrounded by enemies prepared to attack him with their weapons. He then came to a hill, on which the Prophet was standing. Ibn 'Arabi rushed forward and clung to the Messenger of God, who assured him: 'My beloved, *hold fast to me and you will be safe!*' He then devoted himself to the study of the *Hadith*.[23] This episode is reported here as one of Ibn 'Arabi's visions that he hoped would benefit the community by encouraging people to follow the example of the Prophet as contained in *hadith*s. Two other teaching dreams in the same book are recorded in the form of visionary conversations with the Prophet, in which Ibn 'Arabi asked him whether angels were superior to humans and whether animals would be resurrected on the Last Day. The Prophet assured Ibn 'Arabi that angels were indeed superior, but that animals would definitely not be resurrected.[24] The effect of the Prophet's speech in visions of this type is to lend credence to particular doctrinal viewpoints and make it difficult for religious scholars to challenge them. These dialogues appear to be classic instances where 'what the author cannot say on his own authority, he can support with testimony from an outside source through the narration of a dream or vision'.[25] However, such visionary discourse can also be seen as enhancing Ibn 'Arabi's position, since he is the person chosen to receive the Prophet's messages.

In Ibn 'Arabi's later life he claimed a much more extensive contact with the Prophet, asserting that it was Muhammad who transmitted to him his most famous work, *Fusus al-hikam* (The Bezels of Wisdom), at Damascus in the year 1229. (*Fass*, a 'bezel', is the Arabic singular of *fusus* and has the meaning of a setting in which a gemstone is placed on a ring.) The book as a whole offers a condensation of mystical teachings, which can be found more widely dispersed elsewhere in Ibn 'Arabi's writings, especially in the vast *Futuhat*. Each of the 27 chapters contained in the *Fusus* concerns an aspect of God's wisdom as manifested in the life of a particular prophet, beginning with a chapter on 'The wisdom of divinity in the word of Adam.' Thus each prophet acts as the human 'bezel' or 'setting' that serves to contain a gem of divine wisdom. Ibn 'Arabi would often be described by later generations as 'the author of the *Fusus*' (*sahib al-Fusus*) and his critics viciously attacked this work more than any other. The hostility that it attracted is likely to be because all the major ideas associated with the master are expressed in a relatively short space and yet the book does not yield up these ideas to the reader in an easily understandable manner. Consequently, critics could readily fasten on the *Fusus* in their attacks, but often with defective understanding. This is not to say that improved understanding would necessarily deflect all criticisms.

However, Ibn 'Arabi did not see himself as the 'author of the *Fusus*'. In the introduction to the book he writes that the Messenger of God came to him in a vision: 'He had in his hand a book and he said to me, "This is the book of the Bezels of Wisdom; take it and bring it to men that they might benefit from it".'[26] Ibn 'Arabi replied that he would do as he was commanded and asked for God's 'spiritual inspiration' and 'protective support' so as to be 'a transmitter and not a composer, so that those of the Folk [Sufis] who read it may be sure that it comes from the Station of Sanctification and that it is utterly free from all the purposes of the lower soul, which are ever prone to deceive.'[27] Finally, he states that he has only written down what has been revealed to him, but that he is not a prophet and only an heir, one who is bound by the law brought by Muhammad. His many followers down the centuries have been convinced by the sincerity of his belief in the truth of his visionary guidance from the Prophet, placing the *Fusus* on a higher level than a book composed by the human mind of even the greatest Sufi master. Nevertheless, his claims were never sufficient to allay the concerns of his opponents.

Ibn 'Arabi was to have a deep influence on his Sufi successors in his conception of the Muhammadan Light and Perfect Human Being and his encouragement to others to seek a close relationship with the Prophet through visualising him. 'Abd al-Karim al-Jili (d. 1408) is particularly noted for his development of this line of thought, emphasising the role of Muhammad as the Muslim community's link with the Divine and stressing that no spiritual ascension is possible without the Prophet's intervention.[28] Jili gives practical advice on visualising Muhammad, recommending that the worshipper constantly recall the image of the Prophet. This may be an image that has occurred in a dream. Otherwise, it is necessary to bless the Prophet and imagine being present with him or, if one has visited his tomb at Medina, to try to remember it. He advises to

> be as if you were standing at his tomb, in all honor and respect, until his spiritual substance appears to you. If you have not visited his tomb, continue to bless him, and imagine him hearing you, and be entirely respectful, so your blessings will reach him.[29]

Jili was convinced that the Prophet would be able to hear and see the Muslim worshipper who mentioned his name.

African Visions, Fifteenth to Nineteenth Centuries

These views of the need to approach the Prophet through visions appear to have gained momentum in the century following Jili's death. Among the mystics of fifteenth-century North Africa,

Muhammad al-Jazuli (d. 1465) in western Morocco gained a mass following in the tens of thousands, establishing his saintly status as someone who spoke with the Prophet and could assure his devotees of salvation in the afterlife. At his death they bore his coffin with them into battle and believed that it was through him that they were able to repel invasion by the Portuguese.[30] Jazuli established his own branch of the powerful Shadhili Sufi order, which attracted even leading scholars of Fez and became dominant among Moroccan Sufis.[31]

However, visions of the Prophet did not necessarily result in veneration as a saint. The Algerian Muhammad al-Zawawi (d. 1477) was the author of a visionary diary, containing an account of 109 dreams and occasional waking visions, in which he alleged that the Prophet had appeared to him over a period of approximately ten years from 30 November 1447 to 2 April 1457.[32] Although the sheer number of the visions appears impressive at first sight, Zawawi had difficulty in persuading any disciples to appreciate his visionary experience or that he had the qualities of a saint. As Jonathan Katz has observed, Zawawi 'believed himself to be a repository of the Muhammadan light, but this light turned out to be invisible to others'.[33] Katz is of the opinion that Zawawi was indeed a visionary, but lacked a charismatic personality and, unfortunately, suffered instead from a narcissistic personality disorder, which rendered him 'prone to flights of grandiose fantasy'.[34] From this viewpoint he was liable to inflate his own importance by presenting himself as a great saint and intimate of the Prophet, but without having the character and behaviour required to back his claims and gain public recognition.

Zawawi may have been no great saint, but his work is still of interest as marking perhaps the lower end of visionary autobiography by a minor, pedantic jurist with an unwarranted high opinion of himself. For every Ruzbihan or Ibn 'Arabi, there must have been many Zawawis, even though most did not record their visionary encounters. What did these visions of the Prophet mean to this rather ordinary, would-be saint? At first, he does not appear to have been at all confident that the Prophet was actually honouring him with his presence. In his earliest dreams in the Algerian town of Bijaya he feared that it might be Satan who entered his dreaming, despite the *hadith* that assured the believer of the impossibility of such devilish deception. He, therefore, begins his diary with a certain degree of diffidence and perhaps only because the recording of dreams was a practice encouraged in the circle of his Sufi shaykh, Abu 'Uthman Sa'id al-Safrawi al-Tunisi (d. 1448).[35] Very little is known of Safrawi, but both he and his own shaykh apparently laid claim to many sightings of the Prophet. Consequently, there was probably a strong expectation within the group that the Prophet would be seen in the dreams of those who called to mind his image often. Effectively, the practices recommended by Jili were being implemented in the lives of this Sufi circle.

Zawawi recorded 39 visions in a six-month period in Algeria, after which he travelled to the East for a prolonged stay in Mecca and Medina. It might have been expected that he would be favoured with dreams or waking visions of the Prophet in the Holy Cities and especially at Muhammad's tomb in Medina, but there is no testimony in the diary of any such events. The dreams only resume when Zawawi is living in Cairo after his visit to the Hijaz and this is the period of his most dramatic dreaming, over about seven months. In these dreams he believed that he was being given constant assurance of his high spiritual status and was clothed with many wonderful robes, such as the Robe of God's Contentment and the Robe of Taking Charge and Mastery. He became convinced that he would achieve global sovereignty. On one occasion he saw himself entering under the Prophet's robe and that it extended to the far ends of the earth like a tent. Zawawi was led into the middle of the robe where the Prophet told him that one's position in the robe signified one's saintly level. The obvious implication was that he had reached the highest level of sainthood.[36] The lack of followers did not in itself destroy Zawawi's conviction that this was the case, since there was a long-established belief in Sufi circles that saints were ultimately known only to God and might not be recognised by other people.[37]

While belief in hidden saints could obviously be a comfort to those who were unsuccessful in acquiring public recognition, the idea appears to have been widely and sincerely held, including by Ibn

'Arabi. Whether eminent or ordinary, the Sufis of North Africa clung strongly to Ibn 'Arabi's ideas, even when they were simplified for the consumption of the less educated. Veneration of the Prophet in his cosmic role gained in importance as well as the hope that he could be present with those who remembered him and called down blessings on him. One of the most influential figures in promoting these views to the masses was Ahmad al-Tijani (d. 1815). Born in southern Algeria in 1737, Tijani studied in the Moroccan city of Fez, where he was also initiated into three Sufi orders.[38] In 1772–3 he began his journey to the East for pilgrimage, staying for some time in Tunisia and in Egypt along the way and making contact with leading Sufis of the day before travelling on to the Holy Cities.

It was some time after his return to Algeria in 1781–2 that Tijani claimed to have experienced a waking vision of the Prophet, who ordered him to found a new Sufi order and taught him a new prayer, known as the *Jawharat al-kamal* (The Jewel of Perfection).[39] This highly elaborate prayer takes the form of calling on God three times to bless the Prophet and is filled with the light imagery that had long been familiar from Ibn 'Arabi. According to Tijani, the Prophet described himself as

> the most luminous bolt of lightning in the driving storm clouds that fill all seas and vessels exposed to their rain,
>
> Your brilliant light with which You have filled Your created universe, that encompasses all places in existence.[40]

The prayer concludes with an invocation to God to bless the Prophet 'and his people with a blessing that enables us to know Him!' The translator interprets the Arabic emphatic *iyyahu* as 'Him', understanding it as a reference to God, but admitting that it might also apply to His Prophet.[41] Members of the Tijani brotherhood claimed to be able to see God, a view opposed by most Muslim theologians and causing anger in the wider community. They also claimed that the Prophet and first four caliphs of Islam would be present at the Friday group recitation of the prayer.

Ahmad al-Tijani ordered adherents to perform the 'Jewel of Perfection' as a supererogatory prayer 11 times a day, although after his death disputes arose as to whether it should be recited 11 or 12 times.[42] In addition, Tijani required his followers to recite a shorter and simpler prayer of blessing for the Prophet 100 times morning and evening and an extra 50 times as part of further religious rites. He held that this prayer had been sent down from Heaven to a sixteenth-century Egyptian mystic, Muhammad al-Bakri (d. 1545) and that the Prophet had personally assured Tijani that this prayer was beneficial in wiping out the sins of those who recited it.[43] As both prayers had to be performed in addition to the usual formal worship and other formulas of praise and penitence, membership in the new order demanded a great deal of commitment.

Tijani did not stop at claiming to see the Prophet in visions, but also asserted that he, rather than Ibn 'Arabi, was actually the Seal of Muhammadan Sainthood. Sufis acknowledged the existence of a supreme saint in every age, known as the mystical 'pole' (*qutb*), but Tijani described himself as not simply the *qutb* of his age, but the pole of poles (*qutb al-aqtab*), the supreme saint of all ages. It was only logical that he demanded of his followers that they abandon allegiance to all other Sufi shaykhs and adhere to his Tijani Order alone, since he far outranked any living or dead Sufi masters and took his instructions directly from the Prophet. Hence the Tijanis were forbidden from the popular practice of visiting the tombs of saints. Tijani even outdid Ibn 'Arabi in the number of those for whom he allegedly obtained direct entry to Paradise. Where Ibn 'Arabi claimed that God had granted this privilege to his sisters and some others that he looked upon, Tijani made more extensive claims on the grounds that the Prophet had given him this assurance in a vision. Thus all his followers and a wide range of relatives, teachers and others were included among these entrants to Paradise on condition only that they maintained their love for him. Salvation was cancelled for those who became his enemies.[44] Such promises seem to have given confidence to the Tijani membership that they were spiritually superior to non-Tijani Muslims, an attitude that was much criticised by members of other Sufi orders.

Visions of the Prophet were often recounted in support of claims to high spiritual status and sainthood, but they also served to explain a course of action that might otherwise have been contentious. For example, Usuman dan Fodio (d. 1817), one of the great mystics of West Africa, tells of an extraordinary vision that he experienced in 1794 after a period spent in meditation:

> When I reached forty years, five months and some days, God drew me to him, and I found the Lord of djinns and men, our Lord Muhammad – may God bless him and give him peace. With him were the Companions, and the prophets, and the saints. Then they welcomed me, and sat me down in their midst.[45]

There followed a ceremony in which Usuman saw the great saint 'Abd al-Qadir al-Jilani (d. 1166) handing a green embroidered robe and turban to the Prophet, who held them to his breast before passing them on through the line of the Rightly Guided Caliphs to the Prophet Joseph. Joseph then returned them to 'Abd al-Qadir, who was appointed to present them to Usuman. He recalls:

> He ['Abd al-Qadir] sat me down, and clothed me and enturbaned me. Then he addressed me as 'Imam of the saints' and commanded me to do what is approved of and forbade me to do what is disapproved of; and he girded me with the Sword of Truth, to unsheathe it against the enemies of God.[46]

Since Usuman was a prominent shaykh of the Qadiri Order, it was important for him to receive endorsement as 'Imam of the saints' from 'Abd al-Qadir al-Jilani himself as the reputed founding figure of the order. It is also noteworthy that, out of all the prophets, it is Joseph who passes the robe to 'Abd al-Qadir to pass on to Usuman because Joseph is especially associated with the gift of interpreting dreams. The vision appears to have been decisive in persuading Usuman that he had a duty to struggle by all means, including force of arms, to establish Islamic law in the region of Hausaland (in present day northern Nigeria and southern Niger). This and other powerful visions were also of critical importance in convincing his followers that they had divine support to participate in a jihad of the sword against those who claimed to be Muslim while being lax in their implementation of sharia and practising un-Islamic local customs.

The visionary guidance of the Prophet was arguably even more important when laying claim to the rank of Mahdi, the one divinely guided to rule with justice before the end of the world. On 29 June 1881 Muhammad Ahmad b.'Abd Allah, a shaykh of the Sammani Order in the Sudan, declared that he had been appointed by the Prophet in a vision to serve as the chosen Mahdi. Consequently, there was no longer any need for Islamic legal scholars or Sufi masters because he superseded all of them, having superior, God-sent knowledge. Writing in 1882 to the commander of an expedition that was sent against him from Egypt, he stated: 'The Prophet and all possessors of gnosis (*ahl al-kashf*) have informed me that those who question my Mahdi-ship and deny and contradict it, are unbelievers who can lawfully be killed and whose property is booty.'[47] Thus a vision of the Prophet could not only assure Muhammad Ahmad and his supporters of his high status, but could also work to strip opponents of their authority and even of their claim to be Muslims.

Exceptional Visions and Routine Sightings

There is a freshness and immediacy about some medieval mystics' reports of their visions of God and the Prophet, as when Ruzbihan sees God from the roof of his house. We might even speak of 'the ring of truth', but with the usual caveat that it is impossible to know the reality of anyone's experience of this nature. However, the events that the writers claim to recall seem to be in the category of exceptional visions, which have impacted their relationship with the divine in a profound way and awakened in them a greater capacity for insight into the supernatural world. They have also revealed to them inner truths about their own characters and future cosmic role.

By contrast, other accounts appear to be constructed to meet a public expectation of what is normal for a saint and may be regarded as routine sightings. The number of such narratives increases substantially from the fifteenth to nineteenth centuries and may tell us more about the social requirements of sainthood than about the highest levels of the Sufi's journey to God. This seems more likely to be the case with those records that are intended for a wider readership than with those that are apparently limited to a few disciples or others within a small circle of intimates. The pressure to conform to a certain image of sainthood comes to include the demand for accounts of an extraordinary visionary life, and not everyone seems able to resist the temptation to deliver reports of their encounters with the Messenger of God.

CHAPTER 8

CONTACTING THE RIGHTEOUS DEAD

The Visionary Landscape, Thirteenth to Seventeenth Centuries

By the thirteenth century the visionary landscape of the central Islamic lands was becoming covered with the tombs of holy persons: prophets, Shi'i imams and members of the Prophet's family, his Companions, caliphs of Islam, revered scholars and Sufi mystics. Many of these sites were given the designation of *mashhad*, a place of witnessing, where someone had seen the holy one in a dream or waking vision. Although some of these sites assumed far greater importance than others, pilgrims visited even the graves of little-known saints. By the late seventeenth century the scholarly mystic and dream interpreter Nabulusi undertook travels throughout Syria, Palestine, Egypt and the Hijaz, in which hardly a day passed without his visiting one or more minor places of pilgrimage.[1]

Fourteen Pure Ones: The Prophet, Fatima and Twelve Imams
The earliest sites to attract pilgrims were understandably those associated with prophets, especially the Prophet Muhammad, and significant early Muslims, such as relatives and Companions of the Prophet. While some scholars commended visiting graves to pray for the souls of the dead and meditate on the afterlife, others rebuked the

practice as tantamount to illicit worship when it involved asking the righteous dead for their intercession with God and performing acts such as kissing and rubbing the grave or taking soil from the site. However, among the Shi'i community, visits to the tombs of the Imams in Iraq and Iran became regarded as a religious duty and many also visited the graves of other members of the Prophet's family, such as the tomb of the Prophet's daughter Fatima in Medina. In Iraq visitation at the shrines of the Imams 'Ali at Najaf and Husayn at Karbala acquired major significance; it was especially encouraged at times when Shi'i pilgrims were finding it difficult to make the pilgrimage to Mecca, notably during the long period of rivalry between the Safavid Shahs of Iran and the Ottoman Sultans in the sixteenth to eighteenth centuries.

Shi'i authorities attributed to the Imams qualities of a similar character to those ascribed to the Prophet in medieval Sufism, although it is open to debate how early these ideas took hold and how extensively they were shared.[2] According to a certain mystical viewpoint, the Imams participated in the Divine Light that was associated with them from pre-eternity and they were not truly dead, but were able to be present in the spirit with the pious community, to hear the prayers of worshippers and enter into their dreams. The Imams, as sinless and omnipresent beings, were in a strong position to guide the Shi'i faithful on the right path and came to be looked upon as intercessors with God for their followers. Consequently, many believers made the pilgrimage to the grave of an Imam, hoping that he would intercede on their behalf so that their sins might be forgiven. They called on him to free them from debt, poverty and disease, to overcome their enemies and enable them to enter Paradise on the Last Day. In response to the pilgrims' needs, a whole branch of pilgrimage literature arose in order to provide information on the virtues of particular tombs and the best times to visit them, procedures to follow before entering and while staying in the sacred place. Sometimes they would include advice on sleeping near the tomb in order to increase the likelihood of seeing the Imam in a dream. The practice of *istikhara*, seeking a good outcome by performing supplicatory prayers before going to sleep, was thought to be particularly effective at holy graves and has echoes of the practice of incubation at Greek and Roman temples.[3]

The oldest pilgrimage guide to the Najaf tomb of Imam 'Ali was written in the thirteenth century by Ibn Tawus (d. 1293).[4] After seeking to confirm the authenticity of 'Ali's burial at Najaf, the work includes accounts of the miraculous events recorded at the site and a number of visions, in which the Imam allegedly appeared to his visitors. 'Ali was said to protect all those who sought sanctuary at his tomb and would engage in physical combat against enemies who wanted to desecrate the tomb or harm the pious pilgrims under his care.[5] He was also believed to restore stolen property to its owners, for example on an occasion noted in 1188 when a visitor left his sword near the Imam's grave while he completed the rituals associated with the pilgrimage. He returned to find the sword missing, but the Imam came to him in a dream vision three days later and informed him of the house where it could be found.[6] However, the Imam also expected his visitors to live up to their responsibilities, demanding in their dreams that they fulfil their vows and repay their debts.[7]

In view of the fame of 'Ali's mausoleum at Najaf, it is perhaps surprising that the location should be contested. Yet it was not the only site that was claimed as the last resting place of 'Ali b. Abi Talib and it was not only the Shi'a who would claim to be able to identify the grave. The late medieval period saw widespread popular veneration of the Prophet and his family, especially Fatima and 'Ali and their sons Hasan and Husayn, so that visitation of their shrines was not confined to Shi'i pilgrims. The oldest extant account that tells of 'Ali being buried at a village near Balkh in northern Afghanistan dates back to the mid-twelfth century, when a traveller from the Spanish city of Granada wrote of his travels through Central Asia. Towards the end of his book Abu Hamid al-Gharnati recorded extraordinary dream visions that had allegedly occurred a few years before his visit. Al-Gharnati says that he is concluding his work with 'some wonderful stories about the Commander of the Faithful, 'Ali b. Abi Talib'[8] and that a particularly remarkable story concerns the appearance of his tomb in 1135–6 at a village called al-Khayr. He then describes a curious dream:

A number of the village's leading citizens saw the Prophet – on him be peace – in a dream in which he said to them 'My uncle's son, 'Ali b. Abi Talib, is [buried] in this place.' And he pointed out a spot near the village. The dream recurred and the number of people who experienced it increased until more than four hundred people, all of them leading citizens of al-Khayr and another place, had seen it.⁹

The villagers related their experience to the ruler of Balkh, who consulted the city's religious scholars. Most of them conceded that this must be a veridical dream on the basis of the famous *hadith* asserting the truth of dreams of the Prophet, but one jurist disagreed. He protested that it was absurd because 'Ali had been killed at al-Kufa in Iraq, although there was some disagreement as to his exact place of burial. However, the jurist did not go unpunished for his rejection of the Prophet's dream testimony. At midnight he came to the ruler, beaten black and blue and pleading for help. He explained that members of the Prophet's family had visited him in his dream and administered the beating for effectively calling the Prophet a liar. They had dragged him to an open tomb where he found 'Ali sitting. The jurist then begged him for mercy.¹⁰ The dream beating that leaves its marks on the dreamer is familiar from early Christian accounts of punitive angels appearing to sinners in dreams. In addition to the shared dream of the villagers, it suggests that the pre-Islamic heritage of the Balkh area, which had witnessed diverse religious traditions, may have contributed to the visionary narrations current at the time of Gharnati's visit. In any case, Gharnati reports that the ruler was convinced to the point that he ordered a large shrine (*mashhad*) to be built on the site.

Nevertheless, the shrine fell into neglect until it was rediscovered at the end of the fifteenth century. Why it fell out of favour as a place of pilgrimage remains a mystery, but the dream visions had been insufficient to keep belief in 'Ali's burial there alive. A lack of political interest in supporting the shrine and a decline in the rural economy of the area may have played their part in discouraging visitation or it may simply have been the case that the Najaf location had much stronger credentials. The many dreams of the visitors to the first Imam at Najaf could easily outweigh the limited testimony from Afghanistan. However, from the sixteenth century onwards pilgrims were drawn once again to the rediscovered tomb and the important shrine town of Mazar-i Sharif rose to prominence on the site of the old village of al-Khayr.

Although tomb visits were considered especially efficacious in contacting the Imams through dreams, they were by no means the only places where such visionary contacts were thought possible. Mir Damad (d. 1631), one of the most important philosophers and mystics of Safavid Iran, experienced remarkable dream visions, the first of which took place in a mosque in the Iranian city of Qumm in 1602 during the month of Ramadan.[11] This dream occurred in the daytime period of fasting after the afternoon prayer. Mir Damad saw in front of him the figures of the Prophet and Imam 'Ali, both infused with the Divine Light. The Imam then taught him a protective prayer, including the following words: 'The Prophet is before me; Fatima the Radiant is above me, guarding my head; the first Imam is at my right; the eleven other Imams are at my left.'[12] The learning of a prayer is a familiar dream activity, its truth and power being confirmed by the Imam's role as teacher in the presence of the Prophet. The prayer subsequently became popular in Shi'i circles.

Another significant Shi'i visionary was Shaykh Ahmad Ahsa'i (d. 1826), born on the Gulf island of Bahrain into an Arab family, but also resident for many years in Iran. He was a contemporary of the African shaykhs Ahmad al-Tijani and Usuman dan Fodio and, like them, responsible for a movement that was intended to revitalise the faith. It became known after him as the Shaykhi school of Shi'i thought and Ahsa'i and his disciples were prolific in the production of theosophical writings in Arabic and Persian.[13] Among Ahsa'i's works is a short autobiography, composed for the benefit of his son; it includes accounts of the dream visions that he experienced as a youth. In one such vision he dreamt that he entered a mosque and encountered there Hasan (d. 669), the second Imam and son of 'Ali, Zayn al-'Abidin (d. 712/13), the fourth Imam and son of Husayn; and Muhammad al-Baqir (d. 735), the fifth Imam. When he asked the Imams to teach him a prayer, they gave him one, but, despite his best efforts to recite it later, he was unsuccessful in receiving a further vision. Only after he attempted to mould himself spiritually in conformity to its words was he able to embark on a series of visions that brought him into the company of the Prophet, Fatima and all the Imams. The dreams functioned as teaching and initiatory sessions to prepare Ahsa'i on his spiritual path of development.

Similarly, visionary dreams inspired Ahsa'i's first two successors to continue his mission. Sayyid Kazim Reshti (d. 1843) from Resht in northern Iran was led by the dream guidance of Fatima to seek out Ahmad Ahsa'i at his residence in Yazd in south-eastern Iran; Reshti there became Ahsa'i's closest disciple and succeeded him in the leadership of the movement.[14] Muhammad Karim Khan Kirmani (d. 1870), the second successor, was born a member of the Qajar dynasty of the Iranian shahs and has been noted as a prolific author. His brief autobiography includes accounts of his dream visions of the Imams, from whom he claimed to receive all his knowledge and spiritual direction.[15]

At the Graves of the Righteous

A considerable number of holy graves were recognised as belonging to righteous persons from early Islamic history as well as prophets of the pre-Islamic period. However, a large category of the righteous dead were those designated as saints or 'friends of God' (*awliya' Allah*), including many Sufis. Some were figures of international renown, such as 'Abd al-Qadir al-Jilani, whose tomb at Baghdad drew pilgrims from across the Muslim world; he was one of the saints reputed to be most frequently seen in dreams and visions, as noted in the vision of the Qadiri shaykh Usuman dan Fodio. In Egypt Sufi graves were concentrated in large numbers in the great cemetery of al-Qarafa at Cairo, which was also an important place of pilgrimage for international as well as local pilgrims. Along with other Cairene cemeteries, it became the subject of at least 20 pilgrimage guides produced between the middle of the twelfth century and the early seventeenth century, not all of which have survived.[16] During his stay in the city in the fifteenth century the North African Zawawi spent much time there in visiting the graves of saints in the hope and expectation of making contact with them. By contrast, the Syrian cities of Aleppo and Damascus in late medieval times had a smaller number of saintly tombs and these were generally situated close to the central mosque and citadel and in the cemeteries outside the gates. They seem to have attracted fewer international pilgrims.[17]

However, some major Sufi saints were buried in their own mausoleums, often with a mosque attached, famous examples being those of Ibn 'Arabi at Damascus, the poet Jalal al-Din Rumi (d. 1273) at Konya in Turkey and the Indian saints Mu'in al-Din Chishti (d. 1236) at Ajmer and Nizam al-Din Awliya' (d. 1325) at Delhi. The latter shrine gained in popularity soon after Nizam al-Din's burial, being visited by the ruler of the Delhi Sultanate, Muhammad b. Tughluq (1325–51), who ordered the building of the tomb, and later by Firuz Shah (1351–88), who arranged for the construction of the Jama'at Khanah Mosque at the site for the benefit of pilgrims.[18]

Yet other sites saw their fortunes fluctuate depending on patronage or lack of it. A notable example is the case of Ibn 'Arabi's grave, which fell into neglect after his death. However, following the Ottoman conquest of Syria in 1516, Sultan Selim I ordered a mausoleum and mosque to be constructed at the site of the saint's tomb and the building was completed in 1518. Ibn 'Arabi became venerated as the protector saint of the Ottoman dynasty and, as such, drew many Turkish pilgrims to perform pilgrimage to Damascus with his tomb on Mount Qasyun in the district of Salihiyya as the focal point of their visits.[19] Subsequently, other respected Sufis were buried in the vicinity of the great master and attracted further visitation. They included Nabulusi, who described himself as a spiritual son of Ibn 'Arabi and who was buried in his own nearby mausoleum-mosque that he had constructed in 1714, a few years before his death. Another spiritual son was the Amir 'Abd al-Qadir, who fought against the French occupation of Algeria in 1830, but was also devoted to the study of Ibn 'Arabi's works and edited the *Futuhat*; he was buried next to the great master in 1883, although his body was removed to Algeria following the country's independence.[20]

While some pilgrimage sites were the graves of well-known spiritual guides and mystics, others were the burial places of locally recognised personalities or even of alleged righteous figures whose identities were not clearly established. One case from the Mamila cemetery at Jerusalem concerns a much-visited tomb that had no name on the tombstone, although local people thought that it belonged to a saint called al-Wasiti, to whom many miracles were attributed. Mujir al-Din al-'Ulaymi (d.1521) recorded in his sacred history of Jerusalem and Hebron that pilgrims took stones away from the grave, hoping to derive blessing (*baraka*) from them, but found the next day that the stones had been returned to their place at the grave. This confirmed for them the holiness of the site.[21] It was also not uncommon for an esteemed saint to be claimed by supporters of rival sites of burial. For example, despite there being a tomb of the ninth-century mystic Abu Yazid al-Bistami in his native Bistam in northern Iran, further graves of Bistami brought pilgrims to other supposed sites of burial, such as a mausoleum at Rastan in Syria on the way between Hims and Hama and a further reputed grave in Damascus.[22]

Some improbable claims were made on the basis of anecdotal accounts of dreams, asserting that a righteous person's body was buried in a particular place. This led to the creation of numerous 'rediscovered' tombs and, consequently, new places of pilgrimage. In the central Islamic lands these tombs were sometimes said to be those of Companions of the Prophet or members of his family and sometimes those of earlier prophets, but many throughout the Muslim world were those of more recent saints. Stories not infrequently tell of dreamers of low social status (humble villagers, soldiers and sinners), who hear and/or see a holy person and are afraid that they will not be believed. This may indeed be the case. However, the disbelievers often become convinced of a grave's authenticity when they are shown signs (lights, sweet smells, fresh springs, voices) that attest to the truth of the dreamer's account, and the holy grave is then found.[23]

One rediscovered tomb is reported to have been brought to light as a result of a dream on the third night of Ramadan at Mosul, Iraq in

1276. A certain Muhammadun b. al-Aqfasi reported that he had had a vision of a descendant of Husayn b. 'Ali b. Abi Talib and heard the holy one saying that he was calling 'from the bread oven and the drain of the small bathhouse'.[24] On waking, he told one of the village elders about his dream and wondered whether they should try to find the grave. The elder counselled him against such an attempt, but the next night experienced the same dream, in which he heard the voice of the dead man demanding that he excavate the tomb and assuring him that the soil there had curative properties. Local people were not convinced until a blind man rubbed the earth on his eyes and recovered his sight. Then crowds descended on the tomb. However, the identity of this descendant of Husayn was not made known.

Etiquette at the Graves

As the graves of the righteous dead increased from the late medieval period with many rediscoveries and new constructions, pilgrims practised a particular etiquette when seeking to contact the deceased. Visitors to the graves did not conceive of their occupants as truly dead, but understood that their souls were active in the area of the grave and could hear and see the living persons who were making pilgrimage in the hope of being able to communicate with them.[25] Although the most powerful saints were thought to be able to wander far from their tombs, they were also expected to be frequently available to receive their visitors and to come out to greet living saints when they called upon them. Thursdays, Fridays and Saturdays were also judged to be especially propitious for enabling visionary contacts as well as the *mawlid*s or 'birthdays' associated with the earthly deaths of particular saints and their births to new lives with God. In the Indian subcontinent the term *'urs* ('wedding') had come into use at least by the early fourteenth century as a description for these death anniversaries, being a metaphor for the union of the saint's soul with God. Such occasions were considered especially propitious for the pilgrim to see the saint and gain blessings. By the mid-eighteenth century Muhammad Najib Qadiri Nagawri Ajmeri, an Indian Sufi from Awrangabad in the Deccan, wrote a guide for visitors to the saints' festivals across the sub-continent, in which he listed hundreds of anniversaries, giving advice in his introduction on proper behaviour at the tombs.[26]

The most pious pilgrims sought the company of the holy dead out of a desire to improve their own spiritual state by emulating them. They regarded dreams and visions of the saints as a means of learning from them how to draw closer to God in their lives.[27] Indeed it was recommended that visits should be undertaken entirely for the purpose of pleasing God and purifying the pilgrims' hearts. However, according to Ibn 'Uthman, the author of a medieval guide to al-Qarafa cemetery in Cairo, many visitors had less pure intentions, but visited the dead so that the saint's relatives would then feel obliged to visit their own deceased relatives. He claims that this practice 'preoccupies people today, and is so widely acknowledged that people do it openly'.[28] It could hardly be considered conducive to ensuring a beneficial vision of the saintly deceased.

Ibn 'Uthman also instructed pilgrims to treat the deceased with appropriate respect. They were expected to proceed towards the grave from the front and stand facing its occupant as they would when wishing to speak with the living. They should have their back towards the direction of prayer (*qibla*).[29] Presumably this was to avoid any suggestion that they were worshipping the saint. It was important not to walk or sit on the grave and not to kiss the tomb, rub oneself in its soil or roll in the dust. According to Ibn 'Uthman's manual, they were undesirable Christian practices that could not be sanctioned by a Muslim scholar of religion.[30] These concerns were shared by the theologian Ibn Qayyim al-Jawziyya (d. 1350), who was distressed that Muslim pilgrims were 'praying to tombs, circumambulating them, kissing them, touching them (*istilam*), rubbing their cheeks in the soil, worshipping their patrons, seeking aid from them, requesting from them aid, sustenance, health, fulfilling debts, dispelling worries, seeking aid against misfortunes or distress'.[31] Despite some scholarly disapproval, these practices remained common and many stories were told of blessing being imparted by contacts with the holy dead.

Tales were even told of animals rubbing themselves against certain tombs to derive blessing and be cured of illnesses and injuries.[32]

The Persian Sufi author Aziz Nasafi (d. between 1281 and 1300) mentions that the ability to communicate with the spirits of the righteous living and dead is also possessed by animals and he notes: 'Some of the animals inform people before the arrival of each calamity or fortuity which comes to this world. Some people understand and some do not understand.'[33] Thus it was not only humans who could be open to mystical experience and it is not unusual to find tales of saints having their sanctity acknowledged by animals. One interesting case from fourteenth-century Central Asia concerns the effort to establish an appropriate grave site for Sayyid 'Ali Hamadani (d. 1385), a major shaykh of the Kubrawi Order. According to the story, Hamadani was visiting the town known today as Kulab in southern Tajikistan (formerly Khuttalan), when he had a dream of the Prophet telling him that he should find a place for his burial in the nearby forest. The next day he took his followers to the burial site and explained that he was to be buried there three years, one day and one night after he had designated the place. He further charged them to make the pilgrimage to his tomb. Not only was the site sanctioned by the dream vision of the Prophet and the master's command to his followers before his death, but it was given further endorsement by the animals of the forest, which gathered around the shaykh and bowed before him in recognition of his saintliness.[34] They thus showed a natural sensitivity towards the supernatural world that many humans lacked.

Circumambulation of tombs was widely performed as a part of pilgrimage and received scholarly support as well as criticism. Nasafi instructed pilgrims on the best way to approach the deceased saints at their graves:

> The manner of paying pilgrimage and praying is in this way; one must walk around the tomb and be attentive, and at that time, one must be free from everything and make the mirror of the heart clean and pure so that the spirit of the pilgrim can encounter the deceased through the grave.[35]

Nasafi stresses that it is possible through this process of self-purification to summon a vision of the saint's spirit and effectively have one's requests answered, either because the saint is one of those who 'has favour with God' or because the holy one is on the lower level of one who 'has favour near God's esteemed ones'.[36] In this case, the pilgrim would call upon the deceased to ask the favoured saints to intercede with God for a solution to problems in this life and happiness in the afterlife. More than four centuries later Muhammad Najib's Indian manual recommended respectful circumambulation of the grave and advised the visitor to conduct a careful examination of his/her spiritual state in order to promote the likelihood of visionary communication.[37] He also noted that it was important to bring food and drink, sweets and flowers for the saint as well as an offering of money.[38]

Since dreams provided the most usual form of communication with the saints, it was also not uncommon to sleep at the tombs in order to converse with the dead (in the same manner as Shi'i pilgrims sleeping at the tombs of the Imams).[39] Through dreams at the graves and elsewhere the righteous dead were also able to advise visitors on correct behaviour towards them. The grandson of the Egyptian mystical poet 'Umar b. al-Farid (d. 1235) provides a notable example in a story that he narrates in his hagiography of his grandfather. He tells how Ibn al-Farid became spiritually awakened after he met with a greengrocer in Cairo, whom he later came to recognise as one of God's saints. The greengrocer informed him that he would not become enlightened in Egypt, but must travel to the Hijaz. After spending 15 years in the Arabian wilderness, Ibn al-Farid allegedly heard the greengrocer's voice telling him to come back to Cairo where he lay dying and to pray for him. He obeyed the voice and returned to Cairo to find the greengrocer on his deathbed. The saint asked to be buried at a certain place in al-Qarafa cemetery and told Ibn al-Farid that he should wait there for a man who was coming to meet him. Ibn al-Farid again obeyed his spiritual master and, after burying the old saint, he waited until a man came down from Mount Muqattam without his feet touching the ground. In his vision he prayed with the mysterious figure over the saint's body. Then he saw that many white and green birds were praying with them and 'a huge green bird alighted at the foot of the bier, gobbled up the body, and re-joined the other birds, as they flew off singing loudly in praise of God'.[40] The mysterious stranger explained to the puzzled Ibn al-Farid:

> Oh 'Umar, haven't you heard that the spirits of the martyrs are in the stomachs of green birds, which roam where they will in Paradise? They are the martyrs of the sword. As for the martyrs of love, both their spirits and their bodies are in the stomachs of green birds, and this man was among them![41]

The stranger added that he too had been one of these martyrs of love, but had lost his status because he had fallen into sin. He then left Ibn al-Farid, climbed back up the mountain and disappeared.

Why did Ibn al-Farid's grandson find it important to relate this story in the hagiography? It has been suggested that he 'probably included this account to depict spiritual succession as Ibn al-Farid assumed his master's place as a saint of Cairo' and it also served to enhance Ibn al-Farid's saintly status and the holiness of his own place of burial there.[42] These seem reasonable explanations for the inclusion of the story. It is also interesting that the tale draws attention to the virtues of righteousness over religious education and literary merit, since the untutored greengrocer is the master who must be obeyed by the educated poet. The tale depicts the benefits of acting in accordance with visionary instructions, since Ibn al-Farid does everything that he is asked promptly and without questioning.

The domed shrine over Ibn al-Farid's grave in al-Qarafa cemetery became a popular place of pilgrimage with all classes of the Egyptian population as well as international visitors. By the late seventeenth century its popularity apparently reached a peak. The Turkish traveller Evliya Çelebi (d. *c*.1684) visited the tomb in 1670 and observed that up to 6,000 people gathered there on Fridays to pray, recite the Qur'an and listen to Ibn al-Farid's mystical verses. In 1693 Nabulusi also witnessed crowds circumambulating the grave, seeking to contact the spirit of the saint and falling on one another in ecstatic states. However, by the nineteenth century Egypt's modernising rulers and reformist religious scholars ensured that the shrine was starved of funds and that communication with the saintly dead fell into decline.[43]

Ibn al-Farid was supposedly rewarded for believing in the veridical nature of his visions and acting appropriately so that he did not offend his spiritual guide, the greengrocer. His behaviour would have been considered wise by pre-modern Muslims, since there was a popular fear of the consequences of not acknowledging the holy dead, behaving in a respectful manner at their tombs and obeying their wishes. It was thought that failure to follow the correct etiquette could result in angering the saint and risk unwelcome visions and ghostly haunting.[44] During his travels in Palestine in the late seventeenth century, Nabulusi observed that a certain Shaykh 'Ijlin valued courtesy at his grave and became very upset when anyone behaved disrespectfully. He would punish the rudeness of such visitors by sending wind and thunderstorms. On one occasion he became extremely angry with pilgrims who had presumed to cook a sheep's head on his grave and punished them by taking all the meat, leaving them with only the bones.[45]

Many reports also speak of the perils of neglecting to visit a saint's tomb, and this issue was not confined to the tombs of Sufis. Ibn al-Banna' (d. 1079), a religious jurist of Baghdad, recorded a relatively early example in his diary, which contains a number of accounts of dreams. One of the companions of Ibn al-Banna' told him about a dream in which he had seen a deceased scholar:

> He said: 'I saw him in my dream, and I greeted him. He returned my greeting, and took hold of a kerchief which was on my head, with both hands, tied it, and said: "O Abu 'l-'Abbas! What is this rudeness which I have not experienced from you before?"' My informant continued: 'I had stopped visiting his tomb; so I resumed my visits and continued doing so without interruption.'[46]

In this case the dead scholar entered the man's dream in order to rebuke him, but the neglectful visitor escaped lightly and mended his ways. Other tales told of more severe punishment for the discourteous pilgrim and especially for those who attempted to steal from the saint, cheat or abuse the holy one.

The Power to Appear in Dreams

Pilgrims to the holy graves might hope to experience dreams of the dead and seek advice on the proper procedure to facilitate visionary encounters. However, it was widely recognised among the pilgrims that the real power resided with the saints, who would be acknowledged as having the ability to manifest themselves in the dreams of visitors to their tombs. The powerful dead were also thought capable of entering the dreams of the living in other locations and thus continuing their spiritual guidance of disciples; in this way they could also protect and support Muslim rulers and, as noted above, admonish the disrespectful.

Belief that it was possible to enter another's dream by magic is known from ancient Egypt, spells to enable such a feat having been preserved on papyrus in demotic and hieratic Egyptian. Although not common in Greek and Roman magic, the practice was still being recorded in a Greek magical papyrus from Egypt in the fourth century CE.[47] It is unknown whether such a belief was preserved and passed on in a modified form into the Islamic period, but the basic principle is the same; by whatever means, it is understood that those possessed of special powers can command entry into someone else's dream.

Some Sufis were even credited with special influence over rulers due in part to their appearance in the dreams of their protégés. Mu'in al-Din Chishti, who had died in 1236, was said to have entered the dream of Mu'izz al-Din, the future sultan of Delhi (1287–90), in order to command him to invade India, a task he accomplished successfully owing to the miraculous predictive powers of the saint.[48] The great saint was also depicted in paintings as offering the insignia of rule to the major Mughal Emperors Akbar (1556–1605), Jahangir (1605–27) and Shah Jahan (1628–57).[49] The implication is that Mu'in al-Din Chishti was able to enter the emperors' dreams (or waking visions) and assure them of his support for their rule, despite being long since dead to the earthly world.

Mu'in al-Din could also act in his role of spiritual guide many centuries after his death. A famous case concerns Jahanara (d. 1681), daughter of Shah Jahan. Although she had a living Sufi master, Mulla Shah from the Qadiri Order, she also claimed to have received initiation into the Chishti Order through visionary contact with Mu'in al-Din at his tomb in Ajmer during her pilgrimage there in 1643.[50] She writes of him as having taken her hand as the traditional symbolic gesture signifying his acceptance of her as his disciple and observes that, as a result of his spiritual influence, she attained to mystical experiences during her visit to the tomb, which she circumambulated seven times.

Not all masters approved of the practice of seeking initiation from dead saints, but it could provide a means of linking the disciple to an exemplary guide on a higher spiritual level than a living shaykh of lesser attainment. Major living shaykhs would also sometimes seek guidance from great deceased saints, whose spirits they could access through visionary dreams and thus supplement or bypass contemporary guides of lesser status. For instance, Nabulusi was initiated into the Naqshabandi Order by a minor central Asian shaykh, who was passing through Damascus. However, he claimed to have received visionary initiation from the spirit of Khwaja 'Ala al-Din 'Attar (d. 1400), a very important figure in the line of early Naqshabandi masters.[51]

It was not only the dead who were described as entering the dreams of the living, but living Sufi shaykhs might also publicise their power to enter the dreams of their disciples. At times they were even reported as visiting potential disciples in dream form and thus drawing them into their circle as new initiates. To an outside observer the real power may appear to lie with the living shaykhs rather than with the holy dead. They were able to use their authority to control how their own visionary lives were presented and to assert their ultimate superiority by controlling even the content of their disciples' dreams. The visionary landscape might be filled with the righteous dead, but it was the righteous living who were the real masters of that landscape.

CHAPTER 9

VISIONARY TRADITIONS AND THE IMPACT OF MODERNITY

Foreknowing and Spiritual Truth: The Persistence of Tradition

Between 2006 and 2008 Maria Elizabeth Louw, a Danish anthropologist, was conducting fieldwork in Kyrgyzstan, mainly in the capital, Bishkek. During this period she encountered a young woman named Aygul working at a newspaper kiosk in the city and learned that she had migrated there from her home village to live with her aunt in the hope of bettering her financial situation. However, she had been under pressure from family members to return to the village and marry and she was about to give into this pressure. Aygul was forcefully abducted in the village street and taken by car to a house where the kidnappers planned to compel her to marry a son of the family. Although contrary to Kyrgyz law, this practice is sometimes seen as a tradition in the country. Aygul found herself shut in a room overnight and it was then that she experienced a dream vision, in which her grandmother came to visit her and told her to look at herself. She saw that she was dressed in wedding clothes, but, when she looked at her feet, she realised that she had no shoes. Louw remarks that 'according to the Kyrgyz tradition of dream interpretation, shoes are symbols of marriage. When her beloved grandmother drew her attention towards the missing shoes, it might be a sign that it was not her fate to marry the abductor.'[1]

Visionary Traditions and the Impact of Modernity 175

By recounting the dream, Aygul was able to gain the support of her family in order to escape a life as a kidnapped bride, although the abductor's family were reluctant to accept the truth of the dream.[2] Dreams of the dead, and especially of dead ancestors, appear to be widely respected among the Kyrgyz and their words taken seriously as emanating from the 'world of truth', a belief notable in the classical Islamic tradition and persisting elsewhere. Aygul subsequently returned to her work in Bishkek and reported another dream of her grandmother, who 'showed her a big house and told her that it belonged to her'.[3] However, shortly afterwards, when the anthropologist went to look for her at the newspaper kiosk, she was no longer working there and had disappeared.

Following the collapse of the Soviet Union, Kyrgyzstan asserted its independence in 1991. In common with other emergent Central Asian states, it had undergone an extensive process of secularisation and Russification that had left many Kyrgyz insecure as to their religious identity, sometimes grasping hold of traditions that critics were ready to reject as not having a place in authentic Islam. Belief in dream visions and their interpretation as a way of foreknowing are quite commonly seen as representative of a popular religion that is disapproved by the zealously religious. Aygul does not seem to have been particularly attached to folk religious practice, but, like a number of Kyrgyz, self-interpreted her dreams in an effort to make her own life choices in a world that offered her and many other young people very limited control over their future.

It is frequently claimed that anyone can have a veridical dream, a view that was also expressed in pre-modern times, although there were dissenters who held that righteous people, and especially pious male dreamers, were more likely to have dreams that came true. Those who subscribed to such views might have been somewhat sceptical as to the truth of Aygul's dreams. Nevertheless, there are many modern cases of dreams and visions that are reported as occurring without any special preparation by the dreamer, who often lacks religious dedication and may be neglectful of prayer and even sinful. We have already noted in the introduction to this book the case of 'Izz al-'Arab al-Hawari, an Egyptian soldier and lapsed Muslim, who saw members of the Prophet's family heal him while he lay sick in hospital in the 1960s. The miraculous vision had a transformative effect on his life and he became actively involved in Sufi spirituality.[4]

Another remarkable case recorded as taking place in Egypt in the late 1990s was the visionary dream seen by a 70-year-old man from a village near Luxor. Mahmud admitted to anthropologist Amira Mittermaier that he had been a thief for much of his life. Then suddenly in his old age he had a dream in which he saw the Coptic pope and a gathering of people wearing white, whom he understood to be saints. They were performing the Sufi ritual of *dhikr*, proclaiming repeated praises of God. The images of Christian and Muslim sanctity in harmony are unusual in themselves, but so was the thief's response. He became the custodian of a local saint's tomb, sleeping by the grave and spending his days in the cemetery 'on a little bench under a tree, letting his prayer beads run through his fingers, performing *dhikr*'.[5] Visitors donated food and money and gave him a cooler for cold water. These gifts, combined with a small pension from a former government job, enabled him to survive, usually on his own except on Fridays when the saint's tomb was open for pilgrimage visits. He had not prepared himself spiritually to receive this dream, which he understood to be a command from God to guard the tomb.

Some might question the moral value of Mahmud's abrupt change of lifestyle. He gave up stealing, but at the same time deserted his wife and four daughters, who were dependent on him. Was his narration of the dream a way of justifying to himself and others the decision to abandon his this-worldly duties? Of course, it is impossible, as ever, to know whether the dream even happened. However, it does not appear unusual for contemporary Muslims to regard veridical dreams and visions as determining future action to be taken by individuals, whether those individuals are pious or not. By contrast, there are also examples cited of dreams that have been considered authentic divine messages and yet have had no positive, spiritualising effect on the dreamers.[6]

Still other visionary experience is consciously sought by the method previously encountered as *istikhara* and entailing special prayer in preparation for receiving divine guidance while asleep. Many people resort to this practice when making important life choices, for example, in seeking a husband or wife or deciding on a career.[7] Abdemalek Yamani, a Moroccan living in the San Francisco Bay Area in the US, described his own performance of *istikhara* and its results. After supplicatory prayer, he went to sleep and later recounted the following dream:

> There is a big storm. I look up in the sky and I see nothing but dark clouds and lightning. It starts raining hard. I am walking carefully down a strong rocky mountain. The flow of water coming down the mountain is so strong that it easily drags stones and rocks with it. I am scared. I am so scared that I wake up. I become aware that I am dreaming. I decide to go back and continue my dream. In a split second I go back to sleep again and ask, Where am I going? I hear a voice advising me: 'Continue on your way. You will be fine.'[8]

Yamani recalls how he heard the voice encouraging him and his path soon became easier. He felt happy under a clear, cloud-free sky and came upon a beautiful, shallow lake, through which he walked before waking again. He admits that he did not know much about the Muslim tradition of dream interpretation, but self-interpreted the dream to mean that he should change his employer from Nokia to another company.

The dream has some characteristics traditionally associated with a veridical divine communication. It makes a vivid impression on the dreamer, who remembers it in detail with absolute clarity. He wakes in a startled state, a classic sign of a true dream even in antiquity. However, he then proceeds to fall back asleep and consciously resume the dream in a controlled manner, familiar in modern accounts of lucid dreaming. The narration thus appears to have both classical and modern features. It is of interest that this educated migrant, despite a high degree of technological training, was ready to make a significant career move on the basis of a dream. Furthermore, he had so much confidence in the clarity of the dream message that he did not seek out an expert Muslim interpreter for advice on the meaning of the symbolism in this enigmatic dream vision. It seems likely that this reflects an increasingly common situation for contemporary Muslims displaced from traditional environments where dream interpretation and its authorities are a regular part of everyday life.

Similar examples of the personal practice of *istikhara* are reported by Pakistanis living in the UK. Women are often noted as performing the ritual in relation to their own dreams and to those of family members; this is especially common in seeking guidance for marriage. One woman related how she sought guidance through *istikhara* regarding her daughter's choice of marriage partner. She dreamt about a bowl of dates, which looked appetising, but did not taste good.[9] In another case, a Pakistani young woman studying in the UK described how she had carried out *istikhara* in order to decide whether to marry a man whom she had known for five years. Her mother, two of her friends and a male family friend in the US all followed the same course of action. The student's dream turned out to be a nightmare, in which she was driving a car and crashed into a mountain. As her friends and mother also had bad dreams and negative feelings about the man, she became convinced that it would be a mistake to proceed with the marriage.[10]

However, not everyone undertakes *istikhara* on their own or with the help of family and friends. In many Muslim communities individuals will continue the traditional practice of seeking out expert dream interpreters, frequently Sufis, to perform *istikhara* on their behalf and hopefully reach a more reliable conclusion. Such practices seem to be ubiquitous, if varying somewhat in form, across the Muslim world, being observed in places as far apart from one another as Sierra Leone, Bosnia and Pakistan.[11] Two forms of the ritual have been reported in use within a modern Sufi order founded by Shaykh Zindapir (d. 1999) from the North West Frontier Province of Pakistan; the order has a strong following among British Muslims of Pakistani origin, who regard the shaykh as a saint. Pnina Werbner records the description given to her by one of these British Sufis, Hajji Karim, who states that in one form of *istikhara* the shaykh recites Qur'an before going to sleep and then 'sees colours

VISIONARY TRADITIONS AND THE IMPACT OF MODERNITY 179

and signs, which he can interpret as positive or negative. Certain colours such as green and white are positive; others, such as black, red or yellow are negative.'[12] The second form entails the shaykh reciting the *Fatiha*, the opening *sura* of the Qur'an, with repetition and prayer. The shaykh's 'head will tilt either to the left or the right and this will indicate whether the answer is positive or negative'.[13] On the other hand, Rosalind Shaw describes a rather different manner of practising *istikhara* among the Temne in the North East of Sierra Leone. The dream interpreter prepares an amulet 'or simply writes a passage from the Qur'an together with the client's name on a piece of paper, and prays to Allah for the solution to the client's problem before going to sleep with his head resting on the written sheet.'[14] When he wakes, he is able to provide an answer from his God-sent dream, presumably because of the blessed force emanating from the Qur'an, with which he is in physical contact in his sleep.

One case study from Bosnia is of interest because it involves a female dream interpreter performing *istikhara* as a professional service. At the time of being interviewed by anthropologists Iain Edgar and David Henig, Sadeta was already 70 years old and living in the capital, Sarajevo.[15] She had begun to have significant dream visions in 1990 before the outbreak of the 1992–5 war and claimed to have received spiritual guidance in her dreams from a young man dressed in white, whom she identified as a martyr. The martyr instructed her that she was to wear a golden scarf normally worn by those who had performed the *hajj*, even though she had not actually been on the Meccan pilgrimage. She was to help and heal people. She then sought out a religiously educated man, who advised her on the correct way to carry out *istikhara*, dream interpretation and Islamic healing.[16]

Sadeta was widely consulted by young women with regard to their marriage choices, but also, in the context of the war and its aftermath, many people came to ask her for help when they feared that they were victims of sorcery or needing healing from both physical and mental illness. Edgar and Henig remark:

> Her practice is arguably rather simple and intuitive and without recourse to Islamic dream interpretation books such as

the ubiquitous (in Islamic countries and communities) Ibn Sireen volume for interpreting dream symbols. She does not refer to the language of orthodoxy, and to the Qur'an only occasionally, and many if not most of the dream messages were from her perceived dream guide, the handsome young man.[17]

Most, but not all, of Sadeta's clients were women. It is not clear to what extent she was the heir to a specifically feminine type of dream interpretation or one with deep roots in Bosnian tradition. The presence of the martyr spirit guide might be a notably contemporary intrusion, although this figure does seem reminiscent of the young man dressed in white who appeared in the dream visions of Tirmidhi's wife in Central Asia of the late ninth century. Yet there is also the reminder of the Bosnian war that impacted forcefully on Sadeta. It is quite possible that her practice of foretelling through dreams may be the result of her own idiosyncratic approach rather than a method with an established history. It would be interesting to compare her style of interpretation with that of any female counterparts in the area and with the methodology of professional male dream interpreters, religious scholars and Sufis.

Folk traditions appear to have influenced modern dream interpretative practice in settings with a diversity of inherited cultural symbolism. Thus in Kyrgyzstan shoes may be an important dream image associated with marriage, while in Bosnia young women may dream of gardens with flowers or sheep and lambs, which are regularly slaughtered in celebration of a wedding.[18] Among those who are not versed in the Islamic science of oneirocriticism, such folk interpretations may weigh more heavily than the opinions expressed in the classical manuals of dream interpretation. For those who are primarily concerned with seeking knowledge of a happy future in this world, the quest for spiritual truth through dreams and visions is best left to the inspired Sufis. Nevertheless, such a quest continues to be vigorously pursued in Sufi orders. Werbner observes of the Pakistani Shaykh Zindapir: 'He has been guided, like all Sufi saints, only by religious imperatives known to him through visions and dreams.'[19] However, living saints are not alone in laying claim to

Visionary Traditions and the Impact of Modernity 181

spiritual guidance of a visionary nature. A disciple of an Egyptian shaykh asserted that the members of his group were all directed to receive these insights: '[Shaykh Qusi] is an expert in visions. We all see visions. The shaykh has pushed us to a point where we all see. I know people who *have* to see the Prophet twice a day.'[20] Such statements remind us of the many sightings of the Prophet in the dreams of the fifteenth-century North African Zawawi and the notable growth in reports of this type into modern times.

Interactions with Western Modernity

Although there is arguably a powerful continuing impact of scholarly, inspired and folk traditions relating to Muslims' dreams and visions, the force of Western modernity has inevitably been felt across Muslim communities worldwide and affected to some degree individual Muslims' understanding of this visionary experience. Understandably, attitudes to sleeping and waking visions have been affected by personal contacts with non-Muslims as well as printed literature, broadcasting and online discussion of such phenomena. A revision of traditional views and even outright rejection of visionary methods for foreknowing is only to be expected.

Perhaps what is more remarkable is the persistence of inherited beliefs in the face of so much negative opinion expressed by those who are ready to dismiss waking visions out of hand and for whom dreaming is understood as a result of chemical processes within the brain, irrelevant for determining future events. At times non-Muslim researchers have been surprised by the vehemence with which informants have defended the classical Islamic position, insisting that both dreams and visions can have a divine or devilish exterior source. Stephen Lyon recalled his shock at the reaction of a Pakistani friend in rural Punjab, when he related a dream that he experienced during the course of his anthropological fieldwork there. Lyon describes the dream as follows:

> In my dream, I was drinking tea in the local tea-shop called the 'hotel' by villagers. The hotel is small and has only three walls.

Customers sit in charpais and smoke hookahs or water pipes (called locally, chillum) and drink the milky tea freshly prepared while they wait. In my dream I was sitting on a charpai drinking tea when suddenly I fell into a trance and a white glow emanated from around my body. In the trance I began to recite the Qur'an in Arabic. I remained in the trance until I completed the Qur'an and then woke up from my trance with no knowledge of what I had done and no sudden ability to speak Arabic. I interpreted this, rightly in my view, as a response to continual attempts to persuade me to become a Muslim.[21]

Lyon had experienced these conversion attempts as an unwanted pressure, especially when, on occasion, he felt them to be 'aggressive'. Although not accustomed to relating his dreams to other people, he saw no harm in telling a Pakistani friend about it, since he considered him to be 'not overtly religious' and actually 'remarkably tolerant and relaxed about religion'. His friend's reaction, therefore, surprised him. The young Pakistani landlord responded in a quiet and nervous manner, asserting that Lyon 'could not have had that dream if it had not come from God'.[22] It would not have been possible to dream of reciting the whole of the Qur'an in Arabic unless it was a divine message, calling the dreamer to Islam. The friend's advice was to keep silent about the dream, as he was not preparing to embrace the faith. Lyon simply had not appreciated the degree of seriousness with which even lax Muslims take dream visions, especially those involving God, the Prophet and the Qur'an.[23]

Encounters with Freud and Jung

The pre-modern Islamic approach to dreaming was able to assume a shared conception of the phenomenon, one that is challenged today by increasing interaction with those who are unwilling and unable to accept the validity of traditional Muslim interpretative methods. Despite strong attachment to the classical tradition in many Muslim communities, there has been a steady process of infiltration of Western thought on dreaming, often older psychological thought exemplified by Freud, who has become a household name. One Egyptian shop owner remarked that Muslim dream interpreters are liars and ignorant and that today people go to psychologists to have their dreams interpreted.[24] However, it is not unusual to find sections in bookshops containing works on dreams by psychoanalysts placed next to medieval dream manuals. Sometimes there are also attempts to claim that oneirocrits such as Ibn Sirin prepared the way for the modern discoveries of psychoanalysis. It is also not unusual for the introductions to books of Muslim dream interpretation to contain lists of great authorities on dreams, beginning with the classic Muslim authors and ending with Sigmund Freud's *Interpretation of Dreams*.[25]

It is doubtful whether many traditional Muslim dream interpreters are actively acquainted with Freud. However, a case study conducted in Morocco sought to bring several such interpreters face to face with dream reports related by Freud and asked them to provide their own interpretations of the dreams narrated.[26] Field assistants presented the dreams to the interpreters without identifying them as occurring in Freud's works. One of these dream reports was as follows:

> Standing back a little behind two stately palaces was a little house with closed doors. My wife led me along the piece of street up to the little house and pushed the doors open; I then slipped quickly and easily into the inside of a court which rose in an incline.[27]

Freud's interpretation of the dream is that it represents sexual activity and the palaces, little house, street etc. refer to female body parts. The dreamer had allegedly begun to employ a young housekeeper, who had told him 'that she would not necessarily reject overtures on his part'.[28] The dream is not predictive as far as Freud is concerned, but for most of the Moroccan interpreters it offers an insight into character and a means of foreknowing. None of them recognised the dream report as a Freudian narrative. None interpreted it as an account of a sexual dream. Eight out of nine interpreters who listened to the report proceeded to interpret its images as disparate symbols, including some that were meaningful in an Islamic cultural context.[29]

They judged the palaces (or palace in the singular) to have one of the following meanings: paradise, future happiness, a grave, scholars, saints or a saint's sanctuary. Three interpreters identified a link between a palace or palaces and paradise and this does not seem surprising in view of the frequent assertion in Muslim tradition that those most favoured by God, including caliphs and significant early Muslims, have been seen in dreams as rewarded in paradise with residence in palaces.[30] One of the Moroccan interpreters, a religious jurist (*faqih*, Moroccan Arabic *fqih*), understood the palaces to signify 'two learned men or university professors who assist the dreamer (represented by the little house). The small house is a student who comes in search of knowledge or science.'[31] Another interpreter expresses a similar view and it seems to be an interpretation with which an educated male oneirocrit, as the guardian of a store of secret knowledge that the dreamer comes to him in order to access, can feel comfortable.[32]

Generally the interpreters are hopeful of a good outcome for the dreamer, even if he does have to encounter death. However, the woman's role in the dream appears to be minimised in most interpretations, although one does advise the dreamer that he will be happy if he listens to 'his obedient wife's counsel'.[33] Only one of the Moroccan interpreters is a woman and she is the only person to be really negative towards the dreaming husband. Although she understands paradise to be represented by a palace, she sees the little house as a failure, the husband as being cruel to his wife and the dream as 'a bad dream of a rich man who finds himself suddenly deprived of his wealth'.[34] The significance of paradise is not clear in her interpretation, which is jarringly at odds with the opinions of her male counterparts. Interestingly, only one oneirocrit refused to interpret the dream on the grounds that it was not real.[35] Although he did not know the source of the dream report, he had the insight to realise that the field assistant was not recalling his own dream and that it was possibly fabricated. By reacting in this manner, he comes closest to the pre-modern ideal of the expert Muslim dream interpreter, who perceives that a client is laying claim falsely to a dream vision and, therefore, refuses to interpret it.[36]

Although traditional methods of interpretation are still the most widespread, there are some records of contemporary Muslims turning to non-traditional and non-Muslim sources in the search to understand their dreams. A notable example is that of a Muslim young man who landed in New York on the day preceding the attacks of 11 September 2001. Two years later he went to see a Jungian psychoanalyst working in the city, at least partially with the goal of finding an analysis of certain spiritual dreams that he had experienced. The psychoanalyst, Michael Vannoy Adams, notes that his client had been resident in Jerusalem and working for an international relief organisation to help the Palestinians of Gaza.[37]

The young man had been in therapy with an Israeli therapist, but the therapist had apparently not appreciated the high value of this Muslim man's spiritual dreams and not been able to interpret them. The client explained that he had experienced a great deal of internal division between the 'Arab-Islamic part' of his identity and the 'Western part'. In addition to Arabic and English, he spoke Turkish, Hebrew and French and had lived in Europe, Africa and Asia as well as the Middle East and North America. Although he 'was never not a Muslim', he 'aspired to a more inclusive humanity – and a more inclusive spirituality'.[38] He had studied Sufism, but also took an active interest in Jewish and Christian spirituality. As he was actually seeking to escape the conflict between Islam and the West, the timing of his arrival in New York was obviously unfortunate for him and presumably compounded his sense of division and confusion.

Adams analysed three dreams told to him by his client, whom he names 'Nizar', with special reference to the Islamic cultural unconscious, defined by him as 'a dimension of the collective unconscious' that is so central to Jungian discussion of dreaming.[39] He observed the dreams as displaying certain 'cultural complexes', which he identified as sets of 'values about which a culture is especially emotionally sensitive'.[40] These complexes included what Adams terms the Middle Eastern cultural complex, stressing the importance of obedience and submission to God. This complex is shared by Jews, Christians and Muslims, with some variations. In the Islamic case, a submission complex in the Islamic cultural unconscious is viewed as making it difficult for Muslims to focus on the individual out of a concern that such a focus may risk inflating the ego. Inflation of the ego could then lead to the grave sin of *shirk*, which in this case would involve putting the individual on a level with God rather than being humble and submissive in God's presence.

Although all three of Nizar's dreams are of a spiritual character, the first is not specifically Islamic in content, while the third is strikingly so, as Nizar sees himself circumambulating the Ka'ba at Mecca. We shall here consider the second dream, which also contains strong Islamic features and which Nizar described as follows:

> My father is next to me. There are four birds that are killed and cut into pieces. Suddenly, they're resurrected. A pigeon comes to my hand. Then it's as if the sun is just in front of my face. Such a light! It's very realistic. I wake up shocked by the beauty of the light.[41]

From an Islamic perspective, the meaning of the dream can be divined with reference to Qur'an 2:260, where God instructs Abraham to cut four birds into pieces and put parts of them on separate hills. God assures His prophet that the birds will come back to life and fly to him. It is a plain sign from God of His power, even to the point of being able to revive the dead, and that nothing is impossible. Nizar associates this dream vision with his father, whom he recalls as humble and submissive to God, fulfilling the expectations of the Middle Eastern cultural complex. However, Nizar also sees the sun in front of him and its light startles him into wakefulness. Adams notes that, in Jungian discourse, light always represents consciousness. While respecting his father and not wishing to abandon Islamic values, Nizar appreciates that he is undergoing development as an individual and becoming enlightened. The dream is interpreted as helping him to come to terms with his Islamic and Western identities without violating his fundamental beliefs.

Dream Interpretation in Cyberspace

It is unknown how many Muslims may be ready to subject their dreams to any type of Western psychoanalysis, but it is likely to be very few by contrast with the considerable numbers who seek access to traditional forms of Muslim dream interpretation. Nevertheless, accessibility to oneirocrits is evidently a problem and leads to increasing efforts to find information via the internet. Various websites aim to offer user-friendly ways of discovering the kind of interpretations of symbolic images that are familiar from the pre-modern dream manuals.[42] Some traditional interpreters will also provide an online service for clients seeking advice on the meanings of their dreams. Amira Mittermaier recorded the case of Shaykh Nabil, the Egyptian guardian of Ibn Sirin's tomb in Cairo. He received many visitors at the shrine, for whom he offered face-to-face consultations concerning the significance of dreams. However, he also undertook some work for a website that had customers from across the Middle East and not only in Egypt. A journalist brought him the dream reports in a printed version and he wrote his own interpretative comments on each dream. The journalist then collected them from him and put them online.[43]

Critics of online dream interpretation will point to a variety of problems and remark that it is not a good substitute for the oneirocrit interviewing the dreamer in person. During a personal meeting with the dreamer it is possible for the dream interpreter to gain some understanding of his client's character and circumstances. In an online encounter there is much less certainty, even if the dreamer mentions a name, occupation and other details. It is hard, if not impossible, for the interpreter to offer the same quality of advice and to detect fraudulent claims to visionary experience. A phone consultation or access to a handwritten dream report might provide a degree of insight into the significance of a particular dream, but, as Mittermaier notes: 'Typing a dream on a computer keyboard severs the immediate link between dream and dreamer.'[44]

A more sinister use of cyberspace for promoting accounts of dreams, and occasionally waking visions, is provided by the websites of Muslim militants, who employ reports of their martyrs' visionary experiences with propagandist aims.[45] They seek to recruit young Muslim men to join them in jihad by posting online the biographies of their fighters, either as texts or short films. These stories depict the men's visions and dreams of their imminent deaths, which are believed to be reliable predictions, since their impending status as martyrs renders them especially open to receiving veridical messages. In other cases, relatives and friends dream of the deceased martyrs, question them regarding the afterlife and learn of the rewards for their sacrifice.

The reports are usually of literal dreams so that they are readily understandable by the audience without the need for an expert to interpret the meaning. Typically, viewers and readers are assured that the deceased is a martyr and has, therefore, entered Paradise directly, enjoying all the comforts of life that he had forsaken in order to participate in jihad. An early example of this type of relatively unsophisticated account dates from the Bosnian conflict and describes the events surrounding the martyrdom of a Kuwaiti commander of foreign volunteers in 1995. A comrade sees the man named as Abu Muʿadh al-Kuwayti in a dream after he has been killed and asks him a series of questions. Is he really a martyr? What is it like? Abu Muʿadh confirms that he is indeed a martyr and that a window had opened in the sky from Paradise in order to receive all the jihad fighters who were killed on that day. Asked what it feels like, he replies: 'You don't feel a thing. As soon as you are killed, you see two beautiful blonde girls, they come and sit beside you in *jannah* [Paradise] with you.'[46] (He is referring to the beautiful maidens of Paradise, the houris, but this is hardly a traditional description.) Abu Muʿadh assures his comrade that Paradise is all about enjoyment and pleasure. Although he cannot tell the dreamer the exact time of his future martyrdom, he agrees that he will try to come to him in a dream a few days before the event. Many similar reports are recounted on jihadist websites with reference to subsequent wars. The object is evidently to encourage the prospective fighters to view potential martyrdom in a positive light, often as something that they will find easy and with guaranteed rewards.

Militants' reports of enigmatic dreams are rarer and usually contain one or two familiar images that are not hard to decipher. The expectation is that they will be readily understood by someone without specialist knowledge of dream interpretation or access to a skilled interpreter. However, Usama Bin Laden was regarded by his followers in al-Qaeda as an accomplished oneirocrit, who practised the interpretation of their dreams. In 2002 a journalist for Al-Jazeera, Yosri Fouda, interviewed two of those involved in the planning of the attacks on New York and Washington. He recalled the importance that the group attached to dreaming and visionary experience, noting a videotape in which an al-Qaeda spokesman remarked:

> I saw in my dreams that I was sitting in a room with the Sheikh [Bin Laden], and all of a sudden there was breaking news on TV. It showed an Egyptian family going about its business and a rotating strap that said: 'In revenge for the sons of al-Aqsa [that is, the Palestinians], Osama Bin Laden executes strikes against the Americans.'[47]

Bin Laden then gives the interpretation of the one symbolic image, the Egyptian family: 'The Egyptian family symbolises Mohammed Atta, may Allah have mercy on his soul. He was in charge of the group.'[48] The 'rotating strap' replaces the speech of a dream messenger and introduces a distinctive modern element to the oracle. The presentation acts to position Bin Laden at the centre of the operation and lends status to him as an inspired dream interpreter in the eyes of his admirers. To outsiders it obviously appeared as an unsavoury piece of propaganda.

Rejecting and Accepting Dreams and Visions

While belief in the validity of all kinds of visions remains strong among a great many Muslims today, not everyone shares such a belief. In August 2005 I was invited to a lunch gathering in a middle-class suburb of Amman, Jordan. After the meal the conversation among the women turned to the subject of dreams and one of the guests described how a relative had seen a dream vision shortly before he passed away. In the dream a man who had died some time earlier appeared and invited the dreamer to join him in a banquet at which he was the host. The general opinion in the gathering was that this had been a clear sign of the dreamer's imminent death, since he was being invited by someone who had already died. However, the daughter of the dream host objected. Perhaps she was offended at her father being discussed in this way. In any case, she pointed out that it was wrong for them as Muslims to give credence to dreams as a means of foreknowing the time of a person's death or anything else of consequence. As a woman with a scientific education, she was not only inclined to dismiss this type of thinking as ridiculous, but also perceived it as inappropriate for a practising Muslim.

This dismissive attitude towards dream interpretation has also gained ground among both state officials and religious scholars in Egypt. It led to the banning in January 2003 of a popular television programme, in which a scholar from al-Azhar University and a psychologist interpreted viewers' dreams.[49] The state and al-Azhar acted together to denounce the broadcasting of dream interpretation for the masses; the Azhari decree stated that it could result in public confusion and anxiety, while the Ministry of Religious Affairs made the judgement that dream interpretation was nothing but 'idle talk' and was not confirmed to have a place in Islam. It should be replaced by a programme that focused on religion and morals.[50] Thus, at one stroke, a venerable Islamic science was effectively outlawed, despite the large-scale support for it among the Egyptian Muslim population.

However, the rejection of dreams and visions as a means of guidance and foreknowing has had a longer history in Egypt and has exercised a broader influence from there across the Arab lands of the Middle East and sometimes beyond into the wider Muslim world. An early key figure in disseminating a negative perspective in relation to dream interpretation was Rashid Rida (d. 1935). He played an important role among Muslim reformers of the late nineteenth and early twentieth centuries in contesting whatever appeared to him as contrary to reason. Visionary experience of all kinds became an obvious target for his attacks on abuse of the imagination and superstitious beliefs, although he had been open to just such experience himself as a young man growing up in a Sufi religious environment in and around the Syrian city of Tripoli (now in northern Lebanon). After his move to Cairo in 1897, Rida adopted a far more critical attitude towards what he regarded as the excesses of Sufism in his day. He asserted that many Sufis made unreliable claims to receiving veridical dreams and denounced 'their dreams and visions of the dead as devilish delusions'.[51] Rida indicates that an exposure to European thought has made him aware of the need for caution and rationalism, but shows no sign of an active acquaintance with Western psychologists' work on dreaming and his use of reason is erratic at best.

Nevertheless, Rida's ideas reached a wide audience across the Muslim world from Morocco to Indonesia due largely to the publication of the journal *al-Manar*, which stimulated interest in reformist circles. The founder of the Muslim Brotherhood, Hasan al-Banna' (d. 1948), was also closely associated with Rida and stressed the importance of gaining knowledge only through legitimate sources and methods, notably the Qur'an and Hadith, science and reason. Al-Banna', therefore, rejected dreams as a means of acquiring knowledge.[52] Such views have understandably filtered through the powerful Muslim Brotherhood and have furthermore been endorsed by a number of Saudi and Saudi-trained scholars, although not all Saudis subscribe to them (as has been noted in the case of Bin Laden).[53]

Despite the successes of the sceptics in persuading some Muslim activists and government officials of the case against the mass interpretation of dreams, they remain in the minority. They are easily outnumbered by those who do attach significance to dreaming and waking visions. A recent case from Iran illustrates the continuation of traditional beliefs on the subject. In the autumn of 2007 a young man called Abdollah Hosseinzadeh was killed in a street fight. He was 18 years old. In 2014 his distraught mother could not imagine that she would be able to pardon her son's killer, who had been sentenced to death. However, her mind was changed when she experienced dreams that she understood as emanating from the world of truth:

> 'Ten days before the execution was due, I saw my son in a dream asking me not to take revenge, but I couldn't convince myself to forgive,' she told the Guardian. 'Two nights before that day, I saw him in the dream once again, but this time he refused to speak to me.'[54]

The mother held on to her anger towards her son's murderer until the last minute. When the killer was about to be hanged, she slapped him across the face, wept and called on her husband to remove the noose. She admitted that the dreams of her son had been a decisive influence in enabling her to pardon the young man who had killed him.

This 2014 Iranian dream report has some of the classic features of the old epiphany dream narrative. The dreamer 'sees' a deceased relative, who resides in the 'world of truth' and, therefore, brings an authentic message. It is a clear, auditory and visual dream, so needs no special skill in interpretation. Indeed, the report would not have been out of place in Ibn Abi al-Dunya's ninth-century *Kitab al-manam*. It even contains a moral message, appealing for the dreamer to show forgiveness rather than seeking revenge. The second dream performs the ancient function of confirming the truth. However, the dream messenger is silent, apparently out of anger or disappointment at the dreamer's failure to act on the request to forgive. Action is remarkably absent from the reported dreams and their qualities would be considered archaic in much of the modern world, where dream accounts normally describe visual episodes. Admittedly, some medieval scholars and visionaries might have contested the idea that a woman of low social status, the wife of a retired labourer, would be the likely recipient of veridical, epiphany dreams. Yet others would have acknowledged the possibility and perhaps recognised the dreams' veridical nature in view of the virtuous behaviour that the woman's son urged his mother to practise.

If such dreams seem alien in secular society today, they are not uncommon in the Muslim world, for this ancient form of dreaming may function more effectively in present conditions than accounts of enigmatic dreams that depend on inspired or well-trained interpreters. Dreams requiring interpretation may be seen as more vulnerable to decline because it can be argued that fewer religious scholars of high standing devote their efforts to the Islamic science of oneirocriticism and new technology is less conducive to real insight than the traditional face-to-face encounter between dreamer and dream interpreter. Overall, belief in the value of dreams and visions would appear slightly diminished since the pre-modern period, but still strong and acted upon in many instances as a respected means of guidance and foreknowing. Although waking visions are less frequently related, they retain their esteem among the faithful as providing the most direct and truthful method of ongoing divine communication with the human.

NOTES

Preface

1. Muhammad Amanullah, 'Islamic dreaming: an analysis of its truthfulness and influence', in K. Bulkeley, K. Adams and P. M. Davis (eds), *Dreaming in Christianity and Islam: Culture, Conflict and Creativity* (New Brunswick NJ and London, 2009), pp. 106–7; here p. 107.
2. Hidayet Aydar, 'Istikhara and dreams: learning about the future through dreaming', in Bulkeley et al. (eds), *Dreaming in Christianity and Islam*, pp. 131–2.
3. John C. Lamoreaux, *The Early Muslim Tradition of Dream Interpretation* (Albany NY, 2002), p. 4.
4. Ibid., pp. 4–5 for further observations on the desire to link traditional Muslim dream divination with psychoanalysis, either implicitly by listing the names of Muslim authors before that of Freud among the great figures of the field or explicitly by claiming that medieval Muslims had actually pre-empted the findings of modern psychoanalysis.
5. Guy G. Stroumsa, 'Dreams and visions in early Christian discourse', in D. Shulman and G. G. Stroumsa (eds), *Dream Cultures: Explorations in the Comparative History of Dreaming* (New York and Oxford, 1999), p. 189.

Introduction

1. Jonathan G. Katz, *Dreams, Sufism and Sainthood: The Visionary Career of Muhammad al-Zawawi* (Leiden, 1996), p. 210 and n. 14.
2. Katherine P. Ewing, *Arguing Sainthood: Modernity, Psychoanalysis and Islam* (Durham NC, 1997), p. 160.
3. Al-Ghazali, *al-Munqidh min al-dalal* (Beirut, 1959), p. 39 (Arabic) and p. 101 (French trans.).

4. Nile Green, 'The religious and cultural role of dreams and visions in Islam', *Journal of the Royal Asiatic Society*, 3rd series, 13/3 (2003), p. 294.
5. Carl Gustav Jung, *Psychology and Religion* (New Haven CT and London, 1938), p. 7; p. 27.
6. Ibid., p. 41.
7. William V. Harris, *Dreams and Experience in Classical Antiquity* (Cambridge MA and London, 2009), pp. 4–5.
8. Ibid., p. 5 and pp. 91–122.
9. See D. F. Reynolds (ed.), *Interpreting the Self: Autobiography in the Arabic Literary Tradition* (Berkeley, 2001), p. 93 and Louise Marlow (ed.), *Dreaming Across Boundaries: The Interpretation of Dreams in Islamic Lands* (Cambridge MA and London, 2008), pp. 5–6.
10. C. F. Beckingham, 'The *Rihla*: Fact or Fiction?', in I. R. Netton (ed.), *Golden Roads: Migration, Pilgrimage and Travel in Mediaeval and Modern Islam* (Richmond, 1993), p. 86.
11. On this incident see Valerie Hoffman, *Sufism, Mystics and Saints in Modern Egypt* (Columbia SC, 1995), pp. 271–3. For Hoffman, Shaykh 'Izz provided a significant point of contact with Egyptian Sufis and he figures prominently in her book.
12. Ibid., p. 272.
13. Ibid., p. 273.

Chapter 1   Seeing Gods and Angels before the Rise of Islam

1. For comments on the ancient regional dream cultures as contributors to Muslim thought on the subject, see e.g. Sara Sviri, 'Dreaming analyzed and recorded: dreams in the world of medieval Islam', in D. Shulman and G. G. Stroumsa (eds), *Dream Cultures: Explorations in the Comparative History of Dreaming* (New York and Oxford, 1999). On the legacy bequeathed to Muslim writers on dream interpretation see Elizabeth Sirriyeh, 'Arab stars, Assyrian dogs and Greek "angels": How Islamic is Muslim dream interpretation?', *Journal of Islamic Studies* 22/2 (2011), pp. 215–33; for more detail on traces of Artemidorus in Arabic guides to dreams, see John C. Lamoreaux, *The Early Muslim Tradition of Dream Interpretation* (Albany NY, 2002).
2. See Scott Noegel, 'Dreams and dream interpreters in Mesopotamia and in the Hebrew Bible [Old Testament]', in K. Bulkeley (ed.), *Dreams: A Reader on Religious, Cultural and Psychological Dimensions of Dreaming* (New York and Basingstoke, 2001), pp. 45–6 for a brief outline of the problems of classification. On Near Eastern dreaming see further Scott B. Noegel, *Nocturnal Ciphers: The Allusive Language of Dreams in the Ancient Near East* (New Haven CT, 2007).

3. Noegel, 'Dreams and dream interpreters', p. 45.
4. Ibid., p. 46. Noegel argues that the typology of A. Leo Oppenheim is too rigid in making a sharp distinction between symbolic and non-symbolic dreams in the Mesopotamian and wider Near Eastern context. See A. Leo Oppenheim, 'The interpretation of dreams in the ancient Near East with a translation of an Assyrian dream-book', *Transactions of the American Philosophical Society* n.s. 43/3 (1956), pp. 184–90.
5. Curtiss Hoffman, 'Dumuzi's dream: dream analysis in ancient Mesopotamia', *Dreaming* 14/4 (2004), pp. 240–1.
6. Jeremy Black et al., *The Literature of Ancient Sumer* (Oxford, 2004), pp. 78–9.
7. Ibid., p. 79.
8. Oppenheim, 'Interpretation', p. 231. Oppenheim notes that bad dreams were sent to harm humans in the same way as diseases, but their evil effects could be averted by the correct prayers, particularly to the sun-god Shamash and the moon-god Sin. He remarks on a comparable view of evil dreams 'probably everywhere in the ancient Near East'.
9. Black, *Literature of Ancient Sumer*, p. 79.
10. Francesca Rochberg, *The Heavenly Writing: Divination, Horoscopy and Astronomy in Mesopotamian Culture* (Cambridge and New York, 2004), p. 82.
11. Noegel, 'Dreams and dream interpreters', p. 55.
12. Jean-Marie Husser, *Dreams and Dream Narratives in the Biblical World*, trans. Jill M. Munro (Sheffield, 1999), p. 108.
13. Kasia Szpakowska, 'Through the looking glass: dreams in ancient Egypt', in Bulkeley (ed.), *Dreams*, p. 31. For a more detailed study of dreaming in ancient Egypt see Kasia Szpakowska, *Behind Closed Eyes: Dreams and Nightmares in Ancient Egypt* (Swansea, 2003).
14. Szpakowska, 'Through the looking glass', p. 31.
15. Ibid., p. 33 and p. 42 n. 25. This dream book was discovered among documents at the site of an ancient village near the Valley of the Kings and was published in A. H. Gardiner, *Hieratic Papyri in the British Museum*, vol. 3: *The Dream Book* (London, 1935).
16. Husser, *Dreams and Dream Narratives*, p. 66.
17. Ibid. pp. 130–1.
18. Oppenheim, 'Interpretation', pp. 267–9.
19. Rochberg, *Heavenly Writing*, p. 55.
20. Oppenheim, 'Interpretation', p. 280.
21. Rochberg, *Heavenly Writing*, pp. 56–7.
22. Genesis 28:13 and verses 10–22 for the full account. Among numerous discussions of Jacob's dream see Diana Lipton, *Revisions of the Night: Politics and Promises in the Patriarchal Dreams of Genesis* (Sheffield, 1999), pp. 63–114.
23. Oppenheim, 'Interpretation', p. 249, providing a translation of the dream report from an inscription of Assurbanipal in the seventh century BCE.
24. Ibid., p. 189.

25. Husser, *Dreams and Dream Narratives*, pp. 61–2, including a translation of the dream report. See further B. M. Bryan, *The Reign of Thutmose IV* (Baltimore MD and London, 1991). Dates for this pharaoh differ. See e.g. John Baines, 'Society, morality and religious practice', in B. E. Shafer (ed.), *Religion in Ancient Egypt: Gods, Myths and Personal Practice* (London, 1991), p. 202, giving 1400–1390 BCE as the period of his rule.
26. Husser, *Dreams and Dream Narratives*, p. 62.
27. Lipton, *Revisions of the Night*, pp. 80–1.
28. See Robin Lane Fox, *Pagans and Christians* (Harmondsworth, 1986), pp. 102–18 on Greek visions from the age of Homer to the fifth century CE.
29. See William V. Harris, *Dreams and Experience in Classical Antiquity* (Cambridge MA and London, 2009), pp. 24–5.
30. On Aristotle's thought on dreaming see D. Gallop, *Aristotle on Sleep and Dreams: A Text and Translation with Introduction, Notes and Glossary* (Warminster, 1996).
31. Daldis, about 100 km to the north-east of Ephesus, was a little-known town, but Artemidorus appears to have included it in his name out of respect for Apollo, the major deity of Daldis, who inspired him to undertake his work on dreams. See S. R. F. Price, 'The future of dreams: from Freud to Artemidorus', *Past and Present* 113 (1986), p. 10.
32. Lane Fox, *Pagans and Christians*, p. 155.
33. Artemidorus, *The Interpretation of Dreams: Oneirocritica*, trans. Robert J. White (Park Ridge NJ, 1975), p. 22.
34. Ibid., p. 15.
35. Ibid., pp. 20–1.
36. Ibid., p. 23.
37. Ibid., p. 18. See Hanne Lavér Hansen, ' "The truth without nonsense": remarks on Artemidorus' *Interpretation of Dreams*', in R. L. Wildfang and J. Isager (eds), *Divination and Portents in the Roman World* (Odense, 2000), pp. 60–3 for an argument that Artemidorus was not actually a snob, but lived in a place and time where status, usually linked to wealth and a person's social role, mattered above all else.
38. Artemidorus, *Interpretation of Dreams*, trans. White, p. 18.
39. Ibid., p. 16.
40. Harris, *Dreams and Experience*, p. 114.
41. Patricia Cox Miller, *Dreams in Late Antiquity: Studies in the Imagination of a Culture* (Princeton NJ, 1994), p. 86.
42. Artemidorus, *Interpretation of Dreams*, trans. White, pp. 35–6.
43. See Philip S. Alexander, 'Bavli Berakhot 55a–57b: the Talmudic dreambook in context', *Journal of Jewish Studies* 46 (1995), pp. 243–4.
44. See Maurice Simon, *The Babylonian Talmud: Berakhot* (London, 1948) for an English translation.
45. Galit Hasan-Rokem, 'Communication with the dead in Jewish dream culture', in Shulman and Stroumsa (eds), *Dream Cultures*, p. 222.

NOTES TO PAGES 23–33

46. See Alexander, 'Bavli Berakhot 55a–57b', p. 242 for examples of parallels between Artemidorus and the Babylonian Talmud.
47. Ibid., p. 243 on these aspects of dream interpretation 'specific to rabbinic culture'.
48. Ibid., pp. 235–7 and Hasan-Rokem, 'Communication', p. 220.
49. Lane Fox, *Pagans and Christians*, p. 392.
50. Harris, *Dreams and Experience*, p. 74.
51. Guy G. Stroumsa, 'Dreams and visions in early Christian discourse', in Shulman and Stroumsa (eds), *Dream Cultures*, pp. 196–203 on this tripartite division of dreams according to their origin.
52. Ibid., p. 189.
53. On Hermas' visionary experience see Lane Fox, *Pagans and Christians*, pp. 381–9.
54. Lane Fox, *Pagans and Christians*, p. 383.
55. Ibid.
56. Ibid., p. 386.
57. Harris, *Dreams and Experience*, p. 71.
58. Toufic Fahd, *La Divination Arabe: Études Religieuses, Sociologiques et Folkloriques sur le Milieu Natif de l'Islam* (Leiden, 1966), p. 249.
59. Ibid., p. 254.
60. Ibn Hisham, 'Abd al-Malik, *al-Sira al-Nabawiyya*, ed. J. Thabit, M. Mahmud and S. Ibrahim (Cairo, 1996), vol. 1, pp. 30–3 and Fahd, *Divination*, pp. 250–3 on the dream of Rabi'a b. Nasr. See T. Fahd, 'Kahin', in *Encyclopaedia of Islam*, 2nd edn, edited by an editorial committee consisting of H. A. R. Gibb et al. (Leiden, 1960–2009), vol. 4, pp. 420–2 on the function of the *kahin* in pre-Islamic Arabia, including divinatory aspects. Fahd observes that the *kahina*, the female counterpart of the *kahin*, had the role of an ecstatic visionary who was responsible for an oracle. See also T. Fahd, 'Kihana', in *Encyclopaedia of Islam*, 2nd edn, vol. 5, pp. 99–101 on forms of divination that were accepted in the world of Islam and those pre-Islamic forms that were rejected.
61. Lamoreaux, *Early Muslim Tradition*, p. 71.
62. Harris, *Dreams and Experience*, p. 86.
63. See Rotraud E. Hansberger, 'How Aristotle came to believe in God-given dreams: the Arabic version of *De divinatione per somnum*', in L. Marlow (ed.), *Dreaming Across Boundaries: The Interpretation of Dreams in Islamic Lands* (Cambridge MA and London, 2008), pp. 50–77 on the Muslims' adaptation of Aristotle's views on dreams.

Chapter 2 The Prophet as Model Visionary

1. Muhammad Husayn Haykal, *Hayat Muhammad* (Cairo, 1935).
2. Andrew Rippin, *Muslims: Their Religious Beliefs and Practices* (4th edn, London and New York, 2012), p. 212.
3. W. Montgomery Watt, *Muhammad, Prophet and Statesman* (Oxford, 1961), p. 2. This condensed book is based on Watt's classic biography in two volumes,

Muhammad at Mecca (Oxford, 1953) and *Muhammad at Medina* (Oxford, 1956).
4. Fred M. Donner, *Muhammad and the Believers, At the Origins of Islam* (Cambridge MA and London, 2010), p. 51.
5. Matthew 2:2.
6. See Patricia Crone, *Meccan Trade and the Rise of Islam* (Princeton NJ, 1987) for a challenge to the view, notably expressed by Watt in *Muhammad at Mecca*, that Mecca was a key centre of a network of trade in luxury goods, such as frankincense and spices.
7. See J. M. B. Jones, 'Ibn Ishak', in *Encyclopaedia of Islam*, 2nd edn, edited by an editorial committee consisting of H. A. R. Gibb et al. (Leiden, 1960–2009), vol. 3, pp. 810–11 on the differing views of early Muslim scholars regarding the reliability of Ibn Ishaq's narration. For accounts of some dreams and visions concerning the Prophet's birth, in addition to those discussed in this chapter, see Toufic Fahd, *La Divination Arabe: Études Religieuses, Sociologiques et Folkloriques sur le Milieu Natif de l'Islam* (Leiden, 1966), pp. 259–63.
8. 'Abd al-Malik Ibn Hisham, *al-Sira al-Nabawiyya*, ed. J. Thabit, M. Mahmud and S. Ibrahim (Cairo, 1996), vol. 1, pp. 139–40.
9. The idea that the Divine Light passed into Muhammad was to be further elaborated in Shi'i and Sufi thought and extended backwards in time to create the belief that Muhammad was created of pure light from God's primordial light at the very beginning of creation. One of the early advocates of this belief was the Sufi Sahl al-Tustari (d. 896), on whose ideas see Nile Green, *Sufism: A Global History* (Oxford, 2012), pp. 33–6 and Ahmet T. Karamustafa, *Sufism: The Formative Period* (Edinburgh, 2007), pp. 38–43. For a masterful study of Tustari, including his ideas on the Divine Light, see Gerhard Böwering, *The Mystical Vision of Existence in Classical Islam: the Qur'anic Hermeneutics of the Sufi Sahl at-Tustari (d.283/896)* (Berlin, 1980), especially pp. 149–57.
10. Ibn Hisham, *Sira*, vol. 1, p. 140.
11. Ibid., vol. 1, p. 141.
12. New International Version of Luke 1:30–2. For the full account see Luke 1:26–38.
13. M. A. S. Abdel Haleem, *The Qur'an: A New Translation* (Oxford, 2004), p. 444.
14. Ibn Hisham, *Sira*, vol. 1, p. 141.
15. Leonard H. Lesko, 'Ancient Egyptian cosmogonies and cosmology', in B. E. Shafer (ed.), *Religion in Ancient Egypt: Gods, Myths and Personal Practice* (London, 1991), p. 118.
16. Suetonius trans. and quoted in Robin Lorsch Wildfang, 'The propaganda of omens: six dreams involving Augustus', in R. L. Wildfang and J. Isager (eds), *Divination and Portents in the Roman World* (Odense, 2000), p. 44.
17. Asclepiades of Mendes, author of the *Theologoumena*, is thought to have been a contemporary of Augustus and possibly his freedman. See Wildfang, 'Propaganda of omens', p. 47.
18. Ibid., p. 45.
19. Tabari trans. and quoted in Marion Holmes Katz, *The Birth of the Prophet Muhammad: Devotional Piety in Sunni Islam* (London and New York, 2007), p. 40.

20. An ancient example of a shared dream is that described as being experienced by the whole army of the neo-Assyrian ruler Assurbanipal (668–627 BCE), who were afraid to cross the raging torrent of a river, but were given assurance of safety by the goddess Ishtar, who appeared in their dreams. See Scott Noegel, 'Dreams and dream interpreters in Mesopotamia and in the Hebrew Bible [Old Testament]', in K. Bulkeley (ed.), *Dreams: A Reader on Religious, Cultural and Psychological Dimensions of Dreaming* (New York and Basingstoke, 2001), p. 47. See William V. Harris, *Dreams and Experience in Classical Antiquity* (Cambridge MA and London, 2009), p. 42 for examples of shared dreams in the Greco-Roman period. The pattern was continued in Christian Europe.
21. See Katz, *Birth*, pp. 6–62 on the development of Muslim narratives on the birth of the Prophet.
22. For this story see ibid., p. 44.
23. Muhammad Ibn Sa'd, *al-Tabaqat al-kubra*, ed. M 'Ata (Beirut, 1990), vol. 1, p. 152. Ibn Sa'd was the secretary of al-Waqidi (d. 822), author of a famous early chronicle of the Prophet's campaigns. The *Tabaqat* includes important biographical material on Muhammad and his Companions as well as subsequent champions of Islam.
24. Ibid., vol. 1, p. 153.
25. Ibn Hisham, *Sira*, vol. 1, p. 199 and Muhammad al-Bukhari, *al-Jami' al-Sahih*, ed. M. al-Khatib (Beirut, 1991), vol. 4, p. 295.
26. Ibn Hisham: *Sira*, vol. 1, p. 201. On the first two occasions the words translated here as 'I cannot read' (*ma aqra'u*) are somewhat ambiguous and could have the meaning 'What shall I read?' On the third occasion Ibn Hisham's recension of Ibn Ishaq's *Sira* makes a slight change so that the sentence can only mean 'What shall I read?' (*madha aqra'u*) and this is repeated once more, adding further stress to the difference between the two forms of the question. See further the comments by W. Montgomery Watt, *Muhammad at Mecca* (Oxford, 1953), p. 46, noting the importance of the Prophet's statement that he cannot read in stressing his illiteracy and hence the miraculous nature of the Qur'an.
27. Ibn Hisham, *Sira*, vol. 1, p. 202.
28. See ibid., vol. 1, pp. 202–3 and Bukhari, *Sahih*, vol. 4, p. 295.
29. Al-Tabari, *The History of al-Tabari* (Ta'rikh al-rusul wa'l-muluk), vol. 6: *Muhammad at Mecca*, trans. W. Montgomery Watt and M.V. McDonald (Albany NY, 1988), p. 75.
30. Ibid.
31. Ibn Hisham, *Sira*, vol. 1, pp. 145, 146 and 147.
32. Tabari, *History*, vol. 6, pp. 63, 75 and 78.
33. On incubation practices in the ancient Near East see e.g. A. Leo Oppenheim, 'The interpretation of dreams in the ancient Near East with a translation of an Assyrian dream-book', *Transactions of the American Philosophical Society* n.s. 43/3 (1956), pp. 187–8. For references to the practice in classical antiquity, see e.g. Harris, *Dreams and Experience*, pp. 39–40, which notes the particular popularity of visits by sick persons seeking cures, for example at shrines of Asclepius.
34. Tabari, *History*, vol. 6, p. 78.

35. Heribert Busse, 'Jerusalem in the story of Muhammad's night journey and ascension', in U. Rubin (ed.), *The Formation of the Classical Islamic World*, vol. 4: *The Life of Muhammad* (Aldershot and Brookfield VM, 1998), p. 303.
36. See e.g. Mircea Eliade, 'Initiation dreams and visions among the Siberian shamans', in G. E. von Grunebaum and R. Caillois (eds), *The Dream and Human Societies* (Berkeley and Los Angeles, 1966), p. 333, where Eliade notes 'the central theme of an initiation ceremony: dismemberment of the neophyte's body and renewal of his organs; ritual death followed by resurrection'.
37. Tabari, *History*, vol. 6, p. 79.
38. Ibid.
39. See Brooke Olson Vuckovic, *Heavenly Journeys, Earthly Concerns: The Legacy of the Mi'raj in the Formation of Islam* (New York and London, 2005), pp. 43–72 on Muhammad's meetings with the earlier prophets during his ascension, according to some of the fuller accounts of medieval Muslim scholarship. Vuckovic observes the role of these meetings in placing Muhammad within the monotheistic prophetic tradition and delineating him and his community as distinctive from Jews and Christians.
40. Tabari, *History*, vol. 6, p. 78.
41. Ibid. Vuckovic mentions the idea that the *mi'raj* occurred in 'Muhammad's early childhood', although the impression from Tabari is that it took place at a time when the Prophet had reached an adult age at the beginning of his prophetic mission. See Vuckovic, *Heavenly Journeys*, p. 2.
42. See Ibn Hisham, *Sira*, vol. 2, pp. 5–17 on the night journey and ascension.
43. See B. Schrieke—[J. Horovitz], 'Mi'radj: In Islamic exegesis and in the popular and mystical tradition of the Arab world', in *Encyclopaedia of Islam*, 2nd edn, vol. 7, pp. 97–100 on various interpretations of the time and place of events in the *mi'raj* story.
44. See Busse, 'Jerusalem', p. 280 for scholarly views on these three interpretations.
45. Ibid., p. 285.
46. Ibn Sa'd, *Tabaqat*, vol. 1, p. 166.
47. Vuckovic, *Heavenly Journeys*, p. 48 and see pp. 47–50 on the function of Buraq in medieval Islamic narratives. On early Islamic tradition regarding animals as mounts on God-ordained missions, see Suliman Bashear, 'Riding beasts on divine missions: an examination of the ass and camel traditions', *Journal of Semitic Studies* 36/1 (1991), pp. 37–76.
48. Ibn Sa'd, *Tabaqat*, vol. 1, pp. 167–8, here p. 167.
49. Ibn Hisham, *Sira*, vol. 2, p. 9, 10.
50. Busse, 'Jerusalem', p. 284.
51. See e.g. Fazlur Rahman, *Islam* (2nd edn, Chicago and London, 1979), p. 14. Rahman presents a modernist view that these visionary experiences of the Prophet are 'no more than a historical fiction whose materials come from various sources'.
52. Schrieke-[Horovitz], 'Mi'radj', p. 99.
53. Fahd, *Divination*, p. 256.

54. Nile Green, 'The religious and cultural role of dreams and visions in Islam', *Journal of the Royal Asiatic Society*, 3rd series, 13/3 (2003), p. 287.
55. On the nature of the revelation and the Prophet's experience of it, see A. J. Wensinck—[A. Rippin], 'Wahy', in *Encyclopaedia of Islam*, 2nd edn, vol. 11, pp. 53–6 and Daniel A. Madigan, 'Revelation and inspiration', in J. D. McAuliffe (ed.), *Encyclopaedia of the Qur'an* (Leiden, 2001–6), vol. 4, pp. 437–48.
56. Leah Kinberg, 'Dreams and sleep', in *Encyclopaedia of the Qur'an*, vol. 1, p. 530.
57. Kelly Bulkeley, 'Reflections on the dream traditions of Islam', *Sleep and Hypnosis* 4/1 (2002), p. 7.
58. Muhammad b. 'Umar al-Waqidi, *The Kitāb al-Maghāzī of al-Wāqidī*, ed. Marsden Jones (London, 1966), vol. 2, p. 572. The dream is not mentioned by Ibn Hisham or Ibn Sa'd, but Waqidi's version of events was taken up by later commentators on the Qur'an in order to explain the dream referred to in Qur'an 48:27.
59. Bukhari, *Sahih*, vol. 4, p. 302.
60. Ibn Hisham, *Sira*, vol. 3, p. 22.
61. Ibid., vol. 3, pp. 22–3.
62. Waqidi, Maghāzī, vol. 1, p. 209.
63. Ibid.
64. Bukhari, *Sahih*, vol. 4, p. 310.
65. Ibn Hisham, *Sira*, vol. 2, pp. 117–18.
66. I. K. A. Howard, 'The development of the *adhān* and *iqāma* of the *ṣalāt* in early Islam', in G. Hawting (ed.), *The Development of Islamic Ritual* (Aldershot, 2006), p. 223, 222.

Chapter 3   Scholars and Saints in the Path of the Prophet

1. Muhammad al-Bukhari, *al-Jami' al-Sahih*, ed. M. al-Khatib (Beirut, 1991), vol. 4, p. 296. For a discussion of Bukhari's *hadith*s on dreams, see John C. Lamoreaux, *The Early Muslim Tradition of Dream Interpretation* (Albany NY, 2002), pp. 117–20.
2. Muslim b. al-Hajjaj, *Sahih Muslim* (Beirut, 1995), vol. 4, p. 1414. Muslim also records a variant form of the Prophet's saying: 'The righteous *ru'ya* is from God and the bad *ru'ya* from Satan' (p. 1415).
3. On this early Christian view of dreams, see Lamoreaux, *Early Muslim Tradition*, pp. 136–40; Bonnelle Lewis Strickling, 'Early Christians and their dreams', in K. Bulkeley, K. Adams and P. M. Davis (eds), *Dreaming in Christianity and Islam: Culture, Conflict and Creativity* (New Brunswick NJ and London, 2009), pp. 32–42; and Guy G. Stroumsa, 'Dreams and visions in early Christian discourse', in D. Shulman and G. G. Stroumsa (eds), *Dream Cultures: Explorations in the Comparative History of Dreaming* (New York and Oxford, 1999), pp. 199–200.

4. Bukhari, *Sahih*, vol. 4, p. 303.
5. See Stroumsa, 'Early Christian discourse', pp. 196–7.
6. Muslim, *Sahih*, vol. 4, p. 1416; Sulayman Abu Dawud, *Sunan Abi Dawud*, ed. M. al-Khalidi (Beirut, 1996), vol. 3, p. 309; Muhammad Ibn Maja, *Sunan*, ed. B. A. Ma'ruf (Beirut, 1998), vol. 5, p. 409; Muhammad al-Tirmidhi, *al-Jami' al-Kabir*, ed. B. A. Ma'ruf (Beirut, 1996), vol. 4, p. 117.
7. 'Abd al-Malik Ibn Hisham, *al-Sira al-Nabawiyya*, ed. J. Thabit, M. Mahmud and S. Ibrahim (Cairo, 1996), vol. 4, p. 280.
8. Ibid., vol. 4, p. 281.
9. See e.g. Bukhari, *Sahih*, vol. 4, pp. 309–10 on Abu Bakr's interpretation of a dream. According to this *hadith*, the Prophet told Abu Bakr that his interpretation was only partially correct, indicating that, despite his friend's accomplishments, he was less skilled than the Prophet as an oneirocrit.
10. Ibid., vol. 4, p. 297.
11. See e.g. Ibn Maja, *Sunan*, vol. 5, p. 405.
12. See e.g. Bukhari, *Sahih*, vol. 4, pp. 297 and 303, giving the fraction as a forty-sixth; Muslim, *Sahih*, pp. 1415–17, giving a forty-fifth, forty-sixth and seventieth. On the variant fractions in the Arabic tradition see M. J. Kister, 'The interpretation of dreams: an unknown manuscript of Ibn Qutayba's *'Ibarat al-Ru'ya'*, *Israel Oriental Studies* 4 (1974), p. 71 n. 20.
13. See Sara Sviri, 'Dreaming analyzed and recorded: dreams in the world of medieval Islam', in Shulman and Stroumsa (eds), *Dream Cultures*, p. 268 nn. 1 and 3.
14. Bukhari, *Sahih*, vol. 4, p. 303; Abu Dawud, *Sunan*, vol. 3, p. 309; Ibn Maja, *Sunan*, vol. 5, p. 415; Tirmidhi, *Jami'*, vol. 4, p. 117. Muslim, *Sahih*, vol. 4, p. 1415 gives a variant reading: 'the Muslim's dream'.
15. See Fred M. Donner, *Muhammad and the Believers, At the Origins of Islam* (Cambridge MA and London, 2010), pp. 78–82 and p. 246 for further reading.
16. Bukhari, *Sahih*, vol. 4, p. 299.
17. Ibn Sa'd, Muhammad, *al-Tabaqat al-Kubra*, ed. M. 'Ata (Beirut, 1990), vol. 5, pp. 93–5.
18. Ibid., vol. 5, p. 92.
19. Al-Tabari, *The History of al-Tabari* (Ta'rikh al-rusul wa'l-muluk), vol. 23: *The Zenith of the Marwanid House*, trans. M. Hinds (Albany NY, 1990), p. 113.
20. Ibid., vol. 23, p. 114.
21. Ibid., vol. 23, pp. 179–80.
22. Ibid., vol. 23, p. 213.
23. Ibn Sa'd, *Tabaqat*, vol. 5, pp. 90–1.
24. Ibid., vol. 5, p. 93.
25. Lamoreaux, *Early Muslim Tradition*, p. 24 and see pp. 23–4 for some translations and comments on a few of these anecdotes. See also Toufic Fahd, *La Divination Arabe: Études Religieuses, Sociologiques et Folkloriques sur le Milieu Natif de l'Islam* (Leiden, 1966), pp. 310–12 for French translations of the 13 anecdotes.

26. Artemidorus, *The Interpretation of Dreams: Oneirocritica*, trans. Robert J. White (Park Ridge NJ, 1975), pp. 31–2.
27. Ibn Sa'd, *Tabaqat*, vol. 5, p. 93.
28. Ibid.
29. See Elizabeth Sirriyeh, 'Arab stars, Assyrian dogs and Greek angels: How Islamic is Muslim dream interpretation?', *Journal of Islamic Studies* 22/2 (2011), pp. 226–7 on Assyrian precedents.
30. See Ibn Sa'd, *Tabaqat*, vol. 7, p. 143 for a few biographical details.
31. See ibid., vol. 7, pp. 143–54.
32. Fahd, *Divination*, p. 315. More recently Lamoreaux has studied around 100 manuscripts ascribed to Ibn Sirin and concluded that none of them are authentic. See Lamoreaux, *Early Muslim Tradition*, p. 19.
33. Lamoreaux, *Early Muslim Tradition*, p. 22.
34. Ibid., p. 21. The eleventh-century author is Qayrawani, a North African scholar, who produced no fewer than four dream books, one of them being of great length. On these works see ibid., pp. 51–9.
35. Ibid., p. 23, citing a tradition preserved by Qayrawani, according to which Ibn Sirin learned from Ibn al-Musayyab 'six hundred chapters of *The Interpretation of Joseph the Prophet*'. This otherwise unknown work has disappeared, if it ever existed.
36. Kister, 'Interpretation', p. 100, citing an anecdote narrated by Ibn Qutayba (d. 889).
37. Leah Kinberg, 'Qur'an and Hadith: a struggle for supremacy as reflected in dream narratives', in L. Marlow (ed.), *Dreaming Across Boundaries: The Interpretation of Dreams in Islamic Lands* (Cambridge MA and London, 2008), p. 29. On medieval Muslim communication with the dead, see Leah Kinberg, 'Interaction between this world and the afterworld in early Islamic tradition', *Oriens* 29–30 (1986), pp. 285–308.
38. See the excellent edition of the Arabic text with an English introduction by Leah Kinberg, Ibn Abi al-Dunya, *Morality in the Guise of Dreams: a critical edition of* Kitab al-manam *with introduction* (Leiden, New York and Köln, 1994).
39. Ibid., pp. 17–19 and see Kinberg: 'Interaction', pp. 303–4.
40. See Kinberg's introduction to her edition of Ibn Abi al-Dunya, *Morality*, pp. 22–3 on the primarily ethical, rather than political, teachings of the dream narratives relating to caliphs.
41. Ibid., p. 77, 78.
42. Ibid., pp. 75–7, here p. 77.
43. On Kindi's study of swordmaking see Kindi, *Medieval Islamic Swords and Swordmaking: Kindi's treatise 'On Swords and Their Kinds'*, ed., trans. and commentary by R. G. Hoyland and B. Gilmour (Warminster, 2006) and on weather see Kindi, *Scientific Weather Forecasting in the Middle Ages: the writings of al-Kindi: studies, editions and translations*, ed. and trans. G. Bos and C. Burnett (London, 2000).

44. Peter Adamson, 'Al-Kindi and the reception of Greek philosophy', in P. Adamson and R. C. Taylor (eds), *The Cambridge Companion to Arabic Philosophy* (Cambridge, 2004 and online 2011), p. 44 and pp. 42–4 on Kindi's contribution to cosmology and astrology.
45. Ahmad Dallal, 'Science, medicine and technology: the making of a scientific culture', in J. L. Esposito (ed.), *The Oxford History of Islam* (Oxford, 1999), p. 191.
46. Adamson, 'Al-Kindi', p. 45.
47. Ian Richard Netton, 'The origins of Islamic philosophy', in I. R. Netton (ed.), *Islamic Philosophy and Theology: Critical Concepts in Islamic Thought*, vol. 1: *Legacies, Translations and Prototypes* (London and New York, 2007) p. 87.
48. Adamson, 'Al-Kindi', p. 37.
49. Netton, 'Origins', p. 81.
50. Adamson, 'Al-Kindi', p. 37.
51. For the Greek text with English translation see D. Gallop (ed.), *Aristotle on Sleep and Dreams: A Text and Translation with Introduction* (Warminster, 1996). On an Arabic version of this work and its reception see Rotraud E. Hansberger, 'How Aristotle came to believe in God-given dreams: the Arabic version of *De divinatione per somnum*', in Marlow (ed.), *Dreaming Across Boundaries*, pp. 50–77.
52. Hansberger, 'Aristotle', pp. 52–3.
53. For the Arabic text of Kindi's treatise, see his *Risala fi mahiyyat al-nawm wa'l-ru'ya*, in M. Abu Rida (ed.), *Rasa'il al-Kindi al-Falsafiyya* (Cairo, 1950), vol. 1, pp. 283–311.
54. MS Rampur 1752 discussed in Hansberger, 'Aristotle', pp. 54–64 and see pp. 71–2 on Kindi's apparent use of a similar text.
55. Sviri, 'Dreaming analyzed', p. 253.
56. See Ahmet T. Karamustafa, *Sufism: the Formative Period* (Edinburgh, 2007), pp. 1–7 on the term *sufi* and some of the early pious Muslims whom Karamustafa designates as 'renunciants' because of their renunciation of the world. Earlier sources commonly describe the same figures as 'ascetics'.
57. Nile Green, *Sufism, A Global History* (Oxford, 2012), p. 18.
58. Karamustafa, *Formative Period*, pp. 7–26 on the ninth-century Sufis of Baghdad.
59. Green, *Global History*, p. 25.
60. On al-Sulami's *Tabaqat al-Sufiyya*, see Jawid A. Mojaddedi, *The Biographical Tradition in Sufism: The* Tabaqat *Genre from al-Sulami to Jami* (Richmond, 2001), pp. 9–40.
61. Ibid., p. 11.
62. Michael A. Sells, *Early Islamic Mysticism: Sufi, Qur'an, Mi'raj, Poetic and Theological Writings* (New York and Mahwah NJ, 1996), p. 242 and pp. 244–50 for Sells' translation of this *mi'raj* text.
63. Carl W. Ernst, *Words of Ecstasy in Sufism* (Albany NY, 1985), p. 11 and see Sells, *Early Islamic Mysticism*, pp. 214–31 for translated selections concerning Abu Yazid (Bayezid) al-Bistami from Sarraj's *Kitab al-Luma' fi 'l-Tasawwuf*. For the

Arabic text see R. A. Nicholson (ed.), *The* Kitab al-Luma' fi 'l-Tasawwuf *of Abu Nasr 'Abdallah b. 'Ali al-Sarraj al-Tusi* (Leiden and London, 1914). For translations of the biographies of Bistami by Sulami and al-Qushayri (d. 1072) see Sells, *Early Islamic Mysticism*, pp. 234–42.

64. See translation of Sulami giving alternative dates for Bistami's death in Mojaddedi, *Biographical Tradition*, p. 18.
65. Sarraj, *Kitab al-Luma'*, p. 384.
66. Ibid., pp. 385–7 for Arabic commentary on Bistami's description of his vision and Sells, *Early Islamic Mysticism*, pp. 220–2 for an English translation.
67. Ibid., first and second quotations p. 245, third quotation here p. 249.
68. See Leah Kinberg, 'Literal dreams and Prophetic *hadit*s in classical Islam – a comparison of two ways of legitimation', *Der Islam* 70 (1993), pp. 279–300 on the similarities of *hadith*s and edifying dream narratives as means of offering divine guidance.
69. Ibid., pp. 287, 286.

Chapter 4   The Dream Must Be Interpreted

1. Louise Marlow (ed.), *Dreaming Across Boundaries: The Interpretation of Dreams in Islamic Lands* (Cambridge MA and London, 2008), p. 7.
2. See Elizabeth Sirriyeh, 'Arab stars, Assyrian dogs and Greek "angels": How Islamic is Muslim dream interpretation?', *Journal of Islamic Studies* 22/2 (2011), pp. 215–33.
3. Kirmani's full name is given as Abu Ishaq Ibrahim b. 'Abd Allah al-Kirmani, author of a treatise entitled *Dustur fi 'l-ta'bir*. See Toufic Fahd, *La Divination Arabe: Études Religieuses, Sociologiques et Folkloriques sur le Milieu Natif de l'Islam* (Leiden, 1966), p. 316 for the view that Kirmani probably undertook his work on the orders of al-Mahdi.
4. Ibid., p. 315 and John C. Lamoreaux, *The Early Muslim Tradition of Dream Interpretation* (Albany NY, 2002), p. 26.
5. Fahd discovered the first manuscript of the treatise usually called *'Ibarat al-ru'ya* (and sometimes *Ta'bir al-ru'ya*) in the library of the Language, History and Geography Faculty at Ankara University, but in an incomplete form, containing only the introductory section. However, he remained uncertain as to the reliability of its attribution to Ibn Qutayba. See Fahd, *Divination*, p. 317. M. J. Kister discovered a second, fuller copy in the library of the Hebrew University of Jerusalem. He described this manuscript in M. J. Kister, 'The interpretation of dreams: an unknown manuscript of Ibn Qutayba's " 'Ibarat al-Ru'ya"', *Israel Oriental Studies* 4 (1974), pp. 67–103. See Lamoreaux, *Early Muslim Tradition*, pp. 27–8 for the view that the manual is authentic and pp. 29–34 and pp. 188–9 notes 47–89 on the work and its methodology.
6. Kister, 'Interpretation', p. 75.

7. Ibid., p. 99 and Sirriyeh, 'Arab stars', pp. 223–6.
8. Fahd, *Divination*, p. 318 and Lamoreaux, *Early Muslim Tradition*, p. 29. For the first method, compare the quotation from Ibn Qutayba in Abu 'Ali al-Husayn al-Dari, *al-Imam Muhammad b. Sirin: Muntakhab al-kalam fi tafsir al-ahlam*, ed. A. al-Juzu (Beirut, 1986), pp. 35–6. This book is published under the name of Ibn Sirin, although it is falsely attributed to him.
9. Dari, *Muntakhab*, pp. 42–3 and for an English translation see Marcia Hermansen, 'Dreams and dreaming in Islam', in K. Bulkeley (ed.), *Dreams: A Reader on Religious, Cultural and Psychological Dimensions of Dreaming* (New York, 2001), p. 77.
10. Artemidorus, *The Interpretation of Dreams: Oneirocritica*, trans. Robert J. White (Park Ridge NJ, 1975), pp. 35–6.
11. Kister, 'Interpretation', p. 91 and pp. 91–3 for further Qur'anic examples. See also Lamoreaux, *Early Muslim Tradition*, pp. 29–30 on interpretation through Qur'an, *hadith* and proverbs.
12. Dari, *Muntakhab*, pp. 38–9; Fahd, *Divination*, p. 318 and Lamoreaux, *Early Muslim Tradition*, p. 30.
13. Dari, *Muntakhab*, p. 39; Fahd, *Divination*, pp. 318–19 and Lamoreaux, *Early Muslim Tradition*, p. 30.
14. Lamoreaux, *Early Muslim Tradition*, pp. 35 and 83. Sijistani's manual has survived in a number of manuscripts, on which see ibid., pp. 34–5 and pp. 191–2 notes 96–9.
15. Ibid., p. 83. Ibn Sina's dream manual is extant in manuscript form in several copies, on which see ibid., pp. 69–76 and pp. 201–3 notes 140–67. For an early discussion of the manual see Muhammad al-Hashimi, 'On Avicenna's Ta'bir al-Ru'ya', PhD dissertation, School of Oriental and African Studies, London University, 1948. Some of the theoretical introduction has been translated into English in M. A. Muid Khan, 'Kitab Ta'bir-ir-Ruya of Abu 'Ali Ibn Sina', *Indo-Iranica* 9/3 (1956), pp. 15–30 and 9/4 (1956), pp. 43–57.
16. On al-Nabulusi and dreams see Elizabeth Sirriyeh, *Sufi Visionary of Ottoman Damascus: 'Abd al-Ghani al-Nabulusi, 1641–1731* (London and New York, 2005), ch. 4.
17. Lamoreaux, *Early Muslim Tradition*, p. 33.
18. Ibid.
19. For the Arabic text, with an introduction in French, see Toufic Fahd (ed.), *Le Livre des Songes {par} Artémidore d'Ephèse. Traduit du grec en arabe par Hunayn b. Ishaq* (Damascus, 1964).
20. See Manfred Ullmann, 'War Hunain der Übersetzer von Artemidors Traumbuch?', *Die Welt des Islams* n.s. 13 (1971), pp. 204–11 and Toufic Fahd, 'Hunayn Ibn Ishaq est-il le traducteur des *Oneirocritica* d'Artémidore d'Ephèse?', *Arabica* 21 (1974), pp. 270–84.
21. Lamoreaux, *Early Muslim Tradition*, p. 48 and see pp. 48–50 and Sirriyeh, 'Arab stars', pp. 229–30 for examples of Hunayn's adaptations.
22. Fahd (ed.), *Artémidore*, pp. 285, 37.
23. Ibid., p. 287 for the Arabic text and see Sirriyeh, 'Arab stars', p. 229 for an English translation of the passage.

24. See Lamoreaux, *Early Muslim Tradition*, p. 49 for translations of Artemidorus and Hunayn, here pp. 49–50.
25. Artemidorus, *Interpretation of Dreams*, trans. White, p. 112.
26. Fahd (ed.), *Artémidore*, p. 283 and see Sirriyeh, 'Arab stars', p. 230.
27. Kister, 'Interpretation', p. 99.
28. See Ibn Sina quoted in al-Hashimi, 'On Avicenna's Ta'bir al-Ru'ya', p. 15 and Sirriyeh, 'Arab stars', p. 228.
29. See Lamoreaux, *Early Muslim Tradition*, pp. 72–5 for a useful identification of passages from Artemidorus used by Ibn Sina.
30. Lamoreaux has identified over 40 manuscripts of this work. See ibid., p. 60 and p. 198, n. 93 on some of these copies. For a more readily accessible Arabic text, see the manuscript printed in Abu Sa'd al-Dinawari, *Kitab al-ta'bir fi 'l-ru'ya aw al-Qadiri fi 'l-ta'bir*, ed. F. Sa'd (Beirut, 1997). For further discussion of Dinawari and his work, see Lamoreaux, *Early Muslim Tradition*, pp. 59–64.
31. Toufic Fahd, 'al-Dinawari, Abu Sa'id (Sa'd) Nasr b. Ya'qub', in *Encyclopaedia of Islam*, 2nd edn, edited by an editorial committee consisting of H. A. R. Gibb et al. (Leiden, 1960–2009), vol. 2, p. 300.
32. Lamoreaux, *Early Muslim Tradition*, p. 62.
33. Dinawari, *al-Qadiri*, vol. 1, p. 88.
34. Quotation from Aristotle in ibid., vol. 1, p. 88 and trans. in Rotraud E. Hansberger, 'How Aristotle came to believe in God-given dreams: the Arabic version of *De divinatione per somnum*', in Marlow (ed.), *Dreaming Across Boundaries*, p. 70.
35. See Ahmad Dallal, 'Science, medicine and technology: the making of a scientific culture', in J. L. Esposito (ed.), *The Oxford History of Islam* (Oxford, 1999), p. 201 on the Muslims' absorption of Galen's pathology based on the four humours.
36. Hansberger, 'Aristotle', p. 70 and also for the Arabic quotation.
37. Dinawari, *al-Qadiri*, vol. 1, pp. 92, 92–3, 94.
38. Ibid., vol. 1, pp. 151–4 and see Sirriyeh, 'Arab stars', pp. 230–2.
39. Dinawari, *al-Qadiri*, vol. 1, pp. 165–259.
40. Ibid., vol. 1, pp. 165–7.
41. See quotations from the Sufi dream interpreter al-Kharkushi trans. in Lamoreaux, *Early Muslim Tradition*, p. 68.
42. Dari, *Muntakhab*, p. 80.
43. See Lamoreaux, *Early Muslim Tradition*, pp. 90–102 for examples of this homogeneity of interpretation in dream manuals of the ninth to eleventh centuries.
44. See John C. Lamoreaux, 'Some notes on the dream manual of al-Dari', *Rivista degli studi orientali*, 70 (1996), pp. 47–52 on the manual, its dating and identity as an abridgement of Kharkushi's dream book. Lamoreaux favours a date of composition early in the possible period of Dari's activity because he makes no reference to any manuals of the twelfth or thirteenth centuries.
45. On Kharkushi see Lamoreaux, *Early Muslim Tradition*, pp. 64–9, here p. 69.
46. See J. Gaulmier and T. Fahd, 'Ibn Shahin al-Zahiri', in *Encyclopaedia of Islam*, 2nd edn, vol. 3, p. 935. The dream treatise that has disappeared was entitled

al-Kawkab al-munir fi usul al-ta'bir and may have been influenced by a manual known as *al-Badr al-munir fi 'ilm al-ta'bir* by a respected religious jurist, Shihab al-Din al-Maqdisi (d. 1298), noted for his strict adherence to Islamic norms. For a modern edition of Ibn Shahin's surviving manual see Ghars al-Din Khalil Ibn Shahin al-Zahiri, *Kitab al-isharat fi 'ilm al-'ibarat*, ed. S. K. Hasan (Beirut, 1993).

47. Fahd, *Divination*, p. 352 and see pp. 351–2 on the manuscripts.
48. On Nabulusi's life and work see Sirriyeh, *Sufi Visionary* and Samer Akkach, *'Abd al-Ghani al-Nabulusi: Islam and the Enlightenment* (Oxford, 2007).
49. 'Abd al-Ghani al-Nabulusi, *Ta'tir al-anam fi ta'bir al-manam*, ed. H. Tabara (Beirut, 1996), p. 11 and trans. in Sirriyeh, *Sufi Visionary*, p. 72.
50. See Fahd, *Divination*, pp. 338–9 on this manual and Sirriyeh, *Sufi Visionary*, p. 147 n. 55. Ibn Ghannam is also known as Abu Tahir Yahya b. Ghanim al-Maqdisi al-Hanbali.
51. See ibid., pp. 74–5.
52. L. Kopf, 'al-Damiri, Muhammad b. Musa b. 'Isa Kamal al-Din', in *Encyclopaedia of Islam*, 2nd edn, vol. 2, pp. 107–8.
53. Kamal al-Din Muhammad al-Damiri, *Kitab hayat al-hayawan al-kubra*, ed. H. H. Husayn (Cairo, 1274/1857–8), vol. 2, pp. 495–6.
54. See Joseph de Somogyi, 'The interpretation of dreams in Ad-Damiri's *Hayat al-hayawan*', *Journal of the Royal Asiatic Society* 72/1 (1940), pp. 1–20 for translations of some of the interpretations of dreams. De Somogyi identifies certain methods of interpretation that date back at least to Ibn Qutayba.
55. Damiri, *Hayat*, vol. 2, p. 497.
56. Dari, *Muntakhab*, p. 321; Nabulusi, *Ta'tir*, p. 434. Both Damiri and Nabulusi are likely to have been dependent on Dari.
57. Damiri, *Hayat*, vol. 1, p. 25.
58. Ibid., vol. 1, p. 223.
59. Ibid., vol. 1, p. 391. See de Somogyi, 'Damiri's *Hayat*', pp. 13–15 for a number of examples.
60. Damiri, *Hayat*, vol. 1, p. 379. See de Somogyi, 'Damiri's *Hayat*', pp. 12–13 for examples of the opposite and inverted method.
61. Damiri, *Hayat*, vol. 2, p. 7.
62. Ibn Shahin, *Isharat*, p. 517 cites Kirmani on the starling as indicating travelling or a traveller.
63. Damiri, *Hayat*, vol. 2, p. 7.
64. Ibn Shahin, *Isharat*, p. 517.

Chapter 5 Muslims Dreaming of Christians, Christians Dreaming of Muslims

1. Toufic Fahd, *La Divination Arabe: Études Religieuses, Sociologiques et Folkloriques sur le Milieu Natif de l'Islam* (Leiden, 1966), pp. 330–63.

2. John C. Lamoreaux, *The Early Muslim Tradition of Dream Interpretation* (Albany NY, 2002), pp. 3–4, 175–81.
3. Ibid., p. 138.
4. Ibid., p. 152.
5. Maria Mavroudi, *A Byzantine Book of Dream Interpretation: the* Oneirocriticon *of Achmet, and Its Arabic Sources* (Leiden, 2002), p. 61.
6. Steven F. Kruger, *Dreaming in the Middle Ages* (Cambridge, 1992), pp. 7–16.
7. Ibid., pp. 10–11.
8. Abu Sa'd al-Dinawari, *Kitab al-ta'bir fi 'l-ru'ya aw al-Qadiri fi 'l-ta'bir*, ed. F. Sa'd (Beirut, 1997), vol. 1, p. 115.
9. Mavroudi, *Byzantine Book*, p. 243.
10. Philip K. Hitti, *History of the Arabs* (10th edn, Basingstoke, 1970), p. 365.
11. Dinawari, *al-Qadiri*, vol. 2, p. 265.
12. Ibid., vol. 1, p. 353.
13. Ibid., vol. 2, p. 539.
14. Mavroudi, *Byzantine Book*, pp. 337–40.
15. Dinawari, *al-Qadiri*, vol. 1, p. 353.
16. Ibid., vol. 1, p. 354.
17. Abu 'Ali al-Husayn al-Dari, *al-Imam Muhammad b. Sirin:Muntakhab al-kalam fi tafsir al-ahlam* (Beirut, 1986), pp. 428–9.
18. Dinawari, *al-Qadiri*, vol. 1, pp. 353–5.
19. Ibid., vol. 1, p. 356.
20. See C.-E. Ruelle, 'La clef des songes d'Achmet Abou Mazar: fragment inédit et bonnes variantes', *Revue des Etudes Grecques* 7 (1894), pp. 305–12 and Franz X. Drexl, *Achmets Traumbuch: Einleitung und Probe eines kritischen Textes* (Freising, 1909).
21. N. Bland, 'On the Muhammedan science of tabir, or interpretation of dreams', *Journal of the Royal Asiatic Society* 16 (1856), pp. 118–71.
22. Mavroudi, *Byzantine Book*, p. 34.
23. Achmet, *Oneirocriticon*, ed F. X. Drexl (Leipzig, 1925).
24. Karl Brackertz, *Das Traumbuch des Achmet ben Sirin* (Munich, 1986) and Steven M. Oberhelman, *The* Oneirocriticon *of Achmet: A Medieval Greek and Arabic Treatise on the Interpretation of Dreams* (Lubbock TX, 1991).
25. Mavroudi, *Byzantine Book*, pp. 34–5; and Lamoreaux, *Early Muslim Tradition*, p. 141.
26. Oberhelman, Oneirocriticon *of Achmet*, pp. 13–14 suggests that it was compiled at a time between 813, the beginning of al-Ma'mun's caliphate, and c.1075, when extracts of Pseudo-Achmet were copied into other manuscript material. Mavroudi, *Byzantine Book*, pp. 2–3 narrows the dating further to post-843 because of the inclusion of a chapter on icons, which should presumably date from after the ending of iconoclasm in that year.
27. Achmet: *Oneirocriticon*, p. 1, pp. 8–11.
28. Oberhelman, Oneirocriticon *of Achmet*, p. 86. For the Greek text see Achmet, *Oneirocriticon*, pp. 1–2.
29. Ibid., pp. 2–3; here p. 3.
30. Mavroudi, *Byzantine Book*, p. 45.

31. Ibid., pp. 44–5.
32. Achmet, *Oneirocriticon*, pp. 220 and 232.
33. Mavroudi, *Byzantine Book*, pp. 47–51.
34. Oberhelman, Oneirocriticon *of Achmet*, p. 15.
35. Ibid., p. 18.
36. Ibid., p. 19.
37. Mavroudi, *Byzantine Book*, pp. 168–9.
38. Ibid., pp. 235–6.
39. Lamoreaux, *Early Muslim Tradition*, p. 145.
40. Ibid., pp. 150–1 and Mavroudi, *Byzantine Book*, p. 375.
41. Achmet, *Oneirocriticon*, pp. 6–7.
42. Ibid., p. 8.
43. Oberhelman, Oneirocriticon *of Achmet*, p. 90; Greek text in Achmet, *Oneirocriticon*, p. 8.
44. Ibid., p. 15.
45. Compare Chapter 3, p. 68 and see pp. 66–8 for another dream interpreted by Ibn al-Musayyab and having the same significance.
46. Lamoreaux, *Early Muslim Tradition*, p. 151.
47. A. Leo Oppenheim, 'The interpretation of dreams in the ancient Near East with a translation of an Assyrian dream-book', *Transactions of the American Philosophical Society* n.s. 43/ 3 (1956), p. 265.

Chapter 6 'And if a Woman Dreams'

1. J. M. B. Jones, 'Ibn Ishaq and al-Waqidi: the dream of 'Atika and the raid to Nakhla in relation to the charge of plagiarism', in U. Rubin (ed.), *The Formation of the Classical Islamic World*, vol. 4: *The Life of Muhammad*, p. 16.
2. Al-Tabari, *The History of al-Tabari*, vol. 7: *The Foundation of the Community*, trans. W. Montgomery Watt and M. V. McDonald (Albany NY, 1987), p. 36.
3. Ibid., vol. 7, p. 36.
4. Ibid., vol. 7, p. 37.
5. See Toufic Fahd, *La Divination Arabe: Études Religieuses, Sociologiques et Folkloriques sur le Milieu Natif de l'Islam* (Leiden, 1966), pp. 280–1.
6. Muhammad al-Bukhari, *al-Jami' al-Sahih* (Beirut, 1991), vol. 4, p. 300.
7. Ibid., vol. 4, pp. 300–1.
8. Muhammad Ibn Maja, *Sunan*, ed. B. A. Ma'ruf (Beirut, 1998), vol. 5, p. 421.
9. On dreams of Muslim martyrs see David Cook, *Martyrdom in Islam* (Cambridge, 2007), pp. 119–21 and Elizabeth Sirriyeh, 'Dream narratives of Muslims' martyrdom: constant and changing roles past and present', *Dreaming* 21/3 (2011), pp. 168–80.
10. Leah Kinberg and Ibn Abi al-Dunya, *Morality in the Guise of Dreams: a critical edition of* Kitab al-manam *with introduction* (Leiden, New York and Köln, 1994), pp. 180–1; here p. 181.

11. Ibid., p. 58.
12. Ibid., p. 126.
13. Ibid., p. 107.
14. Ibid.
15. See Paul Losensky, trans. with Michael Sells, 'Rabi'a: her words and life in 'Attar's *Memorial of the Friends of God*', in M. A. Sells, *Early Islamic Mysticism: Sufi, Qur'an, Mi'raj, Poetic and Theological Writings* (New York and Mahwah NJ, 1996), pp. 151–70.
16. For reflections on the possible basis for accounts of the legendary Rabi'a and other early Sufi women, see Julian Baldick, 'The legend of Rabi'a of Basra: Christian antecedents, Muslim counterparts', *Religion* 20 (1990), pp. 233–47. Contrast with the traditional picture of Rabi'a presented in Margaret Smith, *Rabi'a the Mystic and Her Fellow Saints in Islam* (Cambridge, 1928).
17. Losensky with Sells trans., 'Rabi'a', p. 155.
18. Ibid., p. 156.
19. Ibid., p. 163.
20. Ibid., p. 165.
21. Ibid., p. 156.
22. Ibid., p. 165.
23. See Munawi trans. in John Renard, *Windows on the House of Islam: Muslim Sources on Spirituality and Religious Life* (Berkeley, Los Angeles and London, 1998), pp. 132–5 and 346–7.
24. See ibid., p. 132, where he notes that 'Rabi'a is one of nearly three dozen women' in Munawi's collection of biographies.
25. Ibid., pp. 346–7, here p. 347.
26. See further Bernd Radtke and John O'Kane, *The Concept of Sainthood in Early Islamic Mysticism: Two Works by Al-Hakim Al-Tirmidhi* (Richmond, 1996).
27. Sara Sviri, 'Dreaming analyzed and recorded: dreams in the world of medieval Islam', in D. Shulman and G. G. Stroumsa (eds), *Dream Cultures: Explorations in the Comparative History of Dreaming* (New York and Oxford, 1999), p. 261.
28. Ibid., p. 261. See also Dwight F. Reynolds, *Interpreting the Self: Autobiography in the Arabic Literary Tradition* (Berkeley, 2001), p. 124.
29. Sviri, 'Dreaming analyzed', p. 264 and see pp. 263–4 for a full translation of this dream account. Compare Reynolds, *Interpreting the Self*, p. 125 for another translation. Sviri notes the ancient association of the myrtle with the righteous (*zaddiq*) in the Jewish tradition and refers to the connection with 'myrtle trees' in Zechariah 1:8–11.
30. Sviri, 'Dreaming analyzed', p. 264.
31. Hagar Kahana Smilansky, 'Self-reflection and conversion in medieval Muslim autobiographical dreams', in L. Marlow (ed.), *Dreaming Across Boundaries: The Interpretation of Dreams in Islamic Lands* (Cambridge MA and London, 2008), pp. 110–11.

32. Sviri, 'Dreaming analyzed', p. 264.
33. Ibid., p. 268.
34. John C. Lamoreaux, *The Early Muslim Tradition of Dream Interpretation* (Albany NY, 2002), p. 83.
35. Ibid., p. 35.
36. Huda Lutfi, 'The construction of gender symbolism in Ibn Sirin's and Ibn Shahin's medieval Arabic dream texts', *Mamluk Studies Review* 9/1 (2005), p. 127.
37. Lamoreaux, *Early Muslim Tradition*, p. 11.
38. A. Leo Oppenheim, 'Mantic dreams in the ancient Near East', in G. E. von Grunebaum and R. Caillois (eds), *The Dream and Human Societies* (Berkeley and Los Angeles, 1966), p. 350.
39. Lutfi, 'Construction of gender symbolism', pp. 128, 129.
40. See Abu Sa'd al-Dinawari, *Kitab al-ta'bir fi 'l-ru'ya aw al-Qadiri fi 'l-ta'bir*, ed. F. Sa'd (Beirut, 1997), vol. 1, pp. 164–259.
41. Ibid., vol. 1, p. 217.
42. Ibid., vol. 1, p. 218.
43. Abu 'Ali al-Husayn al-Dari, *al-Imam Muhammad b. Sirin: Muntakhab al-kalam fi tafsir al-ahlam*, ed. A. al-Juzu (Beirut, 1986), p. 159 and 'Abd al-Ghani al-Nabulusi, *Ta'tir al-anam fi ta'bir al-manam*, ed. H. Tabara (Beirut, 1996), p. 381.
44. Artemidorus, *The Interpretation of Dreams:* Oneirocritica, trans. Robert J. White (Park Ridge NJ, 1975), p. 31.
45. Dinawari, *Qadiri*, vol. 1, pp. 234–5. Dari and Nabulusi reproduce the information, but without disclosing their sources. See Dari, *Muntakhab*, pp. 166–7 and Nabulusi, *Ta'tir*, ed. Y. al-Shaykh Muhammad (Beirut, 1997), pp. 83–4. The image has been cut out from Tabara's family-friendly edition of the work.
46. Dinawari, *Qadiri*, vol. 1, p. 234.
47. Ibid., vol. 1, p. 234 and Artemidorus, *Interpretation of Dreams*, p. 25. See also Dari, *Muntakhab*, p. 167 and Nabulusi, *Ta'tir*, ed. Al-Shaykh Muhammad, p. 83.
48. Artemidorus, *Interpretation of Dreams*, p. 25.
49. M. J. Kister, 'The interpretation of dreams: an unknown manuscript of Ibn Qutayba's *'Ibarat al-Ru'ya'*, *Israel Oriental Studies* 4 (1974), p. 83; Dinawari, *Qadiri*, vol. 1, pp. 169–70 and Ibn Abi al-Dunya, *Morality*, p. 126.

Chapter 7   Envisioning God and His Prophet

1. See D. Gimaret, 'Ru'yat Allah', in *Encyclopaedia of Islam*, 2nd edn, edited by an editorial committee consisting of H. A. R. Gibb et al. (Leiden, 1960–2009), vol. 8, p. 649 for the different theological positions on the subject.
2. Baqli trans. and quoted in Carl W. Ernst, *Ruzbihan Baqli: Mysticism and the Rhetoric of Sainthood in Persian Sufism* (Richmond, 1996), p. 47.

3. On *munajat* see John Renard, *Seven Doors to Islam: Spirituality and the Religious Life of Muslims* (Berkeley and Los Angeles, 1996), pp. 55–6 and C. E. Bosworth, 'Munadjat', in *Encyclopaedia of Islam*, 2nd edn, vol. 7, p. 557.
4. Baqli trans. and quoted in Ernst, *Ruzbihan Baqli*, p. 48.
5. Ibid. The reference here is to Qur'an 107:11.
6. As an introduction to Ibn 'Arabi's life and thought see William C. Chittick, *Ibn 'Arabi: Heir to the Prophets* (Oxford, 2005) and, for a fuller biography, see Claude Addas, *Quest for the Red Sulphur: The Life of Ibn 'Arabi* (Cambridge, 1993). On later Muslims' opposition to Ibn 'Arabi see Alexander D. Knysh, *Ibn 'Arabi in the Later Islamic Tradition: the Making of a Polemical Image in Medieval Islam* (Albany NY, 1999).
7. See Addas, *Quest*, pp. 42–3.
8. Ibn 'Arabi trans. and quoted in Addas, *Quest*, p. 84. *Kitab al-Mubashshirat* survives in manuscripts only, but Addas has translated portions of the work in her biography of Ibn 'Arabi.
9. Ibid., p. 85.
10. Ibid.
11. Ibn 'Arabi, *Sufis of Andalusia: the Ruh al-Quds and al-Durra al-Fakhirah of Ibn 'Arabi*, trans. with introduction and notes by R. W. J. Austin (London, 1971), p. 142.
12. See Elizabeth Sirriyeh, *Sufi Visionary of Ottoman Damascus: 'Abd al-Ghani al-Nabulusi, 1641–1731* (London and New York, 2005), pp. 49–51. The work is preserved in a manuscript at Berlin.
13. Nabulusi trans. and quoted in Barbara von Schlegell, 'Sufism in the Ottoman Arab world: Shaykh 'Abd al-Ghani al-Nabulusi (d.1143/1731)', PhD dissertation, University of California, Berkeley, 1997, p. 71.
14. Sirriyeh, *Sufi Visionary*, p. 8.
15. Marcia K. Hermansen, 'Visions as "good to think": a cognitive approach to visionary experience in Islamic Sufi thought', *Religion* 27/1 (1997), pp. 25–43; here p. 30.
16. Valerie J. Hoffman, 'Annihilation in the Messenger of God: the development of a Sufi practice', *International Journal of Middle East Studies* 31/3 (1999), p. 351.
17. See Gerhard Böwering, *The Mystical Vision of Existence in Classical Islam: The Qur'anic Hermeneutics of the Sufi Sahl al-Tustari (d.283/896)* (Berlin, 1980) on Tustari's contribution to the doctrine of the Muhammadan Light.
18. Ibn 'Arabi trans. and quoted in Hoffman, 'Annihilation', p. 353.
19. Addas, *Quest*, pp. 74–6.
20. Ibid., p. 76.
21. Knysh, *Later Islamic Tradition*, pp. 44–5.
22. Ibid., p. 87 and see pp. 87–111 on Ibn Taymiyya's criticisms of Ibn 'Arabi.
23. Ibn 'Arabi trans. and quoted in Addas, *Quest*, p. 42.
24. Addas, *Quest*, pp. 274–5.
25. Dwight F. Reynolds (ed.), *Interpreting the Self: Autobiography in the Arabic Literary Tradition* (Berkeley, 2001), p. 93.

26. Ibn 'Arabi, *The Bezels of Wisdom*, trans. R. W. J. Austin (Mahwah NJ, 1980), p. 45.
27. Ibid., pp. 45–6.
28. See Hoffman, 'Annihilation', pp. 354–9 on the development of the idea of union with the Prophet and p. 366 n. 6 on the differing dates given for Jili's death between 1402 and 1428. Jumada II 811/November 1408 is the date provided by Jili's son at the end of a manuscript of *al-Insan al-kamil* (The Perfect Human), Jili's best-known work.
29. Jili trans. and quoted in Hoffman, 'Annihilation', p. 357 and, for publication details of the Arabic text, p. 366 n. 16.
30. Jonathan G. Katz, *Dreams, Sufism and Sainthood: The Visionary Career of Muhammad al-Zawawi* (Leiden, New York and Köln, 1996), pp. xiv–xv.
31. Jamil M. Abun-Nasr, *Muslim Communities of Grace: The Sufi Brotherhoods in Islamic Religious Life* (London, 2007), pp. 111–12.
32. Abu 'Abd Allah Muhammad al-Zawawi, *Tuhfat al-nazir wa nuzhat al-manazir*, which survives in a number of manuscripts. See Katz, *Zawawi* for detailed discussion of this work.
33. Katz, *Zawawi*, p. 233.
34. Ibid., p. xv and pp. 22–8 on Zawawi's narcissism.
35. Ibid., p. 5.
36. Ibid., pp. 153–4.
37. Carl W. Ernst, *The Shambhala Guide to Sufism* (Boston, 1997), p. 62.
38. The Qadiri and Nasiri Orders and a minor order established by a certain Ahmad al-Habib b. Muhammad. See Abun-Nasr, *Communities of Grace*, p. 149.
39. Ibid., p. 150 and see the translation of the prayer with commentary in Patrick J. Ryan, 'The mystical theology of Tijani Sufism and its social significance in West Africa', *Journal of Religion in Africa* 30/2 (2000), pp. 211–13.
40. Ibid., p. 211.
41. Ibid., p. 213.
42. Abun-Nasr: *Communities of Grace*, pp. 155 and 225; and Ryan, 'Mystical theology', pp. 216–17.
43. Abun-Nasr, *Communities of Grace*, pp. 154–5.
44. Ibid., pp. 153–4.
45. Usuman dan Fodio trans. and quoted in Mervyn Hiskett, *The Sword of Truth: The Life and Times of the Shehu Usuman dan Fodio* (New York, London and Toronto, 1973), p. 66. The name and title are given here in Hausa, the Arabic form being Shaykh 'Uthman b. Fudi.
46. Ibid., p. 66.
47. Letter from the Mahdi to Yusuf Pasha Hasan al-Shallali trans. and quoted in Rudolph Peters, *Islam and Colonialism: The Doctrine of Jihad in Modern History* (The Hague, 1979), p. 68.

Chapter 8   Contacting the Righteous Dead

1. See Elizabeth Sirriyeh, *Sufi Visionary of Ottoman Damascus: 'Abd al-Ghani al-Nabulusi, 1641–1731* (London and New York, 2005), pp. 108–28 on Nabulusi's travel writings and visits to holy tombs and other shrines.
2. On the origins of views of the Imams, see e.g. Robert Gleave, 'Recent research into the history of early Shi'ism', *History Compass* 7/6 (2009), pp. 1593–605.
3. See T. Fahd, 'Istikhara', in *Encyclopaedia of Islam*, 2nd edn, edited by an editorial committee consisting of H. A. R. Gibb et al. (Leiden, 1960–2009), vol. 4, pp. 259–60 and Hidayet Aydar, 'Istikhara and dreams: learning about the future through dreaming', in K. Bulkeley, K. Adams and P. M. Davis (eds), *Dreaming in Christianity and Islam: Culture, Conflict and Creativity* (New Brunswick NJ and London, 2009), pp. 123–36.
4. See Khalid Sindawi, 'The image of 'Ali b. Abi Talib in the dreams of visitors to his tomb', in L. Marlow (ed.), *Dreaming Across Boundaries: The Interpretation of Dreams in Islamic Lands* (Cambridge MA and London, 2008), pp. 179–201 for a discussion of Ghiyath al-Din Ibn Tawus, *Farhat al-Ghariyy fi ta'yin qabr amir al-mu'minin 'Ali b. Abi Talib fi 'l-Najaf* (Najaf, 1963).
5. Ibid., pp. 190–1.
6. Ibid., pp. 193–4.
7. Ibid., pp. 192 and 194.
8. Gharnati trans. and quoted in R. D. McChesney, *Waqf in Central Asia: Four Hundred Years in the History of a Muslim Shrine, 1480–1889* (Princeton NJ, 1991), p. 27.
9. Ibid.
10. Ibid., pp. 27–8 on the jurist's dream.
11. Henry Corbin, 'The visionary dream in Islamic spirituality', in G. E. von Grunebaum and R. Caillois (eds), *The Dream and Human Societies* (Berkeley and Los Angeles, 1966), pp. 399–402.
12. Ibid., p. 400.
13. Ibid., pp. 402–6 on the dream visions of Ahsa'i and his disciples.
14. Ibid., p. 404.
15. Ibid., pp. 404–5.
16. Christopher S. Taylor, *In the Vicinity of the Righteous: Ziyara and the Veneration of Muslim Saints in Late Medieval Egypt* (Leiden, Boston and Köln, 1999), pp. 5–6.
17. Josef W. Meri, 'A late medieval pilgrimage guide: Ibn al-Hawrani's *al-Isharat ila amakin al-ziyarat* (Guide to Pilgrimage Places)', *Medieval Encounters* 7/1 (2001), p. 5. See Josef Meri, *The Cult of Saints Among Muslims and Jews in Medieval Syria* (Oxford, 2002) and Daniella Talmon-Heller, *Islamic Piety in Medieval Syria: Mosques, Cemeteries and Sermons under the Zangids and Ayyubids (1146–1260)* (Leiden and Boston, 2007), pp. 179–209 on Syrian pilgrimage sites.
18. Iqtidar Husain Siddiqui, 'The early Chishti dargahs', in C. W. Troll (ed.), *Muslim Shrines in India: Their Character, History and Significance* (Delhi, 1992), pp. 18–19.

19. See Ryad Atlagh, 'Paradoxes of a mausoleum', *Journal of the Muhyiddin Ibn 'Arabi Society* 22 (1997), pp. 1–24 on the Ottoman revival of the site.
20. Ibid., pp. 21–2.
21. Al-'Ulaymi cited in Daphna Ephrat, *Spiritual Wayfarers, Leaders in Piety: Sufis and the Dissemination of Islam in Medieval Palestine* (Cambridge MA and London, 2008), pp. 166–7.
22. Elizabeth Sirriya, '*Ziyarat* of Syria in a *rihla* of 'Abd al-Ghani al-Nabulusi (1050/1641–1143/1731)', *Journal of the Royal Asiatic Society*, New Series, 111/2 (1979), pp. 116–17 on these graves, including Nabulusi's description of the Rastan site.
23. Talmon-Heller, *Islamic Piety*, pp. 192–3.
24. See the account by Musa al-Yunini trans. and quoted in Josef Meri, 'Aspects of *baraka* (blessings) and ritual devotion among medieval Muslims and Jews', *Medieval Encounters* 5/1 (1999), pp. 62–3 for the story of the dream and the rediscovery of the tomb.
25. Taylor, *Vicinity*, p. 71.
26. Carl W. Ernst and Bruce B. Lawrence, *Sufi Martyrs of Love: The Chishti Order in South Asia and Beyond* (New York and Basingstoke, 2002), p. 91. Muhammad Najib's *Kitab-e a'ras (Makhzan-e-a'ras)* was published at Agra in 1883.
27. Taylor, *Vicinity*, p. 86.
28. Ibn 'Uthman trans. and quoted in Taylor, *Vicinity*, p. 71.
29. Ibn 'Uthman cited in ibid.
30. Ibn 'Uthman cited in ibid., p. 73.
31. Ibn Qayyim al-Jawziyya trans. and quoted in Meri, 'Aspects of *baraka*', p. 56. Meri notes that *istilam* can mean kissing or wiping as well as touching.
32. Taylor, *Vicinity*, p. 140.
33. Nasafi trans. and quoted in Lloyd Ridgeon, 'Nothing but the truth: the Sufi testament of Aziz Nasafi', PhD dissertation, University of Leeds, 1996, pp. 181–2.
34. Devin DeWeese, 'Sayyid 'Ali Hamadani and Kubrawi hagiographical traditions', in L. Lewisohn (ed.), *The Heritage of Sufism*, vol. 2: *The Legacy of Medieval Persian Sufism (1150–1500)* (Oxford, 1999), p. 149.
35. Nasafi trans. and quoted in Ridgeon, 'Nothing but the truth', pp. 179–80.
36. Ibid., p. 180.
37. Ernst and Lawrence, *Sufi Martyrs of Love*, p. 94.
38. Ibid., p. 93.
39. Meri, 'Aspects of *baraka*', p. 47 and Nile Green, 'The religious and cultural roles of dreams and visions in Islam', *Journal of the Royal Asiatic Society*, 3rd series, 13/3 (2003), pp. 307–8.
40. Th. Emil Homerin, *From Arab Poet to Muslim Saint: Ibn al-Farid, His Verse and His Shrine* (Columbia SC, 1994), p. 37.
41. 'Ali Sibt Ibn al-Farid, 'Dibaja', in Ibn al-Farid, *Diwan*, trans. and quoted in ibid.
42. Homerin, *From Arab Poet to Muslim Saint*, p. 38.
43. See ibid., pp. 78–85 on the visits of Evliya Çelebi and Nabulusi and on the changing fortunes of the shrine from the seventeenth to nineteenth centuries.

44. Green, 'Religious and cultural roles of dreams', p. 307. Green notes a practice of clapping before entering shrines in late nineteenth-century India in order to warn the saint of a visitor's approach and thus avoid the saint's anger at being disturbed without due notice.
45. Elizabeth Sirriyeh, 'The mystical journeys of 'Abd al-Ghani al-Nabulusi', *Die Welt des Islams* 25 (1985), p. 95.
46. Ibn al-Banna' trans. in George Makdisi, 'Autograph diary of an eleventh-century historian of Baghdad—III', *Bulletin of the School of Oriental and African Studies* 19 (1957), p. 36 and see pp. 20–1 for the Arabic text.
47. William V. Harris, *Dreams and Experience in Classical Antiquity* (Cambridge MA and London, 2009), p. 1 and n. 2. Harris notes that the papyrus tells the would-be magician to repeat certain magic words to an oil-lamp and then say: 'Let MM, daughter of NN, see me in her dreams, now, now, quickly, quickly.' In this case, the dreamer is presumed to be female.
48. P. M. Currie, *The Shrine and Cult of Mu'in al-Din Chishti of Ajmer* (Delhi, Bombay, Calcutta and Madras, 1989), p. 92.
49. Ibid., p. 92 n. 74, p. 106 and pp. 106–7 n. 37. See also the frontispiece, showing Mu'in al-Din Chishti presenting the orb and crown to Jahangir, by courtesy of the Chester Beatty Library and Gallery, Dublin. Currie translates the inscription on the orb: 'The key of victory over the two worlds is entrusted to thy hand.'
50. Ernst and Lawrence, *Sufi Martyrs of Love*, pp. 87–90 on Jahanara's visit to Ajmer.
51. Sirriyeh, *Sufi Visionary*, p. 43.

Chapter 9   Visionary Traditions and the Impact of Modernity

1. See Maria Elisabeth Louw, 'Dreaming up futures. Dream omens and magic in Bishkek', *History and Anthropology* 21/3 (2010), pp. 277–92; here p. 279.
2. Ibid., pp. 281–2. Louw observes (p. 290 n. 3) that the practice of bride abduction may also be a method agreed between bride and groom in order to overcome parental objections to a marriage and, in such cases, does not strictly constitute kidnapping.
3. Ibid., p. 288.
4. Introduction, pp. 6–7. See Valerie Hoffman, *Sufism, Mystics and Saints in Modern Egypt* (Columbia SC, 1995) for numerous mentions of Shaykh 'Izz.
5. See Amira Mittermaier, *Dreams That Matter: Egyptian Landscapes of the Imagination* (Berkeley, Los Angeles and London, 2011), pp. 107–9; here p. 108.
6. See ibid., pp. 105–7 on the case of Sharifa, an allegedly worldly young woman, whose dream visions were judged by a respected Egyptian Sufi shaykh as being veridical, but who later earned his disapproval for succumbing to the

temptations of this world. The dreams had not resulted in any reform to her character.
7. See Preface, pp. viii–ix on a Turkish academic who was rejected as a potential husband on the basis of *istikhara*.
8. Abdemalek Yamani, 'Healing and dreams in Islam', in K. Bulkeley, K. Adams and P. M. Davis (eds), *Dreaming in Christianity and Islam: Culture, Conflict and Creativity* (New Brunswick NJ and London, 2009), p. 121.
9. Interview reported during anthropological fieldwork. See Iain R. Edgar, *The Dream in Islam: From Qur'anic Tradition to Jihadist Inspiration* (New York and Oxford, 2011), p. 45.
10. Ibid.
11. See e.g. ibid., pp. 42–53; Rosalind Shaw, 'Dreaming as accomplishment: power, the individual and Temne divination', in M. Jedrej and R. Shaw (eds), *Dreaming, Religion and Society in Africa* (Leiden, 1992), pp. 36–54; Iain Edgar and David Henig, '*Istikhara*: the guidance and practice of Islamic dream incubation through ethnographic comparison', *History and Anthropology* 21/3 (2010), pp. 251–62; and Pnina Werbner, *Pilgrims of Love: The Anthropology of a Global Sufi Cult* (London, 2003), pp. 193–4.
12. Werbner, *Pilgrims of Love*, pp. 193–4.
13. Ibid., p. 194.
14. Shaw, 'Dreaming as accomplishment', p. 47.
15. See Edgar and Henig, '*Istikhara*', pp. 257–61.
16. Ibid., p. 257.
17. Ibid., p. 260.
18. Ibid., p. 256.
19. Werbner, *Pilgrims of Love*, p. 61.
20. Mittermaier, *Dreams That Matter*, p. 224.
21. Stephen M. Lyon, 'Motivation and justification from dreams: Muslim decision-making strategies in Punjab, Pakistan', *History and Anthropology* 21/3 (2010), p. 271. Lyon notes that the *charpai* 'is the four legged cot, cot sofa or bed that serves so many functions across South Asia' (p. 275 n. 3).
22. Ibid., p. 272.
23. See John C. Lamoreaux, *The Early Muslim Tradition of Dream Interpretation* (Albany NY, 2002), pp. 89–90 on the idea that dreams of the Qur'an must necessarily be true. For a modern Iranian Shi'i perspective, see M. Rezvan, '"If somebody dreams about reading the Qur'an, it is a good dream" (on the modern interpretation of the medieval tradition)', *Manuscripta Orientalia* 10/4 (2004), pp. 34–9. According to one Iranian dream manual, reciting the Qur'an aloud predicts good fortune, but there is also a word of warning. If someone has this dream and does not know the text of the Qur'an already, then 'he must start preparing for death, as his hour has come' (ibid., p. 35).
24. Mittermaier, *Dreams That Matter*, p. 8.
25. See also the comments of Lamoreaux, *Early Muslim Tradition*, pp. 4–5 and p. 184 nn. 10–12.

26. Benjamin J. Kilborne, 'Moroccan dream interpretation and culturally constituted defense mechanisms', *Ethos* 9/4 (1981), pp. 294–312.
27. Sigmund Freud, *The Interpretation of Dreams*, Standard Edition (London, 1900–1), vol. 5, p. 397 and quoted in Kilborne, 'Moroccan dream interpretation', p. 300.
28. Ibid.
29. See ibid., pp. 300–5 on the Moroccan interpretations of this dream.
30. See e.g. the account in Chapter 3, pp. 72–3 of a dream reported by Caliph 'Umar II on the Rightly Guided Caliphs sitting with the Prophets Muhammad and Jesus in a palace in Paradise. See also Muhammad al-Bukhari, *al-Jami' al-Sahih*, ed. M. al-Khatib (Beirut, 1991), vol. 4, p. 305 on the Prophet's dream of a palace for the future Caliph 'Umar b. al-Khattab in Paradise.
31. Kilborne, 'Moroccan dream interpretation', p. 300.
32. Ibid., p. 302.
33. Ibid., p. 300.
34. Ibid.
35. Ibid.
36. See e.g. Chapter 3, pp. 66–7, where Ibn al-Musayyab refuses to interpret a dream until the client admits that he was not the dreamer, but was sent by Ibn al-Zubayr to recount the dream.
37. Michael Vannoy Adams, 'The Islamic cultural unconscious in the dreams of a contemporary Muslim man', *Journal of Jungian Theory and Practice* 8/1 (2006), p. 33.
38. Ibid.
39. Ibid., p. 31. On the first use of the expression 'cultural unconscious' in a Jungian context, see Joseph L. Henderson, 'The cultural unconscious', in *Shadow and Self: Selected Papers in Analytical Psychology* (Wilmette IL, 1990), cited by Adams in ibid. Henderson had defined it as 'a dimension between the collective unconscious and the personal unconscious', but Adams redefined it because he regarded the cultural unconscious as an aspect of the collective unconscious.
40. Ibid., p. 32.
41. Ibid., p. 35.
42. The following websites are representative of some that offer Muslim dream interpretation in English: http://www.MyIslamicDream.com; http://www.dreamforth.com; http://www.dreamsabout.net; http://www.dreamtation.com; http://www.understandmydreams.com.
43. Mittermaier, *Dreams That Matter*, pp. 212–16 on Shaykh Nabil's work for the website.
44. Ibid., p. 212.
45. See e.g. Iain R. Edgar, 'The inspirational night dream in the motivation and justification of jihad', *Nova Religio* 11/2 (2007), pp. 59–76 and Elizabeth Sirriyeh, 'Dream narratives of Muslims' martyrdom: constant and changing roles past and present', *Dreaming* 21/3 (2011), pp. 175–9.

46. Reproduced with modification for clarity of language in David Cook, *Martyrdom in Islam* (Cambridge, 2007), p. 178.
47. Yosri Fouda and Nick Fielding, *Masterminds of Terror: The Truth behind the Most Devastating Terrorist Attack the World Has Ever Seen* (Edinburgh and London, 2003), p. 109.
48. Ibid.
49. Mittermaier, *Dreams That Matter*, pp. 32–4.
50. Ibid., p. 33.
51. Elizabeth Sirriyeh, 'Dreams of the holy dead: traditional Islamic oneirocriticism versus Salafi scepticism', *Journal of Semitic Studies* 45/1 (2000), p. 129.
52. Mittermaier, *Dreams That Matter*, p. 45.
53. Ibid., pp. 46–7 on Saudi criticisms of dream interpretation.
54. Saeed Kamali Dehghan, 'A slap, and then forgiveness: mother tells why she saved son's killer from the noose', *The Guardian*, 26 April 2014.

BIBLIOGRAPHY

All references to the *Encyclopaedia of Islam* are to the second edition.

Abu Dawud, Sulayman, *Sunan Abi Dawud*, vol. 3, ed. Muhammad 'Abd al-'Aziz al-Khalidi (Beirut, 1996).
Abun-Nasr, Jamil M., *Muslim Communities of Grace: The Sufi Brotherhoods in Islamic Religious Life* (London, 2007).
Achmet, *Oneirocriticon*, ed. Franz X. Drexl (Leipzig, 1925).
Adams, Michael Vannoy, 'The Islamic cultural unconscious in the dreams of a contemporary Muslim man', *Journal of Jungian Theory and Practice* 8/1 (2006), pp. 31–40.
Adamson, Peter, 'Al-Kindi and the reception of Greek philosophy', in Peter Adamson and Richard C. Taylor (eds), *The Cambridge Companion to Arabic Philosophy* (Cambridge, 2004 and online 2011), pp. 32–51.
Addas, Claude, *Quest for the Red Sulphur: The Life of Ibn 'Arabi* (Cambridge, 1993).
Akkach, Samer, *'Abd al-Ghani al-Nabulusi: Islam and the Enlightenment* (Oxford, 2007).
Alexander, Philip S., 'Bavli Berakhot 55a–57b: the Talmudic dreambook in context', *Journal of Jewish Studies* 46 (1995), pp. 230–48.
Amanullah, Muhammad, 'Islamic dreaming: an analysis of its truthfulness and influence', in Kelly Bulkeley, Kate Adams and Patricia M. Davis (eds), *Dreaming in Christianity and Islam: Culture, Conflict and Creativity* (New Brunswick NJ and London, 2009), pp. 98–110.
Artemidorus, *The Interpretation of Dreams: Oneirocritica*, trans. Robert J. White (Park Ridge NJ, 1975).
Atlagh, Ryad, 'Paradoxes of a mausoleum', *Journal of the Muhyiddin Ibn 'Arabi Society* 22 (1997), pp. 1–24.
Aydar, Hidayet, 'Istikhara and dreams: learning about the future through dreaming', in Bulkeley et al. (eds), *Dreaming in Christianity and Islam*, pp. 123–36.
Baines, John, 'Society, morality and religious practice', in Byron E. Shafer (ed.), *Religion in Ancient Egypt: Gods, Myths and Personal Practice* (London, 1991).
Baldick, Julian, 'The legend of Rabi'a of Basra: Christian antecedents, Muslim counterparts', *Religion* 20 (1990), pp. 233–47.

Bashear, Suliman, 'Riding beasts on divine missions: an examination of the ass and camel traditions', *Journal of Semitic Studies* 36/1 (1991), pp. 37–76.
Beckingham, C. F., 'The *rihla*: fact or fiction?', in Ian Richard Netton (ed.), *Golden Roads: Migration, Pilgrimage and Travel in Mediaeval and Modern Islam* (Richmond, 1993), pp. 86–94.
Black, Jeremy, *The Literature of Ancient Sumer*, translated and introduced by Jeremy Black et al. (Oxford, 2004).
Bland, N., 'On the Muhammedan science of tabir, or interpretation of dreams', *Journal of the Royal Asiatic Society* 16 (1856), pp. 118–71.
Bosworth, C. E., 'Munadjat', in *Encyclopaedia of Islam*, vol. 7, p. 557.
Böwering, Gerhard, *The Mystical Vision of Existence in Classical Islam: the Qur'anic Hermeneutics of the Sufi Sahl al-Tustari (d.283/896)* (Berlin, 1980).
Brackertz, Karl, *Das Traumbuch des Achmet ben Sirin* (Munich, 1986).
Bryan, B. M., *The Reign of Thutmose IV* (Baltimore MD and London, 1991).
Bukhari, Muhammad al-, *al-Jami' al-Sahih*, vol. 4, ed. Muhibb al-Din al-Khatib (Beirut, 1991).
Bulkeley, Kelly, 'Reflections on the dream traditions of Islam', *Sleep and Hypnosis* 4/1 (2002), pp. 4–14.
Bulkeley, Kelly (ed.), *Dreams: A Reader on Religious, Cultural and Psychological Dimensions of Dreaming* (New York and Basingstoke, 2001).
Bulkeley, Kelly, Kate Adams and Patricia M. Davis (eds), *Dreaming in Christianity and Islam: Culture, Conflict and Creativity* (New Brunswick NJ and London, 2009).
Busse, Heribert, 'Jerusalem in the story of Muhammad's night journey and ascension', in Uri Rubin (ed.), *The Formation of the Classical Islamic World*, vol. 4: *The Life of Muhammad* (Aldershot and Brookfield VM, 1998), pp. 279–318.
Chittick, William C., *Ibn 'Arabi: Heir to the Prophets* (Oxford, 2005).
Cook, David, *Martyrdom in Islam* (Cambridge, 2007).
Corbin, Henry, 'The visionary dream in Islamic spirituality', in G.E. von Grunebaum and Roger Caillois (eds), *The Dream and Human Societies* (Berkeley and Los Angeles, 1966), pp. 381–408.
Crone, Patricia, *Meccan Trade and the Rise of Islam* (Princeton NJ, 1987).
Currie, P. M., *The Shrine and Cult of Mu'in al-Din Chishti of Ajmer* (Delhi, Bombay, Calcutta and Madras, 1989).
Dallal, Ahmad, 'Science, medicine and technology: the making of a scientific culture', in John L. Esposito (ed.), *The Oxford History of Islam* (Oxford, 1999), pp. 155–213.
Damiri, Kamal al-Din Muhammad al-, *Kitab hayat al-hayawan al-kubra*, ed. Hasan al-Hadi Husayn (Cairo, 1274/1857–58).
Dari, Abu 'Ali al-Husayn al-, *al-Imam Muhammad b. Sirin: Muntakhab al-kalam fi tafsir al-ahlam*, ed. 'Abd al-Rahman al-Juzu (Beirut, 1986).
Dehghan, Saeed Kamali, 'A slap and then forgiveness: mother tells why she saved her son's killer from the noose', *The Guardian* (26 April 2014).
De Somogyi, Joseph, 'The interpretation of dreams in ad-Damīrī's *Ḥayāt al-Ḥayawān*', *Journal of the Royal Asiatic Society* 72/1 (1940), pp. 1–20.
DeWeese, Devin, 'Sayyid 'Ali Hamadani and Kubrawi hagiographical traditions', in Leonard Lewisohn (ed.), *The Heritage of Sufism*, vol. 2: *The Legacy of Medieval Persian Sufism (1150–1500)*, pp. 121–58.

BIBLIOGRAPHY 225

Dinawari, Abu Sa'd al-, *Kitab al-ta'bir fi 'l-ru'ya aw al-Qadiri fi 'l-ta'bir*, ed. Fahmi Sa'd (Beirut, 1997).
Donner, Fred M., *Muhammad and the Believers, At the Origins of Islam* (Cambridge MA and London, 2010).
Drexl, Franz X., *Achmets Traumbuch: Einleitung und Probe eines kritischen Textes* (Freising, 1909).
Edgar, Iain R., *The Dream in Islam: From Qur'anic Tradition to Jihadist Inspiration* (New York and Oxford, 2011).
———, 'The inspirational night dream in the motivation and justification of jihad', *Nova Religio* 11/2 (2007), pp. 59–76.
Edgar, Iain and David Henig, '*Istikhara*: the guidance and practice of Islamic dream incubation through ethnographic comparison', *History and Anthropology* 21/3 (2010), pp. 251–62.
Eliade, Mircea, 'Initiation dreams and visions among the Siberian shamans', in von Grunebaum and Caillois (eds), *The Dream and Human Societies*, pp. 331–40.
Ephrat, Daphna, *Spiritual Wayfarers, Leaders in Piety: Sufis and the Dissemination of Islam in Medieval Palestine* (Cambridge MA and London, 2008).
Ernst, Carl W., *Ruzbihan Baqli: Mysticism and the Rhetoric of Sainthood in Persian Sufism* (Richmond, 1996).
———, *The Shambhala Guide to Sufism* (Boston, 1997).
———, *Words of Ecstasy in Sufism* (Albany NY, 1985).
Ernst, Carl W. and Bruce B. Lawrence, *Sufi Martyrs of Love: The Chishti Order in South Asia and Beyond* (New York and Basingstoke, 2002).
Ewing, Katherine P., *Arguing Sainthood: Modernity, Psychoanalysis and Islam* (Durham NC, 1997).
Fahd, T., 'al-Dinawari, Abu Sa'id (Sa'd) Nasr b. Ya'qub', in *Encyclopaedia of Islam*, vol. 2, pp. 300–1.
———, 'Istikhara', in *Encyclopaedia of Islam*, vol. 4, pp. 259–60.
———, 'Kahin', in *Encyclopaedia of Islam*, vol. 4, pp. 420–2.
———, 'Kihana', in *Encyclopaedia of Islam*, vol. 5, pp. 99–101.
Fahd, Toufic, 'Hunayn Ibn Ishaq est-il le traducteur des *Oneirocritica* d'Artémidore d'Ephèse?', *Arabica* 21 (1974), pp. 27–84.
———, *La Divination Arabe: Études Religieuses, Sociologiques et Folkloriques sur le Milieu Natif de l'Islam* (Leiden, 1966).
——— (ed.), *Le Livre des Songes [par] Artémidore d'Ephèse. Traduit du grec en arabe par Hunayn b. Ishaq* (Damascus, 1964).
Fouda, Yosri and Nick Fielding, *Masterminds of Terror: The Truth behind the Most Devastating Terrorist Attack the World Has Ever Seen* (Edinburgh and London, 2003).
Freud, Sigmund, *The Interpretation of Dreams*, Standard Edition (London, 1900–1), vol. 5.
Gallop, D., *Aristotle on Sleep and Dreams: A Text and Translation with Introduction, Notes and Glossary* (Warminster, 1996).
Gardiner, A. H., *Hieratic Papyri in the British Museum*, vol. 3: *The Dream Book* (London, 1935).
Gaulmier, J. and T. Fahd, 'Ibn Shahin al-Zahiri', in *Encyclopaedia of Islam*, vol. 3, p. 935.
Ghazali, al-, *al-Munqidh min al-dalal*, Arabic ed. and French trans. (Beirut, 1959).

Gimaret, D., 'Ru'yat Allah', in *Encyclopaedia of Islam*, vol. 8, p. 649.
Gleave, Robert, 'Recent research into the history of early Shi'ism', *History Compass* 7/6 (2009), pp. 1593–605.
Green, Nile, 'The religious and cultural role of dreams and visions in Islam', *Journal of the Royal Asiatic Society*, 3rd series, 13/3 (2003), pp. 287–313.
_____, *Sufism: A Global History* (Oxford, 2012).
Hansberger, Rotraud E., 'How Aristotle came to believe in God-given dreams: the Arabic version of *De divinatione per somnum*', in Louise Marlow (ed.), *Dreaming Across Boundaries: The Interpretation of Dreams in Islamic Lands* (Cambridge MA and London, 2008), pp. 50–77.
Hansen, Hanne Lavér, '"The truth without nonsense": remarks on Artemidorus' *Interpretation of Dreams*', in Robin Lorsch Wildfang and Jacob Isager (eds), *Divination and Portents in the Roman World* (Odense, 2000), pp. 57–65.
Harris, William V., *Dreaming and Experience in Classical Antiquity* (Cambridge MA, 2009).
Hasan-Rokem, Galit, 'Communication with the dead in Jewish dream culture', in David Shulman and Guy G. Stroumsa (eds), *Dream Cultures: Explorations in the Comparative History of Dreaming* (New York and Oxford, 1999), pp. 213–32.
Hashimi, Muhammad al-, 'On Avicenna's Ta'bir al-Ru'ya', PhD dissertation, School of Oriental and African Studies, London University, 1948.
Hermansen, Marcia, 'Dreams and dreaming in Islam', in Kelly Bulkeley (ed.), *Dreams: A Reader on Religious, Cultural and Psychological Dimensions of Dreaming* (New York and Basingstoke, 2001), pp. 73–92.
Hermansen, Marcia K., 'Visions as "good to think": a cognitive approach to visionary experience in Islamic Sufi thought', *Religion* 27/1(1997), pp. 25–43.
Hiskett, Mervyn, *The Sword of Truth: The Life and Times of Shehu Usuman dan Fodio* (New York, London and Toronto, 1973).
Hitti, Philip K., *History of the Arabs*, (10th edn, Basingstoke, 1970).
Hoffman, Curtiss, 'Dumuzi's dream: dream analysis in ancient Mesopotamia', *Dreaming* 14/4 (2004), pp. 240–51.
Hoffman, Valerie J., 'Annihilation in the Messenger of God: the development of a Sufi practice', *International Journal of Middle East Studies* 31/3 (1999), pp. 351–69.
_____, *Sufism, Mystics and Saints in Modern Egypt* (Columbia SC, 1995).
Homerin, Th. Emil, *From Arab Poet to Muslim Saint: Ibn al-Farid, His Verse and His Shrine* (Columbia SC, 1994).
Howard, I. K. A., 'The development of the *adhān* and *iqāma* of the *ṣalāt* in early Islam', in G. Hawting (ed.), *The Development of Islamic Ritual* (Aldershot, 2006), pp. 219–28.
Husser, Jean-Marie, *Dreams and Dream Narratives in the Biblical World*, trans. Jill M. Munro (Sheffield, 1999).
Ibn 'Arabi, *Sufis of Andalusia: the Ruh al-Quds and al-Durra al-Fakhirah of Ibn 'Arabi*, trans. with introduction and notes by R. W. J. Austin (London, 1971).
Ibn 'Arabi, *The Bezels of Wisdom*, trans. R. W. J. Austin (Mahwah NJ, 1980).
Ibn Hisham, 'Abd al-Malik, *al-Sira al-Nabawiyya*, ed. Jamal Thabit, Muhammad Mahmud and Sayyid Ibrahim (Cairo, 1996).
Ibn Maja, Muhammad, *Sunan*, vol. 5, ed. Bashshar 'Awwad Ma'ruf (Beirut, 1998).

BIBLIOGRAPHY

Ibn Sa'd, Muhammad, *al-Tabaqat al-kubra*, vols 1, 5 and 7, ed. Muhammad 'Abd al-Qadir 'Ata (Beirut, 1990).
Ibn Shahin al-Zahiri, Ghars al-Din al-Khalil, *Kitab al-isharat fi 'ilm al-'ibarat*, ed. Sayyid Kasrawi Hasan (Beirut, 1993).
Jones, J. M. B., 'Ibn Ishak', in *Encyclopaedia of Islam*, vol. 3, pp. 810–11.
_____, 'Ibn Ishaq and al-Waqidi: the dream of 'Atika and the raid to Nakhla in relation to the charge of plagiarism', in Rubin (ed.), *The Formation of the Classical Islamic World*, vol. 4: *The Life of Muhammad*, pp. 11–21.
Jung, Carl Gustav, *Psychology and Religion* (New Haven CT and London, 1938).
Kahana-Smilansky, Hagar, 'Self-reflection and conversion in medieval Muslim autobiographical dreams', in Marlow (ed.), *Dreaming Across Boundaries*, pp. 99–130.
Karamustafa, Ahmet T., *Sufism: The Formative Period* (Edinburgh, 2007).
Katz, Jonathan G., *Dreams, Sufism and Sainthood: The Visionary Career of Muhammad al-Zawawi* (Leiden, 1996).
Katz, Marion Holmes, *The Birth of the Prophet Muhammad: Devotional Piety in Sunni Islam* (London and New York, 2007).
Khan, M. A., 'Kitab Ta'bir-ir-Ruya of Abu 'Ali Ibn Sina', *Indo-Iranica* 9/3 (1956), pp. 15–30 and 9/4 (1956), pp. 43–57.
Kilborne, Benjamin J., 'Moroccan dream interpretation and culturally constituted defense mechanisms', *Ethos* 9/4 (1981), pp. 294–312.
Kinberg, Leah, 'Dreams and sleep', in *Encyclopaedia of the Qur'an*, vol. 1, pp. 531–46.
_____, Ibn Abi al-Dunya, *Morality in the Guise of Dreams: a critical edition of Kitab al-manam with introduction* (Leiden, New York and Köln, 1994).
_____, 'Interaction between this world and the afterworld in early Islamic tradition', *Oriens* 29–30 (1986), pp. 285–308.
_____, 'Literal dreams and Prophetic *hadits* in classical Islam – a comparison of two ways of legitimation', *Der Islam* 70 (1993), pp. 279–300.
_____, 'Qur'an and Hadith: a struggle for supremacy as reflected in dream narratives', in Marlow (ed.), *Dreaming Across Boundaries*, pp. 25–49.
Kindi, *Medieval Islamic Swords and Swordmaking: Kindi's treatise 'On Swords and Their Kinds'*, ed., trans. and commentary by Robert G. Hoyland and Brian Gilmour (Warminster, 2006).
_____, *Risala fi mahiyyat al-nawm wa 'l-ru'ya*, in *Rasa'il al-Kindi al-falsafiyya*, vol. 1, ed. M. Abu Rida (Cairo, 1950), pp. 283–311.
_____, *Scientific Weather Forecasting in the Middle Ages: the writings of al-Kindi: studies, editions and translations* by Gerrit Bos and Charles Burnett (London, 2000).
Kister, M. J., 'The interpretation of dreams: an unknown manuscript of Ibn Qutayba's *'Ibarat al-Ru'ya'*, *Israel Oriental Studies* 4 (1974), pp. 67–103.
Knysh, Alexander D., *Ibn 'Arabi in the Later Islamic Tradition: the Making of a Polemical Image in Medieval Islam* (Albany NY, 1999).
Kopf, L., 'al-Damiri, Muhammad b. Musa b. 'Isa Kamal al-Din', in *Encyclopaedia of Islam*, vol. 2, pp. 107–8.
Kruger, Steven F., *Dreaming in the Middle Ages* (Cambridge, 1992).
Lamoreaux, John C., 'Some notes on the dream manual of al-Dari', *Rivista degli studi orientali* 70 (1996), pp. 47–52.
_____, *The Early Muslim Tradition of Dream Interpretation* (Albany NY, 2002).
Lane Fox, Robin, *Pagans and Christians* (Harmondsworth, 1986).

Lesko, Leonard H., 'Ancient Egyptian cosmogonies and cosmology', in Shafer (ed.), *Religion in Ancient Egypt*, pp. 88–122.

Lipton, Diana, *Revisions of the Night: Politics and Promises in the Patriarchal Dreams of Genesis* (Sheffield, 1999).

Losensky, Paul, trans. with Michael Sells, 'Rabi'a: her words and life in 'Attar's *Memorial of the Friends of God*', in Sells, *Early Islamic Mysticism*, pp. 151–70.

Louw, Maria Elisabeth, 'Dreaming up futures. Dream omens and magic in Bishkek', *History and Anthropology* 21/3 (2010), pp. 277–92.

Lutfi, Huda, 'The construction of gender symbolism in Ibn Sirin's and Ibn Shahin's medieval Arabic dream texts', *Mamluk Studies Review* 9/1 (2005), pp. 123–61.

Lyon, Stephen M., 'Motivation and justification from dreams: Muslim decision-making strategies in Punjab, Pakistan', *History and Anthropology* 21/3 (2010), pp. 263–76.

Madigan, Daniel A., 'Revelation and inspiration', in *Encyclopaedia of the Qur'an*, vol. 4, pp. 437–48.

Makdisi, George, 'Autograph diary of an eleventh-century historian of Baghdad – III', *Bulletin of the School of Oriental and African Studies* 19 (1957), pp. 13–48.

Marlow, Louise (ed.), *Dreaming Across Boundaries: The Interpretation of Dreams in Islamic Lands* (Cambridge MA and London, 2008).

Mavroudi, Maria, *A Byzantine Book of Dream Interpretation: the Oneirocriticon of Achmet, and Its Arabic Sources* (Leiden, 2002).

McChesney, R.D., *Waqf in Central Asia: Four Hundred Years in the History of a Muslim Shrine, 1480–1889* (Princeton NJ, 1991).

Meri, Josef W., 'A late medieval pilgrimage guide: Ibn al-Hawrani's *al-Isharat ila amakin al-ziyarat* (Guide to Pilgrimage Places)', *Medieval Encounters* 7/1 (2001), pp. 3–78.

―――, 'Aspects of *baraka* (blessings) and ritual devotion among medieval Muslims and Jews', *Medieval Encounters* 5/1 (1999), pp. 46–69.

―――, *The Cult of Saints Among Muslims and Jews in Medieval Syria* (Oxford, 2002).

Miller, Patricia Cox, *Dreams in Late Antiquity: Studies in the Imagination of a Culture* (Princeton NJ, 1994).

Mittermaier, Amira, *Dreams That Matter: Egyptian Landscapes of the Imagination* (Berkeley, Los Angeles and London, 2011).

Mojaddedi, Jawid A., *The Biographical Tradition in Sufism: The Tabaqat Genre from al-Sulami to Jami* (Richmond, 2001).

Muslim b. al-Hajjaj, *Sahih Muslim*, vol. 4 (Beirut, 1995).

Nabulusi, 'Abd al-Ghani al-, *Ta'tir al-anam fi ta'bir al-manam*, ed. Hanan Tabara (Beirut, 1996).

―――, *Ta'tir al-anam fi ta'bir al-manam*, ed. Yusuf al-Shaykh Muhammad (Beirut, 1997).

Netton, Ian Richard, 'The origins of Islamic philosophy', in Ian Richard Netton (ed.), *Islamic Philosophy and Theology: Critical Concepts in Islamic Thought*, vol. 1: *Legacies, Translations and Prototypes* (London and New York, 2007), pp. 79–99.

Nicholson, Reynold Alleyne, *The* Kitab al-Luma' fi 'l-Tasawwuf *of Abu Nasr 'Abdallah b. 'Ali al-Sarraj al-Tusi* (Leiden and London, 1914).

Noegel, Scott, 'Dreams and dream interpreters in Mesopotamia and the Hebrew Bible [Old Testament]', in Bulkeley (ed.), *Dreams*, pp. 45–71.

Noegel, Scott B., *Nocturnal Ciphers: The Allusive Language of Dreams in the Ancient Near East* (New Haven CT, 2007).

Oberhelman, Steven M., *The* Oneirocriticon *of Achmet: A Medieval Greek and Arabic Treatise on the Interpretation of Dreams* (Lubbock TX, 1991).
Oppenheim A. Leo, 'Mantic dreams in the ancient Near East', in von Grunebaum and Caillois (eds), *The Dream and Human Societies*, pp. 341–50.
_____, 'The interpretation of dreams in the ancient Near East with a translation of an Assyrian dream-book', *Transactions of the American Philosophical Society* n.s. 43/3 (1956), pp. 179–373.
Peters, Rudolph, *Islam and Colonialism: The Doctrine of Jihad in Modern History* (The Hague, 1979).
Price, S. R. F., 'The future of dreams: from Freud to Artemidorus', *Past and Present* 113 (1986), pp. 3–37.
Radtke, Bernd and John O'Kane, *The Concept of Sainthood in Early Islamic Mysticism: Two Works by Al-Hakim al-Tirmidhi* (Richmond, 1996).
Rahman, Fazlur, *Islam*, (2nd edn, Chicago and London, 1979).
Renard, John, *Seven Doors to Islam: Spirituality and the Religious Life of Muslims* (Berkeley and Los Angeles, 1996).
_____, *Windows on the House of Islam: Muslim Sources on Spirituality and Religious Life* (Berkeley, Los Angeles and London, 1998).
Reynolds, Dwight F. (ed.), *Interpreting the Self: Autobiography in the Arabic Literary Tradition* (Berkeley, 2001).
Rezvan, M., '"If somebody dreams about reading the Qur'an, it is a good dream" (on the modern interpretation of the medieval tradition)', *Manuscripta Orientalia* 10/4 (2004), pp. 34–9.
Ridgeon, Lloyd, 'Nothing but the truth: the Sufi testament of Aziz Nasafi', PhD dissertation, University of Leeds, 1996.
Rippin, Andrew, *Muslims: Their Religious Beliefs and Practices* (4th edn, London and New York, 2012).
Rochberg, Francesca, *The Heavenly Writing: Divination, Horoscopy and Astronomy in Mesopotamian Culture* (Cambridge and New York, 2004).
Rubin, Uri (ed.), *The Formation of the Classical Islamic World*, vol. 4: *The Life of Muhammad* (Aldershot, 1998).
Ruelle, C.-E., 'La clef des songes d'Achmet Abou Mazar: fragment inédit et bonnes variantes', *Revue des Études Grecques* 7 (1894), pp. 305–12.
Ryan, Patrick J., 'The mystical theology of Tijani Sufism and its social significance in West Africa', *Journal of Religion in Africa* 30/2 (2000), pp. 208–24.
Schrieke, B. –[Horovitz, J.], 'Mi'radj: In Islamic exegesis and in the popular and mystical tradition of the Arab world', in *Encyclopaedia of Islam*, vol. 7, pp. 97–100.
Shafer, Byron E. (ed.), *Religion in Ancient Egypt: Gods, Myths and Personal Practice* (London, 1991).
Shaw, Rosalind, 'Dreaming as accomplishment: power, the individual and Temne divination', in M.C. Jedrej and Rosalind Shaw (eds), *Dreaming, Religion and Society in Africa* (Leiden and New York, 1992), pp. 36–54.
Sells, Michael A., *Early Islamic Mysticism: Sufi, Qur'an, Mi'raj, Poetic and Theological Writings* (New York and Mahwah NJ, 1996).
Shulman, David and Guy G. Stroumsa (eds), *Dream Cultures: Explorations in the Comparative History of Dreaming* (New York and Oxford, 1999).

Siddiqui, Iqtidar Husain, 'The early Chishti dargahs', in C.W. Troll (ed.), *Muslim Shrines in India: Their Character, History and Significance* (Delhi, 1992), pp. 1–24.

Simon, Maurice, *The Babylonian Talmud: Berakhot* (London, 1948).

Sindawi, Khalid, 'The image of 'Ali b. Abi Talib in the dreams of visitors to his tomb', in Marlow (ed.), *Dreaming Across Boundaries*, pp. 179–201.

Sirriya, Elizabeth, '*Ziyarat* of Syria in a *rihla* of 'Abd al-Ghani al-Nabulusi (1050/1641–1143/1731)', *Journal of the Royal Asiatic Society*, New Series, 111/2 (1979), pp. 109–22.

———, 'Arab stars, Assyrian dogs and Greek 'angels': How Islamic is Muslim dream interpretation?', *Journal of Islamic Studies* 22/2 (2011), pp. 215–33.

———, 'Dream narratives of Muslims' martyrdom: constant and changing roles past and present', *Dreaming* 21/3 (2011), pp. 168–80.

———, 'Dreams of the holy dead: traditional Islamic oneirocriticism versus Salafi scepticism', *Journal of Semitic Studies* 45/1 (2000), pp. 115–30.

———, 'Muslims dreaming of Christians, Christians dreaming of Muslims: images from medieval dream interpretation', *Islam and Christian-Muslim Relations* 17/2 (2006), pp. 207–21.

———, *Sufi Visionary of Ottoman Damascus: 'Abd al-Ghani al-Nabulusi, 1641–1731* (London and New York, 2005).

———, 'The mystical journeys of 'Abd al-Ghani al-Nabulusi', *Die Welt des Islams* 25 (1985), pp. 84–96.

Smith, Margaret, *Rabi'a the Mystic and Her Fellow Saints in Islam* (Cambridge, 1928).

Szpakowska, Kasia, *Behind Closed Eyes: Dreams and Nightmares in Ancient Egypt* (Swansea, 2003).

———, 'Through the looking glass: dreams in ancient Egypt', in Bulkeley (ed.), *Dreams*, pp. 29–43.

Strickling, Bonnelle Lewis, 'Early Christians and their dreams', in Bulkeley et al. (eds.), *Dreaming in Christianity and Islam*, pp. 32–42.

Stroumsa, Guy G., 'Dreams and visions in early Christian discourse', in Shulman and Stroumsa (eds.), *Dream Cultures*, pp. 189–212.

Sviri, Sara, 'Dreaming analyzed and recorded: dreams in the world of medieval Islam', in Shulman and Stroumsa (eds.), pp. 252–73.

Tabari, *The History of al-Tabari* (Ta'rikh al-rusul wa 'l-muluk), vol. 6: *Muhammad at Mecca*, trans. and annotated by W. Montgomery Watt and M.V. McDonald (Albany NY, 1988).

———, *The History of al-Tabari* (Ta'rikh al-rusul wa 'l-muluk), vol. 7: *The Foundation of the Community*, trans. and annotated by W. Montgomery Watt and M. V. McDonald (Albany NY, 1987).

———, *The History of al-Tabari* (Ta'rikh al-rusul wa'l-muluk), vol. 23: *The Zenith of the Marwanid House*, trans. and annotated by Martin Hinds (Albany NY, 1990).

Talmon-Heller, Daniella, *Islamic Piety in Medieval Syria: Mosques, Cemeteries and Sermons under the Zangids and Ayyubids (1146–1260)* (Leiden and Boston, 2007).

Taylor, Christopher S., *In the Vicinity of the Righteous: Ziyara and the Veneration of Muslim Saints in Late Medieval Egypt* (Leiden, Boston and Köln, 1999).

Tirmidhi, Muhammad al-, *al-Jami' al-kabir*, vol. 4, ed. Bashshar 'Awwad Ma'ruf (Beirut, 1996).

Ullmann, Manfred, 'War Hunain der Übersetzer von Artemidors Traumbuch?', *Die Welt des Islams* n.s. 13 (1971), pp. 204–11.

von Grunebaum, G. E. and Roger Caillois (eds), *The Dream and Human Societies* (Berkeley and Los Angeles, 1966).
von Schlegell, Barbara, 'Sufism in the Ottoman Arab World: Shaykh 'Abd al-Ghani al-Nabulusi (d.1143/1731)', PhD dissertation, University of California, Berkeley, 1997.
Vuckovic, Brooke Olson, *Heavenly Journeys, Earthly Concerns: The Legacy of the Mi'raj in the Formation of Islam* (New York and London, 2005).
Waqidi, Muhammad b. 'Umar al-, *The* Kitab al-Maghazi *of al-Waqidi*, ed. Marsden Jones (London, 1966).
Watt, W. Montgomery, *Muhammad at Mecca* (Oxford, 1953).
_____, *Muhammad at Medina* (Oxford, 1956).
_____, *Muhammad, Prophet and Statesman* (Oxford, 1961).
Wensinck, A.J. –[Rippin, A.], 'Wahy', in *Encyclopaedia of Islam*, vol. 11, pp. 53–6.
Werbner, Pnina, *Pilgrims of Love: The Anthropology of a Global Sufi Cult* (London, 2003.)
Wildfang, Robin Lorsch, 'The propaganda of omens: six dreams involving Augustus', in Wildfang and Isager (eds), *Divination and Portents in the Roman World*, pp. 43–55.
Wildfang, Robin Lorsch and Jacob Isager (eds), *Divination and Portents in the Roman World* (Odense, 2000).
Yamani, Abdemalik, 'Healing and dreams in Islam', in Bulkeley et al. (eds), *Dreaming in Christianity and Islam*, pp. 111–22.

INDEX

al-'Abbas, 119–21
'Abbasids, 74, 84, 89, 104, 117
'Abd Allah b. 'Abd al-Muttalib, 35–6
'Abd Allah b. Zayd, 56
'Abd Allah b. al-Zubayr, 64, 66–7
'Abd al-Malik, Caliph, 46, 64, 66–8, 115–16
'Abd al-Qadir, Amir, 164
Abraham, 44, 48, 51–2, 84
Abu Bakr al-Siddiq, Caliph, 47, 51, 54, 61
  as dream interpreter, 65, 83
  in dreams, 72, 73
Abu Dawud, 58
Abu Dharr, 42
Abu Hurayra, 61
Abu Jahl, 120–1
Abu Mukhallad, 105
Abu Talib, 50
Abyssinia, 27, 35
Achilles, 17
Achmet, son of Sereim, *see* Pseudo-Achmet
Adams, Michael Vannoy, 185–6
adhan, 56–7
Afghanistan, 160
Agamemnon, 18
ahlam, 49, 59

Ahsa'i, Shaykh Ahmad, 162–3
'A'isha bint Abi Bakr, 48, 53–4
Ajmer, 164, 173
Ajmeri, Muhammad Najib Qadiri Nagawri, 166–7
Akbar, Emperor, 172
Aleppo, 164
Algeria, 152, 153
'Ali b. Abi Talib, 64, 160–1
  in dreams, 72, 73
  see also Imam 'Ali
'Ali Zayn al-'Abidin, 8; *see also* Imam Zayn al-'Abidin
Amina bint Wahb, 35–8
angels
  in Arabic translation of Artemidorus, 90
  biblical, 16, 36–7
  in Christian dreams and visions, 25–6
  in Muslim dreams and visions, 84, 125, 142, 143
  in the Prophet's dreams and visions, 42–5
  status, 148
  in Sufi dreams and visions, 2, 80, 130–1
Apollo, 37, 90

Arabia, pre-Islamic, 26–7, 35
Aristotle, 18, 75–6, 92, 93–4
Artemidorus, 19–22, 23, 90–5, 99, 111, 134–7
  Hunayn b. Ishaq's 'translation' of, 89–92, 94, 111
  Oneirocritica of, 19, 23, 89
Asclepiades, 37
Asma' bint Abi Bakr, 65, 83, 133
Astrampsychus, 111
astrology, 74
Athena, 17, 90
Atia, mother of Augustus, 37
'Atika, 119–21
Atta, Mohammed, 189
'Attar, Farid al-Din, 126–9
'Attar, Khwaja 'Ala al-Din, 173
Augustus, Emperor, 37–8
awliya' Allah, 78, 163; *see also* saints; *wali Allah*
Aygul, Kyrgyz dreamer, 174–5
al-Azhar, 190

Babylonian Talmud, 23, 70, 91
Badr, battle of, 51–2, 119, 120–1
al-Bakri, Muhammad, 154
al-Banna', Hasan, 191
Baqli, Ruzbihan, 141–2, 146
baraka, 165
Baram, 110, 111
Bin Laden, Usama (Osama), 189–90
Bishkek, 174, 175
al-Bistami, Abu Yazid, 78–80, 165
Bosnia, 179–80
al-Bukhari, 39, 58–9, 122
Buraq, 46–7
bushra, 49
Byzantine Empire, 35, 103–4, 117

Cairo, 152, 163, 167, 169, 187
caliphs, 61, 64, 67
  in dreams, 66–7, 72–3, 142, 155
Chishti, Mu'in al-Din, 164, 172–3
Chosroes, 38

Christianity, 31, 104–8
  Waraqa as convert to, 41
Christians
  as dreamers and visionaries, 24–6
  dreaming of Muslims, 112–16
  Muslim dreams of, 105–8
Constantine, Emperor, 24
Constantius II, Emperor, 24

Damascus, 97, 143, 145, 164, 165
al-Damiri, Kamal al-Din, 98–101
Daniel, 12, 84, 92, 111
al-Dari, Abu 'Ali (Pseudo-Ibn Sirin), 95–6, 98, 107, 133, 134, 135–6
dead, the
  in dreams, 70–1, 106, 124–5, 158–75, 190, 191–2
al-Dinawari, Abu Sa'd, 92–4, 99, 104–8, 117, 134–8
divination
  under 'Abbasids, 74
  ancient Mesopotamian, 14
  Arab, 103
  pre-Islamic, 26–7
  Christian views of, 103–4
Divine Light, 159, 162; *see also* God: Light of
dream interpretation
  ancient Egyptian, 13–14, 68
  ancient Mesopotamian, 14–15, 68, 116
  in Artemidorus' *Oneirocritica*, 19–22, 66, 134–6, 137
  biblical, 12–13
  Christian, 103–4, 105, 107, 108–16, 117
  Freudian, 183
  Jewish, 23–4, 66, 70, 86
  Jungian, 185–7
  Kyrgyz, 174–5
  in the medieval West, 104
  Moroccan, 183–5

INDEX

Muslim, 28, 30–1, 63–70, 83–108, 132–8, 178–80, 182–5, 187, 189–90
  the Prophet's, *see* Muhammad the Prophet
  women's, 179–80
Dumuzi, 10–12

Edgar, Iain, 179
Egypt, 6, 96, 134, 163, 176, 190
  ancient, 13, 17, 172
Egyptians
  in *Oneirocriticon* of Pseudo-Achmet, 109–10, 111
enhypnion, 20
Evliya Çelebi, 170
Ewing, Katherine, 1

al-Farabi, 75
Fatima bint 'Abd al-Malik (wife of 'Umar II), 72
Fatima bint Ibn al-Muthanna, 144
Fatima, daughter of the Prophet, 159, 160, 163
Firuz Shah, 164
Fouda, Yosri, 189
Freud, Sigmund, 183

Gabriel, 32, 40–1
Galen, 19, 93
al-Gharnati, Abu Hamid, 160–1
al-Ghazali, 2, 71
Gideon, 121
God
  dreams from, 24–5, 30–1, 51–2, 181–2
  in Hunayn b. Ishaq's 'translation' of Artemidorus' *Oneirocritica*, 90
  Light of, 38, 147; *see also* Divine Light
  in Muslims' dreams and visions, 88, 99, 121, 128–9, 140–6, 153, 182
  Wisdom of, 149

hadith, 58–60, 80–1, 100, 122–3, 147, 148, 191
Halima, 38–9
Hamadani, Sayyid 'Ali, 168
Hamza, 55
al-Hasan al-Khallal, 105
Hasan b. 'Ali, 123, 160; *see also* Imam Hasan
Hausaland, 155
Haykal, Muhammad Husayn, 33
Henig, David, 179
Hermas, 25–6
Hoffman, Valerie, 6, 7
Horus, 14
Hosseinzadeh, Abdollah, 191
Hudaybiyya, 52, 53
Hunayn b. Ishaq, 89–91, 105
Husayn b. 'Ali b. Abi Talib, 8, 123, 160; *see also* Imam Husayn

Ibn Abi al-Dunya, 71–3, 123–6
Ibn 'Arabi, 130, 140, 143–5, 146, 147–50, 164
Ibn al-Banna', 171
Ibn al-Farid, *see* 'Umar b. al-Farid
Ibn Ghannam, 97
Ibn Hisham, 32, 55
Ibn Ishaq, 32
  on 'Atika's dream, 119
  on birth of the Prophet, 35–6, 37
  on the Prophet at Mecca, 39–41, 42–3, 48
  on the Prophet at Medina, 54–5, 56, 61
Ibn Ishaq, Hunayn, *see* Hunayn b. Ishaq
Ibn Maja, 123
Ibn al-Musayyab, 61, 63–8, 69, 83, 84
Ibn Qayyim al-Jawziyya, 71, 167
Ibn Qutayba, 70, 84–9, 91, 138
Ibn Sa'd, 39, 46–8, 65, 68
Ibn Shahin, Ghars al-Din Khalil, 96, 102
Ibn Sina (Avicenna), 28, 75, 88, 91–2

Ibn Sirin, 59–60, 68–70, 84, 95, 109
  (Ibn Sireen), 180
  tomb of, 187
Ibn Tawus, 160
Ibn Taymiyya, 148
Ibn 'Uthman, 167
Ibn al-Zubayr, *see* 'Abd Allah b.
  al-Zubayr
'Ijlin, Shaykh, 171
Iliad, 17
imams, 83, 158–60, 162–3
Imam 'Ali, 159, 160, 162; *see also* 'Ali b.
  Abi Talib
Imam Hasan, 162; *see also* Hasan b. 'Ali
Imam Husayn, 159; *see also* Husayn b.
  'Ali b. Abi Talib
Imam Muhammad al-Baqir, 162
Imam Zayn al-'Abidin, 162; *see also* 'Ali
  Zayn al-'Abidin
Inana, 10
Indians
  in *Oneirocriticon* of Pseudo-Achmet,
    109–10
Iran
  dreams in modern, 191
  tombs in, 159, 165
Iraq
  tombs in, 159, 165
Ishtar, 16
isra, 46, 49; *see also* Muhammad the
  Prophet: night journey of
istikhara, 159–60, 176–9
'Izz al-'Arab al-Hawari, 6–8

Jabriyya, 108
Jacob, 16, 49–50
Jahanara, 173
Jahangir, Emperor, 172
Jahmasb, 94, 99
Jama'at Khanah Mosque, Delhi, 164
al-Jazuli, Muhammad, 151
Jerusalem, 45–6, 47, 131, 165
Jesus
  ascension of, 45, 48
  birth of, 34, 36
  in dreams and visions, 44, 73, 112,
    148
Jews, 23–4, 106, 108
  Christian dreams of, 113–14
al-Jilani, 'Abd al-Qadir, 155, 163
al-Jili, 'Abd al-Karim, 150
John Philoponus, 75
Jordan, 190
Joseph, 12, 49–50, 84, 111, 155
Judaism, 105, 108, 113
al-Junayd, 77, 78
Jung, Carl, 3

Ka'ba, 44, 45
  in dreams, 52, 115, 120, 125, 186
Kadizadeli movement, 146
Karbala, 159
Khadija, 41, 50
al-Kharkushi, Abu Sa'd al-Wa'iz, 96
al-Khayr, Afghanistan, 161, 162; *see also*
  Mazar-i Sharif
al-Kindi, 74–7
Kirmani, 84, 88
Kirmani, Muhammad Karim Khan,
  163
Kulab, Tajikistan, 168
al-Kuwayti, Abu Mu'adh, 188
Kyrgyz, 174–5
Kyrgyzstan, 174, 175

Leo VI, Emperor, 104
Louw, Maria Elisabeth, 174
Lyon, Stephen, 181–2

magi, 34, 113, 114; *see also* Zoroastrians
Mahdi, 146, 156
Mahmud, Egyptian dreamer, 176
majdhub, 4
Mamila cemetery, Jerusalem, 165
al-Ma'mun, Caliph, 109, 115, 116
manam, 49
martyrs, 123
  in dreams, 124, 188

Index

Marwan I, 115
Mary, 36–7
Masjid al-Aqsa, 46
*mawlid*s, 166; *see also 'urs*
Mazar-i Sharif, 162
Mecca, 35, 46, 50, 52, 53
   in dreams, 52, 115, 120, 186
Medina, 51, 54, 63–4
   Prophet's mosque at, 68, 116
   Prophet's tomb at, 150, 152
   tomb of Fatima at, 159
Midian, 121
Mir Damad, 162
mi'raj, 43, 46; *see also* Muhammad the Prophet: ascension of
   of Bistami, 79–80
Mittermaier, Amira, 176, 187
Morocco, 151
Moses, 44, 47, 48, 148
Mosul
   dream of tomb at, 166
Mount Hira', 39
Mount Muqattam, 169
Mount Qasyun, 164
Mu'awiya I, Caliph, 72
Muhammad Ahmad b. 'Abd Allah (the Sudanese Mahdi), 156
Muhammadan Light, 147, 150, 151, 199 n.8
Muhammad Najib, 169; *see also* Ajmeri, Muhammad Najib Qadiri Nagawri
Muhammad b. Sirin, *see* Ibn Sirin
Muhammad b. Tughluq, 164
Muhammad the Prophet, 31, 123, 124
   ascension of, 2, 43–6, 48
   death of, 61
   as dream interpreter, 53–6, 63, 65, 122, 123
   dreams and visions of, 2, 3, 32, 39–56
   in Muslims' dreams and visions, 62–3, 73, 127–8, 146–56, 161, 162, 163, 181

night journey of, 2, 45–8
   and the Qur'an, 50, 51–3
   and the supernatural, 32–4
Mu'izz al-Din, sultan of Delhi, 172
munajat, 142
al-Munawi, 'Abd al-Ra'uf, 129
Muslim b. al-Hajjaj, 58

Nabil, Shaykh, 187
al-Nabulusi, 'Abd al-Ghani, 97, 135–6, 145, 158, 170, 171, 173
   tomb of, 210
Najaf, 159, 160
Nasafi, Aziz, 168–9
Neo-Platonism, 75
Nestor, 18
Nizam al-Din Awliya', 164
Nizar, Arab dreamer in New York, 185–7
Nut, 37

Octavius, 37
Odysseus, 17
Odyssey, 17
oneiros, 20

Pakistan, 1, 178
Palestine, 158, 171
Palestinian Talmud, 23
Perfect Human Being, 147, 150
Persia, Sasanian, 35, 38, 74
Persians
   in *Oneirocriticon* of Pseudo-Achmet, 109–10, 111
Pharaoh, 12, 50, 111
Plotinus, 75
prophets
   in dreams and visions, 142, 147, 155
Pseudo-Achmet, 108–9, 117
   Oneirocriticon of, 104, 109, 111, 112, 114

Ptolemy, 19
Punjab, 181

Qadari, 108
al-Qadir, Caliph, 92, 108
Qarafa cemetery, Cairo, 163–4, 167, 169, 170
al-Qastallani, Qutb al-Din, 148
Qur'an
  dream terms in, 49, 59
  in dreams, 182
  dreams interpreted through, 49–50, 86, 99, 180, 186
  on Prophet's dreams, 51–2, 52–3
  reading of, 6–7, 70, 124, 125, 143, 170, 178–9
  revelation of, 48–9
Qusi, Shaykh, 181
qutb, 154

Rabi'a b. Nasr, king of Yemen, 27
Rabi'a of Basra (Rabi'a al-'Adawiyya), 126–9
Ra-Harakhty, 17
Ramadan, 39
Rastan, 165
Reshti, Sayyid Kazim, 163
Rida, Rashid, 190–1
Rumi, Jalal al-Din, 164
ru'ya, 1, 49, 59
Ruzbihan, *see* Baqli, Ruzbihan

Sadeta, Bosnian dream interpreter, 179–80
al-Safrawi, Abu 'Uthman Sa'id (al-Tunisi), 152
saints, 142, 147–8, 151, 152, 163
  graves of, 154, 163–72, 176
  imam of the, 155
  seal of the, 130
  see also awliya' Allah; *wali Allah*
sainthood, 141, 146, 152, 157

Seal of Muhammadan Sainthood; *see also* saints: seal of the
sakinah, 42, 43
Salihiyya, 164
al-Salimi, Abu 'Abd Allah, 96
al-Sarraj, Abu Nasr, 78, 79
Satan, 29, 59
Selim I, Sultan, 164
Seth, 14
Shah Wali Allah of Delhi, 146
Shams Umm al-Fuqara', 144
Shaykhi school, 162
Sierra Leone, 179
al-Sijistani, Abu Ahmad Khalaf b. Ahmad, 87, 92
Stoics, 25
Sufis, 77–8, 145
  as guides in dreams, 172–3
  shaykhs, 1, 143, 152, 154, 156, 163, 168, 178–9, 181
  tombs of, 163–72; *see also* saints: graves of
al-Sulami, Abu 'Abd al-Rahman, 78
Sulayman, Caliph, 64, 67, 116
al-Suyuti, 71
Syrbacham, 110

al-Tabari, 38, 42–5, 119
al-Tabari, 'Ali b. Sahl Rabban, 105
Tarphan, 110, 111
al-Tawhidi, Abu Hayyan, 131
Tertullian, 25
Thutmose IV, Pharaoh, 17
al-Tijani, Ahmad, 153–4
al-Tirmidhi, al-Hakim, 130
  wife of, 130–2
al-Tunisi, Abu 'Uthman Sa'id al-Safrawi, *see* al-Safrawi, Abu 'Uthman Sa'id

Uhud, 54–6
al-'Ulaymi, Mujir al-Din, 165

INDEX

'Umar b. 'Abd al-'Aziz ('Umar II), Caliph 72–3
'Umar b. al-Farid, 169–71
'Umar b. al-Khattab, Caliph, 56, 57, 61, 72, 73
Umayyads, 64, 67, 72
Umm al-'Ala', 122
Umm al-Fadl, 123
'urs, 166; *see also mawlids*
Usuman dan Fodio, 155–6
'Uthman b. 'Affan, Caliph, 64, 83
'Uthman b. Maz'un, 122–3

wali Allah, 148; *see also* saints; *awliya' Allah*
Walid, Caliph, 64, 67

al-Waqidi, 52, 55–6, 63, 119
Waraqa, 41
al-Wasiti, 165
Werbner, Pnina, 178

Yamani, Abdemalek, 177–8
Yazid II, Caliph, 67

al-Zawawi, Muhammad, 141, 151–2, 163–4
Zeus, 18
Zindapir, Shaykh, 178, 180
Zoroastrianism, 105, 111, 113
Zoroastrians, 35, 38, 48, 94, 106, 114; *see also* magi
Zuhayr, 48

www.ingramcontent.com/pod-product-compliance
Lightning Source LLC
Chambersburg PA
CBHW050137240426
43673CB00043B/1705